Neurological Physiotherapy
Bases of evidence for practice

D1500549

Neurological Physiotherapy

Bases of evidence for practice

Treatment and management of patients described by specialist clinicians

Edited by

Cecily Partridge PhD

University of Kent at Canterbury

Chief Collaborators

CHRISTINE BITHELL, University of Kingston, SUSAN EDWARDS, lately National Hospital for Neurology and Neurosurgery, London, and JENNIFER FREEMAN, University of Plymouth

TOURO COLLEGE LIBRARY
Main Campus Midtown
WITHDRAWN

W

WHURR PUBLISHERS
LONDON AND PHILADELPHIA

MT

© 2002 Whurr Publishers Ltd

First published 2002 by
Whurr Publishers Ltd
19b Compton Terrace, London N1 2UN, England
325 Chestnut Street, Philadelphia PA19106, USA

All rights reserved. No part of this publication may be reproduced, stored in a retrieval system, or transmitted in any form or by any means, electronic, mechanical, photocopying, recording or otherwise, without the prior permission of Whurr Publishers Limited.

This publication is sold subject to the conditions that it shall not, by way of trade or otherwise, be lent, resold, hired out, or otherwise circulated without the Publisher's prior consent, in any form of binding or cover other than that in which it is published, and without a similar condition including this condition being imposed upon any subsequent purchaser.

British Library Cataloguing in Publication Data

A catalogue record for this book is available from the British Library.

ISBN 1 86156 225 X

Printed and bound in the UK by Athenaeum Press Limited, Gateshead, Tyne & Wear.

7/12/04

Contents

Acknowledgements

Because we wanted this book to be of interest to clinicians we decided the central focus of each chapter would be a Case Report based on details from a real patient. We are most grateful to the clinicians who provided these reports. They were: Cherry Kilbride, Jennifer Freeman, Jan Glover, Louise Lockley, Claire Dunsterville, Ebba Bergström, Susan Edwards, Laura Buckholtz and Nikki van der Heiden. We are also grateful to the patients themselves who agreed to their details' being used, though of course their identities have been protected.

The following physiotherapists, who are each recognized specialists in their own area of neurological practice, were invited to prepare and describe the treatment and management of a patient presented in the Case Report:

Ebba Bergström MPhil, National Spinal Injuries Unit, Stoke Mandeville, UK
Karen Bridgewater PhD, University of South Australia
Maggie Campbell SRP, UK
Susan Edwards FCSP, London, UK
Jennifer Freeman PhD, University of Plymouth, UK
Fiona Jones MSc, Brighton University, UK
Diane Madras PhD, Creighton University, USA
Anne Moseley PhD, The University of Sydney, Australia
Elia Panturin MEd, Tel Aviv University, Israel
Suzanne Roberts MCSP, Whittington Hospital, London, UK
Margie Sharpe PhD, Flinders University of South Australia
Margaret Schenkman PhD, University of Colorado, Denver, USA
Paulette van Vliet PhD, University of Nottingham, UK

Cecily J. Partridge

Acknowledgements

Introduction

The starting point for this book series was work in other disciplines such as psychology, where books are frequently produced under titles such as Recent Advances or New Horizons. These excellent series provide the interested professional reader with a way of keeping up to date with recent work in their discipline or profession. We felt that this could be useful for physiotherapists. The first problem we encountered was that we did not have a baseline from which to advance. To rectify this we came together as a small group of physiotherapists with an interest in neurological physiotherapy to discuss and develop ideas about the extent of the bases of evidence for current practice. Christine Bithell, Susan Edwards, Jennifer Freeman and I formed the Core Group that has guided the work.

It is widely acknowledged that there is a gap between researchers and clinicians in the healthcare professions. The language of research is often seen by clinicians as turgid and complex, and their interests differ from those of researchers. Clinicians are focused on meeting patients' needs; researchers on the other hand are often more concerned with subjects, statistical analyses, obtaining research funding and publishing their work in learned journals. Yet unless research results are read by clinicians and influence practice, and the problems of practice are addressed in research, the profession will not develop a sound evidence base, and patients will not receive optimal physiotherapy.

To capture the interest of both clinicians and researchers we decided that the central focus of each chapter would be a Case Report of a patient drawn from the practice of neurological physiotherapists. It was difficult to select from the vast array of neurological conditions treated by physiotherapists, but we decided, in the first instance, to present those conditions seen most frequently. We divided them between single-incident events and those where the prognosis was for progressive deterioration. Specialists in different fields of neurology and from different philosophical backgrounds were invited to describe the treatment and management they would offer to the patient described in the report; they were also asked to provide references, wherever possible, to support their choice of treatment.

In medicine evidence is usually presented as a hierarchy, with the randomized controlled trial (RCT) as the pinnacle. A number of authors have, however, challenged the fact that RCTs can provide precise and unambiguous guidance for practice (Feinstein, 1995; Charlton, 1997; Goodman, 1998, 1999). These authors maintain that as most RCTs are conducted on unrepresentative populations of heterogenous patients, interpretation of results in relation to individual patients is usually far from straightforward (Goodman, 1999).

Recognizing the complexity of rating the strength of the evidence available we examined the physiotherapy neurological literature and on the basis of this and the rating scales used in medical hierarchies we asked the authors to rate the references they cited on a six-point scale. However, there appeared to be considerable overlap and we have now collapsed these to three major categories which seemed to represent the current state of research in neurological physiotherapy.

The categories are as listed below. We considered that reviews constituted a separate category, and these were marked as **R**.

A Based on the results of sound research, quoting the results of a research project, often a clinical trial, where treatment effects on patients have been evaluated, to include single-case design studies (this would be indicated in the text), also sound qualitative research – for example exploring patients' opinions.

B Theory-based work, often laboratory investigations in, for example, biomechanics, psychology or neurophysiology. Here results help to inform physiotherapy practice but have not evaluated treatment of patients.

C Statements provided by authority figures but not backed by experimental work. Also citations from textbooks and consensus statements.

Most references in the text have one of these initials attached after the date; where these are missing the references mentioned do not fit the categories provided. We removed all ratings of scales of measurement, as of themselves they do not provide evidence; they do so only when used in research.

As the authors are all specialists in their own fields we are using their ratings of the articles cited, and cannot be responsible for the categories they have selected. However, we hope readers will be interested to look up some of the references and make their own judgements.

It is usual to aim for consistency in style and layout between different sections in a book but as we started to collect the Case Reports we realized that the variability of the patients was such that they could not all be presented in the same way. The chapters too, because the specialists were working within very different philosophies, showed considerable variation. We therefore decided that this variability was indeed a strength and not a weakness.

References

Charlton BG (1997) Restoring the balance: evidence based medicine put in its place. Journal of Evaluation in Clinical Practice 387–98.

Feinstein AR (1995) Meta-analysis: statistical alchemy for the 21st century. Journal of Clinical Epidemiology 48: 71–9.

Goodman NW (1998) Anaesthesia and evidence based medicine. Anaesthesia 53: 353–68.

Goodman NW (1999) Who will challenge evidence based medicine? Journal of the Royal College of Physicians 33: 249–51.

Cecily J. Partridge

Section 1
Single Incident Neurology

Stroke

Case report – Mrs LM

Background

Mrs LM was a 29-year-old married woman who lived with her husband and 2-year-old daughter. At the time of the incident she was 37 weeks pregnant with a second child. She led a physically active life, looking after her family and undertaking all household activities. She enjoyed an active social life, and was involved in all her daughter's activities. She was temporarily living with her parents, having had to rent out their privately owned one-bedroom flat as a result of financial difficulties. Her husband was a self-employed carpenter.

Mrs LM was found unconscious at home by her husband. She was admitted to a local hospital where an emergency caesarean section (of a healthy baby boy) was undertaken. Immediately following surgery Mrs LM was transferred to the intensive care unit of a specialist neurological hospital.

Main Diagnosis

Arterio-venous malformation (AVM) bleed. Large left fronto-temporal bleed extending to the frontal basal ganglia, with minimal blood in the fourth ventricle.

Main Incidents

Intensive Care Unit (days 1–9)

Days 1–4: On admission patient paralysed, sedated, intubated and ventilated.
Respiratory status: No complications.
Neurological status: Intracranial pressures ranging from 10 to 25 mm (consistently resting at levels >20 mm). Neurological status unable to be assessed due to sedation/paralysis.

Days 5–9: Surgery (day 5).
Craniotomy performed for evacuation of haematoma and clipping of AVM. Post-surgery Mrs LM remained intubated, ventilated, sedated and paralysed for 24 hours.
Respiratory status: No complications throughout this period. Gradual reduction in ventilatory assistance over the following week – extubated on day 9.

Neurological status:

- Consistently agitated and restless (optimal positioning and limb care difficult).
- Spontaneous left-sided movement observed, nil movement on right.
- Tightness of tendo Achilles tendons bilaterallly (R >L) was recorded at day 9 (although full range achievable).
- Neglecting right side.
- Mute.
- Swallowing difficulties with pooling of secretions in the mouth.

Transferred to Ward (day 10)

- Continues to be disoriented with severe problems with midline orientation.
- Requires maximum support of two therapists to maintain sitting on bed edge and standing at bedside.
- In sitting and standing Mrs LM pushes strongly into extension of both trunk and head. Also pushes through ball of left foot, and has 'overactive left side'.
- Marked weakness of trunk and right arm and leg (nil active movement right arm).
- 'Associated reactions/movements' observed in right arm in standing.
- Tightness of right pectorals and rhomboids.

Day 15:

- Attending gym on daily basis. Sitting for short periods in wheelchair with contoured back support.
- Remains aphasic, speech therapists suggest there may be an element of dyspraxia contributing to speech problems.
- Pain at end of range supination of forearm, and wrist extension on the right.

Day 27:

- Oriented.
- Gastrostomy inserted.
- Spontaneous vocalization beginning with single words.
- Able to walk approximately10 steps with bandage with two therapists to control foot in dorsiflexion.
- Stiffness/reduced extensibility of soft tissues in trunk and left shoulder girdle musculature.
- Pressure sore on left heel.

Transferred to Rehabilitation Unit (day 33)

Impairments, restriction of activity and participation:

- Dense right hemiplegia.
- Left-sided 'overactivity/overcompensation'.
- Impaired balance reactions.
- Mild right hemisensory loss.
- Soft tissue shortening of left hip flexors, persistent tightness of bilateral tendo Achilles and plantar fascia of feet, tightness of right teres major/ latissimus dorsi/pectoralis major/upper trapezius.
- Right ankle unstable and swollen.
- Pain in low back and right upper limb.
- Pressure sore left heel.
- Poor concentration, easily distractible.
- Emotional lability.
- Aphasia (expressive and receptive) – unable to make more than basic sounds, difficulty understanding complex conversation.
- Dysphagia and dyspraxia.
- Dependent for all transfers, bed mobility, wheelchair mobility for all personal and domestic care and on gastrostomy for nutrition.
- Bladder (catheterized) and bowel dysfunction (diarrhoea).
- Poor exercise tolerance.
- Unable to participate actively in parenting role (husband caring for both children).
- Unsatisfactory social and housing set-up.

Discharged Home ($5\frac{1}{2}$ months post-incident)

Impairments, restrictions in activity and participation:

- Right arm densely hemiplegic and non-functional.
- Paresis right leg.
- Impaired balance reactions.
- Persistent soft tissue tightness in right tendo Achilles (though full range achievable).
- Dependent for some domestic tasks and parenting duties.
- Difficulty with walking out of doors and using public transport.

Early Rehabilitation of a Stroke Patient (1)

PAULETTE VAN VLIET

Introduction

A substantial amount of research now exists which is relevant to the treatment of neurological patients, and it is important that physiotherapy treatment is based on this research. This chapter will therefore draw on current research from the sciences relevant to physiotherapy, as well as the results of pragmatic trials of treatment in a clinical setting.

There is no evidence at present that one overall approach is superior to another. The approaches that have been compared for efficacy in controlled trials include the Bobath, proprioceptive neuromuscular facilitation, and functional (traditional) approaches (Dickstein et al., 1986 **A**; Loggigian et al., 1983 **A**; Lord and Hall, 1986 **A**). These trials have some problems in their design. For example, the study of Loggigian et al. was the only one of the three that randomized adequately, and all three studies arguably had insufficient power to detect differences, owing to small numbers. A single-case design was used by Wagenaar et al. (1990 **A**) to compare neuro-developmental (a modernized version of Bobath) and Brunnström methods of treatment, and also found no substantial differences. It is possible that differences do exist between the effectiveness of these approaches, but were not demonstrated in these studies.

Elements of treatment packages have been investigated with more success. In randomized controlled trials, training of weight distribution via auditory feedback has improved symmetry of body-weight distribution in sit-to-stand (Enghardt et al., 1993 **A**), and visual feedback about weight-bearing in the standing position has improved standing balance (Sackley and Lincoln, 1997 **A**). EMG biofeedback has been shown to facilitate recovery of arm function (Crow et al., 1989 **A**). In another randomized controlled trial, repeated pressing movements with the arm (in a position contrary to the typical pattern of spasticity) to push the body backwards in a rocking chair resulted in a better outcome on the Fugl-Meyer test (Feys et al., 1998 **A**). An enhanced therapy regimen for the arm, which included more intensive therapy, encouragement for the patient and relatives to be active participants in the rehabilitation, facilitation of learning new skills and self-directed exercise programmes, was found to improve strength, range and speed of movement in another randomized controlled trial (Sunderland et al., 1992 **A**). Task-specific training of reaching beyond arm's length in sitting was shown to improve outcome compared with a control placebo treatment by Dean and Shepherd (1997 **A**). There is also evidence that home exercise programmes (Turton and Fraser, 1990 **A**) and forced use of the affected arm by restraint of the intact arm in chronic patients (Taub et al., 1993 **A**) improve outcome of upper limb function.

Given this evidence, there is good reason to incorporate these elements of active learning, including feedback and task-specific training, into our management of patients. One must have a framework in which to use these elements and in this chapter I shall describe management of the patient within the context of the framework developed by Carr and Shepherd (1987a **C**, 1987b **C**, 1989 **C**, 1994 **C**). This is chosen because it is based on current information available from the movement sciences and it incorporates the above-mentioned interventions, which are supported by experimental evidence.

General Principles

The overall aim of my treatment would be to retrain the patient's motor control so that her motor performance is as close to normal as possible, since normal performance is the most efficient. At a later stage it may be necessary to alter this aim and adopt a more functional approach. Whilst motor control is being regained, it is essential to preserve muscle length and joint integrity, which are both at risk while the patient is unable to move normally.

A problem-solving approach is used, which can be summarized in four steps (Carr and Shepherd, 1987a, p. 31 **C**).

- The task to be trained is analysed by comparing the patient's motor performance with a normal model, which is based on findings from studies of the biomechanics of the task.
- Practice of either the missing component(s) of the task or the whole task occurs, with the therapist and patient identifying the goal to be achieved, and instructions, feedback, manual guidance and structuring of the environment are used to facilitate relearning of motor control.

- The movement or part of a movement which is initially assessed is reassessed under the same conditions at the end of the training.
- The therapist encourages transference of training to the patient's everyday setting by making it possible for them to practise in context, communicating with staff and relatives and organizing self-monitored practice for the patient.

Some of the key principles of the motor training are:

- The patient is encouraged to be an active learner in the rehabilitation process.
- A sound analysis of biomechanics and motor control of normal and abnormal movement underpins training.
- Training is task specific, because movements are normally organized so they are specific to a particular goal and set of environmental conditions.
- Active motor control, particularly the control of force and timing of muscle activity, is believed to minimize the clinical signs of spasticity.

Treatment and Management: Early Intervention

Early intervention aims to maintain optimal respiratory function, preserve integrity of the musculoskeletal system and start the process of regaining motor control.

Respiratory Function

Mechanical ventilation and paralysis will have adverse effects on respiratory function, including decreased functional residual capacity, microatelectasis, decreased lung compliance, increased secretions and a tendency towards infection (Ada et al., 1990 **C**). The respiratory status of the patient must therefore be assessed and treated appropriately, with due care so that any techniques used do not cause secondary brain damage, for example, by raising intracranial pressure (Frost, 1985 **C**). Techniques may include modified postural drainage, vibrations, rib springing, chest percussion and suction with humidification. Any intervention would be based on an analysis of the patient's pulmonary, cardiovascular and neurological status (Ada et al., 1990 **C**).

Preserving Integrity of the Musculoskeletal System

Positioning

In the earliest stage, when Mrs LM was sedated and unable to move, I would position her to prevent the development of contractures and reflex hyperexcitability. Hypertonia, the increased resistance to passive movement, may develop due to altered mechanical properties of muscle (Dietz and Berger, 1983 **A**) as well as hyperexcitable reflexes. In a study by O'Dwyer et al. (1996 **A**) of 24 stroke patients, hypertonia was associated with contracture but not with reflex hyperexcitability and it was suggested that contracture may actually potentiate hypertonia.

To preserve muscle length, the muscles at risk of developing contractures are identified and these are put in a lengthened position for part of the day. For example, pectoralis major (which remained persistently tight in Mrs LM) and biceps brachii are muscles normally at risk in stroke patients owing to the typical resting posture of the flaccid arm in sitting, with the arm adducted and the elbow flexed, and the hand resting on the lap. Muscle atrophy resulting from disuse occurs faster and to a greater degree in muscles immobilized in a shortened position (Gossman et al., 1986 **B**), so this is another reason to position muscles in their lengthened position. To lengthen these muscles, in supine, the patient's arm could be supported on a table in abduction, with the elbow extended. At the same time, a round heavy can could be placed into the hand (taped on if necessary) to maintain length of the finger flexors and the adductor muscles of the thumb.

For the lower limb, length of soleus and gastrocnemius could be maintained by keeping bedclothes off the feet with a bed cradle or by pleating the sheets, and by putting the lower legs in splints to maintain dorsiflexion for some of the day, providing the plantar flexors are not hypertonic. Short-leg plaster casts with the ankles in the plantargrade position, as described by Ada and Scott (1980 **C**), would be advisable if hypertonus is already present as other methods will not hold the feet in position and so will not prevent muscle shortening. Mrs LM's restlessness might mean plasters would not be suitable. I would monitor the plasters closely to check for circulatory problems and would leave the first casts on for four to five days, then remove to check the condition of the leg. The limitation of casts on ankle movement when Mrs LM starts to activate the tibialis anterior and begins to stand would be considered before reapplication. If the hips are constantly externally rotated, I would use sandbags or pillows along the sides of the legs to obtain a position of neutral rotation. To avoid shortening of neck flexors, Mrs LM could lie supine without a pillow some of the time.

There is as yet no clear evidence in humans as to how long the limb should be positioned to prevent muscle-length changes. It is known in mice, however, that a half-hour stretch daily is sufficient to prevent loss of sarcomeres and retain extensibility of connective tissue (Williams, 1990 **B**). It is also known that the biochemical changes which result in changes to sarcomere numbers begin after only 24 hours of immobilization (Gossman et al., 1982 **B**). Once established, length changes are reversible for up to six weeks in animal studies (Gossman et al., 1982 **B**). Therefore, it is essential to prevent changes early and, in the absence of evidence in humans, I would use a prolonged stretch for half an hour per day. The stretch would normally be a greater than resting length, the amount of stretch depending on Mrs LM's comfort and the tightness of the muscle. One study of children with cerebral palsy demonstrated that to prevent short soleus muscles shortening further, at least six hours per day was needed with the muscle at greater than its resting length (Tardieu et al., 1988 **B**). I would therefore consider half an hour to be a minimum time.

Passive Range of Motion Exercises

Slow, passive range of motion exercises, avoiding any forceful movements at the end of range, could be useful at this stage to maintain extensibility of connective tissues. I would use everyday movements such as reaching the hand to the back of the head or reaching towards the ceiling, as these would be a safe way to perform passive movements and are less likely to cause myositis ossificans, which can result from forceful movements at the end of range (Ada et al., 1990 **C**). Whilst performing movements with the arm, I would encourage Mrs LM to try to actively do the movements, such as protracting the shoulder to reach towards the ceiling, or to someone's hand. Accessory joint mobilizations (Maitland, 1979 **C**) could be performed if necessary, to maintain range.

Standing and Sitting

As soon as Mrs LM's intracranial pressure, heart rate and blood pressure were stable, I would commence standing with physical assistance. This has benefits for the patient's level of awareness, respiratory function, kidney, bladder and bowel functions. It will also help preserve muscle length and joint integrity in the lower limb and will start to reintroduce the patient to postural adjustments and the normal standing position. Loading of the bones will occur in the standing position, which is essential to prevent resorption (Ada et al., 1990 **C**) and compression of joint cartilage, which is necessary for its nutrition. In this position, I would encourage Mrs LM to extend her hips and knees and keep her head up, conveying this by visual or physical demonstration if necessary.

Sitting would also be commenced at this time to encourage head control and postural adjustments in sitting.

I would encourage interactions between staff, relatives and Mrs LM to occur on the right side some of the time to encourage the patient not to neglect that side. I would ascertain from the speech therapist the best way of communicating with Mrs LM.

After Transfer to Ward

General Approach

Once Mrs LM has been transferred to the ward and is ready to start more active movement with the therapists, my approach would be to organize treatment around functional movements needed in everyday life, such as supine to sitting, balance in sitting, sit-to-stand, standing and reaching activities with the arm. My comments are mainly restricted to the approach I would take initially, given Mrs LM's problems at this time. Training strategies would obviously change in accordance with changing performance. The movement is analysed by comparing the patient's performance with normal biomechanics and motor control of that movement. Carr and Shepherd (1987a **C**) list the invariant kinematic features of each functional activity. These are derived from studies of the biomechanics of these movements. The therapist observes which of these invariant kinematic features are missing or are not performed normally and notes the particular compensatory movements the patient makes. A decision is made about Mrs LM's main problems and training is aimed at improving these particular problems. There is growing evidence that dyscontrol after stroke is due more to underactivation of muscles rather than overactive or 'spastic' antagonist muscles interfering with the activation of agonists (Burke, 1988 **B**; Fellows et al., 1994 **A**; Sahrmann and Norton, 1977 **A**). The emphasis is therefore on training the underactivated muscles that are needed to perform the task. Mrs LM is expected to be able to decrease compensatory activity as she improves the ability to generate force in the muscles that are underactive.

A problem-solving approach to training is used throughout, where observation and analysis are followed by training, re-evaluation and progression. The movement or part of a movement which is initially assessed is reassessed under the same conditions at the end of the training. Where possible, any change in performance is measured objectively. If necessary, part of the skill may be practised first, followed by practice of the whole task that was initially observed. Wherever possible, I would choose a strategy where Mrs LM could elicit the desired muscle activity herself, with no, or minimal, manual guidance. She is then more likely to execute the movement in the correct temporo-spatial sequence. This is hard to achieve through handling. She will also receive more normal feedback from the periphery, in the absence of manual guidance, and will be better prepared for practising these movements on her own.

Patients are likely to recover faster if they perceive themselves to be in control of their rehabilitation (Partridge and Johnston, 1989 **A**). It would therefore be made as clear as possible to the patient that the responsibility for her rehabilitation is jointly between her and the therapist. Until the patient had more language, this may be difficult to explain but it can be communicated in other ways; for example, by giving her choice in the organization of her day, deciding on treatment goals together, with the therapist's guidance, and expecting her to work on practising movements when the therapist is not present. Overall progress would be measured by the Motor Assessment Scale (Carr et al., 1985), which I would use every two weeks or so.

Balance in Sitting

At this stage, Mrs LM requires the support of two therapists to sit. The invariant kinematic features of sitting include hip flexion to 90 degrees with trunk extension (including anterior tilt of the pelvis), head and neck extension, and foot placement under the knees. Because she is pushing strongly into extension in sitting, I would work first on obtaining active hip flexion, with extended head, neck and trunk. This could be done, for example, by encouraging the patient to reach for an object in front of her with the left arm, which may also discourage the tendency to push herself backwards with this arm. Support may be needed initially from a therapist seated in front, with the patient's extended arms resting on her shoulders. The object needs to be placed high enough to require some trunk extension in order to grasp it, and is moved further away systematically as practice continues. Varying the distance and direction systematically during practice has been shown to be effective in improving extent of reach by Dean and Shepherd (1997 **A**). The object should be something meaningful to the patient, such as one of her personal belongings, and preferably a bright colour, to hold her attention.

Regarding the problems with midline orientation, I would note the side to which the patient was tending to fall to most, and work on eliciting the appropriate postural adjustments for moving to that side. Postural adjustments are anticipatory and ongoing (Belenkii et al., 1967 **B**; Horak et al., 1984 **A**) and are specific to the task being performed (Cordo and Nashner, 1982 **B**), so training would occur in conjunction with movements in sitting, rather than in isolation. For example, if the patient was tending to fall to the right, pillows could be placed on the right side and she could be guided towards this side until her elbow rests on the pillows (Carr and Shepherd, 1987a, p. 95 **C**). I could facilitate the appropriate adjustment by manual guidance under the elbow, encouraging lateral flexion of the trunk to the opposite side. She should then be instructed to regain the midline sitting position, while the therapist facilitates this again with her hands. As a progression from this, the patient could practise reaching to the right side, as illustrated in Carr and Shepherd (1987b, p. 44 **C**).

Standing

Standing practice would continue daily, which is important both for retraining the ability to be in this position and also for maintaining length of muscles such as soleus, gastrocnemius, iliopsoas, psoas major and hamstrings. Because Mrs LM was pushing into plantar flexion, I would try the following training strategy to encourage standing with dorsiflexed ankles. From a sitting position on a high plinth, two therapists on either side assist the patient to stand by helping her to extend hips and knees. Standing from a high seat requires less vertical force generation at the knee and hip (Ellis et al., 1984 **B**; Murray et al., 1967 **B**). A table is placed in front, at hip height, so that the hips will touch the table if the ankles are sufficiently dorsiflexed. The goal is to move the body forward by dorsiflexing the ankles, until the hip touches the table. The table is a visible means of support and Mrs LM will want to be close to it. The appropriate set of postural responses might be elicited more easily if she was doing an everyday task which would normally require ankle dorsiflexion, such as reaching forward for an object at shoulder height, so I would also try this. This is an example of structuring the environment to achieve the goal. If Mrs LM does not understand what is required, visual demonstration can be given before she attempts it herself, by the therapist herself doing the movement to the table (the patient views from the side). Or, she can be manually assisted to do the movement a few times to give her the idea. The right lower limb was described as markedly weak. A calico splint around the right knee to help to hold it extended (Carr and Shepherd, 1987a, p. 118 **C**) might allow her to stand with less help while practising.

In addition, at this stage, the weakness in the gluteus maximus and hamstrings for hip extension, and the quadriceps for knee extension, needs to be addressed. It may be difficult for Mrs LM to work on these components in standing, and if so, part of the skill would be practised in another position. I would choose a strategy which is task specific. For example, practice of unilateral hip extension in a supine position, with the affected foot over the side of the bed, could commence to elicit activity in the hip extensors and increase their strength and endurance. With the hip extensors working unilaterally, at around 0 degrees of hip extension, and the body straight, they are activated in a similar way to that in standing. Practice of knee extension could occur in a sitting position, with the therapist simulating weight-bearing by giving firm pressure through the heel towards the extended knee, while the patient practises eccentric and concentric contractions of the quadriceps (Carr and Shepherd, 1987a, p. 136 **C**) or by static quadriceps contractions if very weak. Both of these components also need to be practised in the context in which they are needed, that is, standing. Whole-skill practice is more task specific and so is more likely to improve performance of the skill (Carr and Shepherd, 1987a **C**) but in patients with difficulty eliciting movement components, part-skill practice can be necessary. When practising components of a skill, I would choose a movement that closely resembles the way in which the muscles would work in the whole skill. I would expect this to result in better transference of training as several studies have demonstrated the specificity training effects (Gonnella et al., 1981; Rasch and Morehouse, 1957 **B**; Sale and McDougall 1981 **B**). For example, the knee extension exercise above involves weight-bearing in the relevant knee joint range for standing.

Sit-to-stand

The biomechanics of sit-to-stand would be analysed according to the invariant kinematic features (Carr and Shepherd, 1987a, p. 102 **C**) and training would accordingly aim at improving the main missing component(s). Practice would occur from a high plinth. Mrs LM could then do more herself and thus need less manual help from the therapists. The height chosen would be measured and practice would occur from this height until it was judged that the height could be lowered. Once she could sit-to-stand independently, the height of the plinth could be used as an objective measure of change in performance. Normal sit-to-stand requires overlap of the pre-extension (hip flexion and ankle dorsiflexion) and extension phases (thighs off to standing) (Vander Linden et al., 1994; Carr and Shepherd 1987a **C**). For example, the head reaches its maximum horizontal velocity just prior to thighs off so that this momentum can be transferred to extension at thighs off (Vander Linden et al., 1994; Schenkmann et al., 1990 **B**). For this reason, I would try to train the component in a way that involved both of these phases. For example, if the main problem was decreased hip flexion with an extended trunk, one way to train this is as follows. A curtained screen would be placed in front of Mrs LM, and the goal of moving her head to touch the curtain, and then pushing down and back through her heels at the end of the movement, is conveyed to her.

Upper Limb Training

As there was no movement in the right upper limb at this stage, I would try to elicit activity in the arm in various positions. In doing this, I would be considering factors such as the type of contraction required, the relationship of the arm to gravity, and the changed length–tension relationship of individual muscles. For the same neural input, optimal force production is greatest for eccentric contractions, then isometric and then concentric contractions (Albert, 1991 **C**), so it may be easier for Mrs LM to produce an eccentric contraction at this early stage. For example, in the supine position, an eccentric contraction of triceps brachii might be elicited in the outer range, with the upper arm held at 90 degrees to the horizontal, as she tries to control the movement of the hand to the head. Also, when a concentric contraction is immediately preceded by an eccentric contraction, elastic energy is stored and potentiates the concentric contraction (Cavanagh et al., 1968 **B**). Using this principle, when the patient can do an eccentric triceps contraction, it could be used to potentiate the concentric contraction. Finger extension might be more easily elicited in a position of finger flexion, as the fingers are likely to have been resting in a flexed position for much of the day. Muscles adapt to the length at which they are kept by changing their number of sarcomeres (decreased in the case of a muscle in a shortened position) so the peak tension in the finger extensors may now be produced in a lengthened position (Gossman et al., 1982 **B**). I would be particularly interested in obtaining some activity in the external rotators of the shoulder. Infraspinatus and teres minor are both external rotators and part of the rotator cuff, which is crucial in providing stability at the gleno-humeral joint. The rotator cuff forms a force couple with the deltoid at the shoulder, in elevation of the arm (Nordin and Frankel, 1989 **B**). External rotation is also significantly and negatively correlated with shoulder pain (Bohannon, 1988 **A**).

Since tightness of right pectorals and rhomboids has developed, the arm would be positioned to specifically stretch these muscles for some time during the day, and training of protraction (serratus anterior) and shoulder abductors (for example, middle deltoid as a prime mover and supraspinatus as a stabilizer) would be a priority.

There is some activity in the left upper limb, and it is described as being 'overactive'. As recovery of movement occurs, repetition of incorrect movements and length–tension changes can result in a muscle imbalance, where some muscles are easier to activate than others and are therefore used frequently and sometimes inappropriately. Other muscles, however, remain underactivated. To prevent this muscle imbalance developing further, I would identify the underactive muscles and work on increasing activation of these, in a way that discourages compensatory 'overactivity'. For example, to encourage forward flexion (for which the anterior deltoid is the prime mover) whilst discouraging internal rotation at the shoulder, the patient could be positioned side-lying with her arm extended on a table in front of her. A target object would be placed in the direction of forward flexion and Mrs LM encouraged to move the arm along the table to touch the object, or knock it off the table. The arm will not move easily if it is pressing into the table, so, to achieve the goal, she cannot use internal rotation.

Pain in Supination

Regarding the pain at the end of range of supination and wrist extension, I would perform a subjective and objective assessment of the joints and muscles that might contribute (Maitland, 1979 **C**). I would consider tightness of pronators or joint stiffness at radio-ulnar joints (inferior and superior) as possible causes of pain on supination and tightness of long finger flexors and wrist flexors and stiffness of wrist joint and carpal bones as likely causes of the pain on wrist extension, because of the period of virtual immobilization of the right arm. If the pain is caused by these problems, stretching of tight muscles and training of supination and wrist extension would be needed. Positive joint signs would be treated with the appropriate accessory joint mobilizations (Maitland, 1979 **C**). Strategies for training supination could include pouring water from one container to another, with assistance, in the direction of supination, or trying eccentric and isometric contractions in different parts of the range.

Self-monitored Practice

As soon as it seems practical, relatives would be encouraged to practise with Mrs LM specific exercises set by the therapist. Skill in performance increases as a direct function of the amount of practice. The study by Feys et al. (1998 **A**) is an example of how repetitive practice of movements can result in improved outcome. The average physiotherapy training session, which must be divided into treatment of several different problems, is unlikely to allow enough time for learning to take place, although performance may change. Therefore, it is logical to require the patient to practise outside the treatment sessions. Small but significant improvements in ADL and function have been found with higher intensities of rehabilitation (Kwakkel et al., 1997 **A**). Self-monitored practice is one way in which higher intensity of rehabilitation can be managed. In an observation of a stroke rehabilitation ward, Keith et al. (1980 **A**) demonstrated that much of a patient's day is spent alone, doing little. Much of this time could be used productively in practice. In the case of Mrs LM, the relatives could help by positioning her hand, palm down over the edge of the wheelchair arm, to allow her to practise wrist extension. The relative could hold her own hand in an appropriate place and encourage her to move her hand up towards her own. To ensure compliance and that practice is done correctly, the exercises would be recorded in the patient's own practice book and the relatives would be asked to record in the book the exercises done. Polaroid photographs of the exercises would be used when needed. A detailed discussion of ways of ensuring that practice takes place and is done correctly can be found in Ada and Canning (1990 **C**).

Walking

Preparation for walking has already begun with practice of hip and knee extension and standing. As soon as Mrs LM could manage it, stepping forward and back with the left leg would be performed in order to improve the ability to dorsiflex the ankle whilst lengthening the right plantar flexors, and to accustom her to bearing weight through the right leg. This proved to be particularly important in this case, as dorsiflexion was limited at day 27 and tightness in the right tendo Achilles remained at five and a half months. Initial training would aim to ensure that the hip and knee extensors are activated strongly enough to support the weight of the body in standing. Once able to stand, training would continue to depend on the therapist's analysis of Mrs LM's standing each day. In general, I would aim for improving the ability to transfer the weight to one leg, whilst maintaining a degree of knee and hip extension which was within her current abilities. Measurable feedback about weight transference would be indicated by bathroom scales under the feet and given orally via the therapist, or by auditory feedback from a pressure-sensitive device. The goal would be set so as to be achievable but challenging. It might be, for example, to maintain 30% of body weight on the leg, with the knee within five degrees of full extension, for one minute. Mrs LM's ability to do movements while standing, with the appropriate postural adjustments, would also be practised. This may start with looking up to the ceiling, which requires a slight anterior movement of the centre of mass, and progress to turning to look behind, then reaching for objects at the side, in front and behind.

A stepping exercise using a block has been shown to be helpful to stroke patients (Nugent et al., 1994 **A**). The patient starts with the affected leg on a block, then lifts the unaffected leg up on to the block by extending the affected hip and knee. There was a dose–response relationship between an increased number of repetitions of this exercise and improved walking outcome on the Motor Assessment Scale. This exercise could be introduced even at an early stage, as it was in this study.

Organization of Daily Treatment

In a typical 45-minute to one-hour session, I would aim to work on about three different problems identified from different functional activities. At around day 27, these might be hip and knee extension for standing, hip flexion for sit-to-stand and forward flexion for reaching in the right upper limb. This is purely a hypothetical choice, as the problems would be identified and would change based on ongoing analysis of Mrs LM's problems.

Other Factors Affecting Learning

Mrs LM was said to have poor concentration and was easily distractible. Learning will be adversely affected by poor concentration so a strategy would be worked out to improve concentration, in conjunction with a neuropsychologist, if one is available. Mrs LM would be treated in a quiet room, and the number of tasks to be learned would be reduced. As concentration improved, she would gradually be exposed to more distractions during treatment. The time for which Mrs LM concentrated on the task she was learning could be measured daily, and a chart made to show change in the time she was able to concentrate. The chart is displayed where she can check on progress herself.

Exercise Tolerance

Poor exercise tolerance is a consequence of the period without regular exercise. A decrease in cardiovascular fitness can be partially prevented, and improved by including exercise in the patient's rehabilitation programme specifically for that purpose. For Mrs LM, practice of sit-to-stand from a high chair or plinth could be used when she was able to do this independently with someone standing by. The practice could be supervised by a physiotherapy helper, or relative, who can remind the patient about the quality of the movement. The number of repetitions will depend on her cardiovascular response, which can be monitored by heart rate, and also on the quality of the performance. Forty to 50 repetitions of sit-to-stand per day would not be unusual when using this framework for treatment (Canning, 1987 **A**).

Training in the Later Stages

Motor skills can be classified as 'closed', where the movement is performed under invariant conditions each time, or 'open', where conditions change between attempts (Gentile, 1987 **C**). It appears that much of physiotherapy in the rehabilitation gym tends to train closed motor skills. For example, sit-to-stand is practised from a plinth most of the time. In real life, open skills are needed, so therapy needs to incorporate learning open skills. To this end, sit-to-stand would be practised from different types and heights of seats, and also under different conditions such as standing up in order to walk out of the door, or to reach for a box of tissues. This would require Mrs LM to problem-solve about the best solution for each situation. This type of training has been shown to be more successful in training normal individuals to transfer their learning to movements in different contexts than practice in unvarying situations (Shea and Morgan, 1979 **B**). The factors present while walking in the real world, such as talking while walking, avoiding stationary and moving objects, and walking on a moving object (for example, a bus), could be introduced into the latter stages of walking training.

The involvement of the patient as an active learner would have prepared her well for carrying out a home exercise programme. Leading up to Mrs LM's discharge, this programme would be demonstrated to her and updated regularly as performance changes. A home visit would help to establish what objects and furniture could be used within the programme. There is reason to expect the home programme to improve outcome, according to a study by Turton and Fraser (1990 **A**).

Implications

In summary, patients are not passive recipients of treatment, but have an active learning role in their rehabilitation. Accordingly, therapists have a role as trainer, facilitating patients' learning of motor skills. Empowering stroke patients in this way allows them to do more practice for themselves outside the training sessions and may result in faster recovery of motor control. An important skill for therapists involves choosing training strategies at a level which allows the patient to practise the desired movement without too much compensatory activity from inappropriate muscles. To achieve this, the therapist must draw on their broad range of knowledge, including areas such as muscle biology, as well as knowledge more closely associated with neurological conditions.

This chapter has tried to describe a treatment approach that is grounded in scientific findings. In response to a general demand for evidence-based treatments, physiotherapy treatment is rightly moving on from a stage where praxis-based treatment was considered satisfactory. More studies are obviously needed to evaluate the effectiveness of components of treatment approaches and the approaches as a whole. For now, we can concentrate on incorporating those interventions that have been demonstrated to be effective. In doing so, we need to be careful to note the limitations of the existing research. For example, can the interventions shown to be effective in patients more than one year after stroke, such as the forced-use paradigm, be applied earlier to patients as effectively? Whatever interventions therapists decide to adopt in their own practice, they need to examine the theoretical and experimental evidence to ensure there is a sound basis for their use.

References

Ada L, Scott D (1980) Use of inhibitory, weight-bearing plasters to increase movement in the presence of spasticity. Australian Journal of Physiotherapy 26(2): 57–61.

Ada L, Canning C, Paratz J (1990) Care of the unconscious head-injured patient. In Ada L, Canning C. Key Issues in Neurological Physiotherapy. London: Heinemann Medical, pp 248–86.

Albert M (1991) Eccentric Muscle Training in Sports and Orthopaedics. London: Churchill Livingstone, p 12.

Belenkii VY, Gurfinkel VS, Paltsev YI (1967) Elements of control of voluntary movements. Biophysics 12: 135–41.

Bohannon RW (1988) Relationship between shoulder pain and selected variables in patients with hemiplegia. Clinical Rehabilitation 2: 111–17.

Burke D (1988) Spasticity as an adaptation to pyramidal tract injury. In Waxman SG (Ed) Advances in Neurology, 47: Functional Recovery in Neurological Disease. New York: Raven Press, pp 401–23.

Canning C (1987) Training standing up following stroke – a clinical trial. In Proceedings of the Tenth International Congress of the World Confederation for Physical Therapy, Sydney, pp. 915–19.

Carr JH, Shepherd RB, Nordholm L, Lynne D (1985) Investigation of a new motor assessment scale for stoke. Physical Therapy 65: 175–80.

Carr JH, Shepherd RB (1987a) A Motor Relearning Programme for Stroke. London: Heinemann Physiotherapy.

Carr JH, Shepherd RB (1987b) A motor learning model for rehabilitation. In Carr JH, Shepherd RB (Eds) Movement Science: Foundations for Physical Therapy in Rehabilitation. London: Heinemann Physiotherapy, pp 93–154.

Carr JH, Shepherd RB (1989) A motor learning model for stroke rehabilitation. Physiotherapy 75(7): 372–80.

Carr JH, Shepherd RB (1994) Reflections on physiotherapy and the emerging science of movement rehabilitation. Australian Journal of Physiotherapy 40th Jubilee Issue: 39–47.

Cavanagh GA, Dusman B, Maragia R (1968) Positive work done by previously stretched muscle. Journal of Applied Physiology 24: 21–32.

Crow JL, Lincoln NB, Nouri FM, de Weerdt W (1989) The effectiveness of EMG biofeedback in the treatment of arm function after stroke. International Disability Studies 11: 155–60.

Cordo PJ, Nashner LM (1982) Properties of postural adjustments associated with rapid arm movements. Journal of Neurophysiology 47: 287–302.

Dean CM, Shepherd RB (1997) Task-related training improves performance of seated reaching tasks after stroke. Stroke 28(4): 722–8.

Dickstein R, Hockerman S, Pillar T, Shaham R (1986) Stroke rehabilitation: three exercise therapy approaches. Physical Therapy 66: 1233–8.

Dietz J, Berger W (1983) Normal and impaired regulation of muscle stiffness in gait. A new hypothesis about muscle hypertonia. Experimental Neurology 79: 680–7.

Ellis MI, Seedhom BB, Wright V (1984) Forces in the knee joint whilst rising from a seated position. Journal of Biomedical Engineering 6: 113–20.

Enghardt M, Ribbe T, Olsson E (1993) Vertical ground reaction force feedback to enhance stroke patients' symmetrical body-weight distribution while rising/ sitting down. Scandinavian Journal of Rehabilitation Medicine 25: 41–8.

Fellows SJ, Kaus C, Thilmann AF (1994) Voluntary movement at the elbow in spastic hemiparesis. Annals of Neurology 36(3): 397–407.

Feys HM, De Weerdt WJ, Selz BE, Cox Steck GA, Spichiger R, Vereeck LE, Putman KD, Van Hoydonck GA (1998) Effect of a therapeutic intervention for the hemiplegic upper limb in the acute phase after stroke. Stroke 29: 785–92.

Frost EAM (1985) Management of head injury. Canadian Anaesthesia Society Journal 32(3): 532.

Gentile AM (1987) Skill acquisition: action, movement and neuromotor processes. In Carr JH, Shepherd RB (Eds) Movement Science: Foundations for Physical Therapy in Rehabilitation. London: Heinemann Physiotherapy, pp 93–154.

Gonella C, Hale G, Ionta M, Perry JC (1981) Self-instruction in a perceptual motor skill. Physical Therapy 62(12): 1799–1808.

Gossman MR, Rose SJ, Sahrmann SA (1986) Length and circumference measurements in one-joint and multijoint muscles in rabbits after immobilisation. Physical Therapy 66(4): 516–20.

Gossman MR, Sahrmann SA, Rose SJ (1982) Review of length-associated changes in muscle. Physical Therapy 62(12): 1799–1808.

Horak FB, Esselman P, Anderson ME, Lynch MK (1984) The effects of movement velocity, mass displaced and task uncertainty on associated postural adjustments made by normal and hemiplegic individuals. Journal of Neurology, Neurosurgery and Psychiatry 47: 1020–8.

Keith RA (1980) Activity patterns of a stroke rehabilitation unit. Social Science in Medicine 14A: 575–80.

Kwakkel G, Wagenaar RC, Koelman TW, Lankhorst GJ, Koetsier JC (1997) Effects of intensity of rehabilitation after stroke. Stroke 28(8): 1550–6.

Loggigian MK, Samuels MA, Falconer J, Zagar R (1983) Clinical exercise trial for stroke patients. Archives of Physical Medicine and Rehabilitation 64: 364–7.

Lord JP, Hall K (1986) Neuromuscular reeducation versus traditional programs for stroke rehabilitation. Archives of Physical Medicine and Rehabilitation 67: 88–91.

Maitland GD (1979) Peripheral Manipulation. Sydney: Butterworths.

Murray MP, Seireg A, Scholtz RC (1967) Center of gravity, center of pressure, and supportive forces during human activities. Journal of Applied Physiology 23: 831–8.

Nordin M, Frankel VH (1989) Basic Biomechanics of the Musculoskeletal System. London: Lea & Febiger, p 242.

Nugent JA, Schurr KA, Adams RD (1994) A dose–response relationship between amount of weight-bearing exercise and walking outcome following cerebrovascular accident. Archives of Physical Medicine and Rehabilitation 75: 399–402.

O'Dwyer N, Ada L, Neilson P (1996) Spasticity and muscle contracture following stroke. Brain 119: 1737–49.

Partridge C, Johnston M (1989) Perceived control of recovery from physical disability: measurement and prediction. British Journal of Clinical Psychology 28: 53–9.

Rasch PT, Morehouse LE (1957) Effect of static and dynamic exercise on muscular strength and hypertrophy. Journal of Applied Physiology 11: 29–34.

Sackley CM, Lincoln NB (1997) Single blind randomised controlled trial of visual feedback after stroke: effects on stance symmetry and function. Disability and Rehabilitation 19(12): 536–46.

Sahrmann SA, Norton BJ (1977) The relationship of voluntary movement to spasticity in the upper motor neurone syndrome. Annals of Neurology 2: 460–5.

Sale D, MacDougall D (1981) Specificity in strength training: a review for the coach and athlete. Canadian Journal of Applied Sports Science 6: 87–92.

Schenkmann MA, Berger RA, Riley PO, Mann RW, Hodge WA (1990) Whole-body movements during rising to standing from sitting. Physical Therapy 70: 638–48.

Shea JB, Morgan RL (1979) Contextual interference effects on the acquisition, retention, and transfer of a motor skill. Journal of Experimental Psychology: Human Learning and Memory 5(2): 179–87.

Sunderland A, Tinson DJ, Bradley EL, Fletcher D, Langton Hewer R, Wade DT (1992) Enhanced physical therapy improves recovery of arm function after stroke. A randomised controlled trial. Journal of Neurology, Neurosurgery, and Psychiatry 55: 530–5.

Taub E, Miller NE, Thomas AN, Cook EW, Fleming WC, Nepomuceno CS, Connell JS, Crago JE (1993) Technique to improve chronic motor deficit after stroke. Archives of Physical Medicine and Rehabilitation 74: 347–54.

Tardieu C, Lespargot A, Tabary C et al. (1988) How long must the soleus muscle be stretched each day to prevent contracture? Developmental Medicine in Child Neurology 30: 3–9.

Turton A, Fraser C (1990) The use of home therapy programmes for improving recovery of the upper limb following stroke. British Journal of Occupational Therapy 53(11): 457–62.

Vander Linden DW, Brunt D, McCulloch MU (1994) Variant and invariant characteristics of the sit-to-stand task in healthy elderly adults. Archives of Physical Medicine and Rehabilitation 75: 653–60.

Wagenaar RC, Meijer OG, Wieringen CWv, Kuik DJ, Hazenberg JG, Lindeboom J et al. (1990) The functional recovery of stroke: a comparison between neuro-developmental treatment and the Brunström method. Scandinavian Journal of Rehabilitation Medicine 22: 1–8.

Williams PE (1990) Use of intermittent stretch in the prevention of serial sarcomere loss in immobilised muscle. Annals of the Rheumatic Diseases 49: 316–17.

Early Rehabilitation of a Stroke Patient (2)

Elia Panturin

Introduction

The treatment described for this patient is based on the Bobath concept. This approach to therapy and rehabilitation comes from the work of Berta and Karel Bobath who, in the 1940s, started to develop treatment based on an understanding of normal movement behaviour, on their clinical experience, and on the scientific knowledge at the time.

It is a problem-solving approach to the assessment and treatment of people (adults and children) with disturbances of function, movement and tone caused by a lesion or lesions of the central nervous system. New models of motor control and a greater understanding of the neurosciences, evolved during the past 50 years, provide the rationale for current practice.

A 24-hour interactive process is developed between the patient, the interdisciplinary team, appropriate family members and carers, by addressing their biological and psychosocial needs. Preventive aspects are always stressed and guidance offered.

Treatment is based on an understanding of the components of function and normal movement. The goal is to optimize function through an ongoing process of assessment and treatment directed to the underlying impairments. Integrating improved control in functional activities and participation in daily life is crucial, and includes assessing the patient's function at home with family and friends at work and leisure.

The focus of treatment is symptomatic and characterized by facilitating the missing components of normal patterns of function, movement and posture while avoiding reactions interfering with efficiency, success and quality of performance. The treatment, preferably performed in the person's natural surroundings, is holistic, yet specific when addressing a particular element. The active participation of the individual together with the specific handling of the therapist, which is gradually withdrawn, is necessary in order to achieve independence. Follow-up treatment, when indicated, may need to continue for the rest of the patient's life.

The theoretical framework of the Bobath concept is always evolving and is constantly enriched by new information and knowledge from the movement sciences and the International Bobath Instructors Training Association (IBITA).

General Principles

- Treat the patient as a whole person.
- The physiotherapist works as part of a large inter-disciplinary team. Without co-operation of the team and the family members throughout, the rehabilitation process will not be effectual.
- The rehabilitation process should start immediately after admission to hospital (Perry, 1998 **C**) and the treatment is symptomatic and functional (Vliet et al., 1995 **A**; Pobl and Dunn, 1998 **C**). Each symptom observed *always* originates from more than one cause.
- Aims of treatment must be functional and specific, with emphasis on *quality* of performance (Le Vere, 1980 **C**; Bobath, 1990 **C**). The functional outlook should focus on individual lifestyle (Bernstein, 1967 **C**; Carr and Shepherd, 1987 **C**; Mulder, 1994 **C**; Dunn et al., 1994 **C**; Haley et al., 1994 **C**; Pobl and Dunn, 1998 **C**).
- Evaluation and treatment are a continuum. Re-examine the patient during and after each treatment to determine whether the desired effect is being achieved. The therapist may choose to work on a particular element of a specific function and not on the function as a whole but it must be remembered that, at the end of a treatment, these elements should be combined within the desired function while retaining specific details.
- Treat primary impairments in order to prevent development of secondary impairments, which may lead to further limitation of function.
- Rehabilitation continues 24 hours per day (Shumway-Cook and Wollacott, 1995 **C**), and the nearer to normal the stimuli given, the more the gains achieved, for example correct positioning in bed and in sitting.
- Although the concept of constraint induced movement and learned non-use (Miltner et al., 1999) were originally used in the treatment of chronic hemiplegia (Wolf et al., 1989 **A**; Taub et al., 1993 **B**, 1994 **A**), it should be remembered that 'learned non-use' should be avoided from the early stages of rehabilitation (Bobath, 1990 **C**). There is neurological

evidence supporting the influence of treatment on the plasticity of the nervous system (Bach-y-Rita, 1987 **C**; Held, 1987 **C**; Fisher, 1992 **C**; Kidd et al., 1992 **C**; Lee and Van Donkelaar, 1995).
- A large part of the treatment should take place in the patient's natural surroundings: in the ward, rehabilitation department and at home (Bernstein, 1967 **C**; Mulder, 1994 **C**; Gentile, 1987 **C**; Park et al., 1994 **A**).
- A desired movement can often be achieved by changing the environment, for example rearranging the furniture to produce a narrow passage demanding side walking to navigate it successfully (Gentile, 1987 **C**; Perry, 1998 **C**).
- Treatment is through problem-solving and, as Bernstein said in 1967(**C**), 'learning is repetition without repetition'.
- Giving feedback is an integral part of treatment. Real, informative feedback should be used and reduced with time (Carr and Shepherd, 1987 **C**; Schmidt, 1975 **C**; Winstein, 1987 **C**, 1991 **C**; Winstein et al., 1996 **A**).

Treatment

- The treatment is based on knowledge and understanding of normal function and movement. Normal movement demands the ability to control selected movements, such as movements between the upper and lower trunk or between trunk and extremities.
- It is important to understand the function of the dynamic stabilizing muscles and their influence on other muscles. For example, the abdominal muscles and the function of the serratus anterior muscle, or the importance of the trunk muscles for function of the upper and lower extremities (Hodges and Richardson, 1996 **A**).The good side may be involved (Arsenault et al., 1987 **A**; Thilman et al., 1990 **A**; Yi-Chung Pai et al., 1994 **A**; Desrosiers et al., 1996 **C**).
- It is important to understand the motor and sensory influence of the base of support on posture and movement. The muscles of the hips and lower trunk, when sitting, and of the feet, when standing, need to receive motor and sensory input.
- Closed kinematic chain (CKC)[1] and open kinematic chain (OKC)[2] movements should be used in treatment. CKC movements are important for enhancing the dynamic stability of the stabilizers of the upper

---

[1]CKC: The distal part of the body is fixed on a stable surface and the body moves round it.

[2]OKC: The distal parts of the body such as the hands and feet move freely in space.

and lower extremities (Brouwer and Ambury, 1994 **B**; Ryerson and Levit, 1997 **C**). Usually, using CKC movements away from pathological patterns reduces spasticity and facilitates normal movement (Davies, 1985 **C**; Bobath, 1990 **C**).

- Proximal parts of the body, such as the trunk, influence function of the extremities (Tokizane et al., 1951 **B**; Wyke, 1979 **C**; Bobath, 1990 **C**). The abdominal muscles, particularly the transverse abdominus, and deep trunk muscles contract before lifting the arm or leg (proactive response) (Hodges et al., 1996 **A**; Hodges and Richardson, 1997 **A**). Range of movement of the trunk is of similar importance when considering the patient's ability to function (Schenkman et al., 1996 **A**).
- Strengthening of muscles must be functional, specific and of good quality (Davies, 1985 **C**; Bobath, 1990 **C**; Vliet et al., 1995 **B**). Treatment should include concentric, eccentric and isometric muscle contractions. Functions can be used as tools for strengthening muscles.
- Movement of one part of the body can be influenced by movements in another distant part (Davies, 1990 **C**; Panturin, 1998 **C**).
- If, despite normal range, patients have difficulty in reaching a specific position, they may first be brought to that position passively, helping them to learn and control this position both motorically and perceptually. Once acquired, the patient can practise moving out and coming back into this position.
- Initially it will be difficult to control many degrees of freedom, therefore, at this stage, the therapist should limit them. Examples include: using the right hand with elbow resting on the table to neutralize the effect that the trunk and shoulder girdle have on the function of the hand. During the first stages of standing, it is often very difficult to cope with many degrees of freedom, such as joints and muscles, or the effect of the surroundings on perception. Therefore it is recommended to stand the patient close to a table with or without back splints (Davies, 1990 **C**; Edwards, 1996 **C**).
- Good muscle control demands proprioceptive awareness. Proprioception of the trunk can be facilitated by working actively towards the end range of movement (Wilson et al., 1986 **C**).
- In the beginning, weak postural muscles need to be isometrically strengthened in the inner range. Later, eccentric contraction can be introduced.
- Frequently the affected muscles of patients suffering damage to their CNS contract quickly and are unable to sustain contraction (Gardiner, 1996 **C**). Therefore treatment should include maintaining muscle contraction while moving, and fixing should be avoided.

- Treatment must include automatic and voluntary movements (Davies, 1985 **C**; Bobath, 1990 **C**) and should include placing and holding (Bobath, 1990 **C**).
- Before every passive or active movement the joint should be placed in its anatomical position. Improved range of movement achieved passively should immediately be controlled actively.
- To improve or preserve range of motion of joints or soft tissues, various techniques can be used, such as: myofacial therapy or general treatment using movements of the nervous system – neurodynamics (Davies, 1994 **C**; Panturin, 1998 **C**).
- Attention to the midline is important. One of the causes of deviation from the midline was explained by Karnath et al. (1994 **B**): afferent visual, vestibular and proprioceptive input which converge to the neural generation of an egocentric, body-centred image.
- Throughout treatment the good quality of function and movement must be maintained, avoiding spasticity, compensations, fixations and associated reactions (AR) (Davies, 1994 **C**).

Days 1–4 (ICU before Surgery)

Rehabilitation of Mrs LM should start immediately and the aim, at this stage, is to prevent complications. Treatment will, to an extent, be determined by the intercranial pressure, which will be constantly monitored. Elevating the head, shoulders and upper trunk to just above 30° may help prevent an undesired rise in the intercranial pressure. Minimal stimuli should be present at this time in the surroundings – which should be kept quiet and darkened. The head should be moved as little as possible, therefore position changes are carried out using the log-rolling technique, taking care to stabilize the head and shoulders. Besides helping to prevent pressure sores, from which Mrs LM suffered, position changes also enhance lung ventilation. Passive movements should be carried out slowly and gently. Regarding the respiratory care, there were no complications described in this case. During this stage however, good hygienic care of the tubus is essential; any complication developing should be detected early and treated accordingly (Dean and Frewnfelter, 1996; Brimioulle et al., 1997 **A**; Dean, 1997 **B**).

Days 5–9 (ICU Post-surgery)

Positioning and Changing Position

As Mrs LM is restless and disoriented she needs to be given more environmental reference points in bed, such as surrounding her with firm packs which will help her to feel where she is in space (Affolter, 1987 **C**; Davies, 1994 **C**). Position changing continued by log-rolling to prevent complications, taking into account the intercranial pressure. When this is normal the bed can be level while the patient is side lying. In this position, on either side, the back should be supported, the lower leg placed with the hip and knee in flexion, and the upper leg placed behind the lower leg, supported on a pillow, with some hip extension and knee flexion. This gives relative extension to the hip, an essential component of movement when standing and walking, and good airing of the genital area. The persistent tightness of both Achilles tendons may be improved with inhibitory casting (Conine et al., 1990 **A**; Davies, 1990 **C**; Edwards, 1996 **C**; Moseley, 1993 **A**). As the signs of right unilateral neglect develop, and providing that Mrs LM is now permitted to move her head, the bed should be placed so that the centre of the room is to her right (Herman, 1992 **C**; Riddoch et al., 1995 **C**). If this causes Mrs LM to be more restless the change should be carried out gradually.

Respiratory System

The physiotherapist's evaluation should include inspection, palpation and auscultation. This case study states that Mrs LM displayed no respiratory problems throughout her hospitalization. Her restlessness, spontaneous movements of the left side and the specific movements provided by the therapist may all have helped to prevent respiratory complications from developing.

Movement

Mrs LM's haemodynamic state will dictate the rate of progress, which will also depend on her medical condition, her consciousness level and her ability to learn and concentrate. At this stage she may need several short treatments each day, with repeated explanations given in short, clear, simple sentences. *All movements should be performed slowly*. Maximum stimulation to her right side should now be given, encouraging the staff and visitors to stand to her right, place the night table to the right and feed her from the right (if she is allowed to move her head). It is also advisable to give sensory stimuli to the right side, such as feeling objects of different materials and size (Herman, 1992 **C**; Riddoch et al., 1995 **C**).

Active and assisted active movements of trunk and extremities will be introduced, while continuing to perform passive movements to preserve the ranges. When she is permitted to move her head, neck movements should be introduced. All these movements should be integrated into *functional activities*. Motor and sensory treatment of the mouth should be started now, taking for granted that hygienic care is being performed (Davies, 1994 **C**).

Standing

Besides its importance in everyday life, standing aids the function of internal organs and systems, helps to maintain a full range of motion of the joints of the lower extremities, reduces spasticity, affords sensory stimulation, and is of psychological importance (Davies, 1990 **C**; Richardson, 1991 **C**; Edwards, 1996 **C**).

Standing Mrs LM on a tilt table, or leaning her forward on a high table with long back splints applied to both legs, or sitting her up as soon as permitted, is very important. Of course, this will depend on her haemodynamic status and the doctor's decision.

Days 10–33 (On the Ward)

As the treatment programme is a continuum, part of the following will have been initiated immediately following surgery, and continue throughout rehabilitation and after discharge.

As Mrs LM has poor concentration and exercise tolerance, short but frequent therapy sessions during the day are recommended. Therapy should be given in a restful, quiet atmosphere.

Respiratory System

Because of her swallowing difficulties, weakness (particularly of the abdominal muscles), spasticity and the fact that she had been artificially ventilated, Mrs LM had the potential to develop respiratory failure and my aim would be to prevent this. It is worth remembering here that movements, especially of the trunk (including extension of the thoracic spine), sitting and standing all help to prevent respiratory complications (Annoni et al., 1990 **C**; Davies, 1990 **C**).

Aphasia

This should be treated by a speech therapist.

Function and Movement

From the beginning, the aim of my assessment would be functional, choosing, together with Mrs LM, tasks relevant to her present condition, in the ICU, medical ward, rehabilitation department or at home. I would assess each component and treat whatever is missing or preventing good quality performance. For example:

- movements in bed, including: pelvic lifting, turning – with trunk rotation – in both directions (also the first stage of sitting on the side of the bed), movements of the lower limbs, using her hands – one at a time and both together – for feeding, washing and grooming;

- for functions while sitting – such as dressing or holding the baby – Mrs LM needs good trunk control, midline orientation and sitting control;
- propelling and transferring to and from the wheelchair;
- standing and walking to the toilet.

Besides the importance of function itself, it must be remembered that while performing each particular function Mrs LM will be strengthening muscles, encouraging selective movements of the trunk and limbs, inhibiting increased tone and fixation, and receiving sensory (proprioceptive and tactile) stimulation. For example:

- While turning to the paretic side, with hip or shoulder leading, Mrs LM is working the left side of her body selectively, using rotation of the trunk (an important element for developing normal movement), strengthening abdominal muscles and reducing spasticity (Tokizane et al., 1951 **B**; Wyke, 1979 **C**; Dewald, 1987 **C**; Bobath, 1990 **C**; Schenkman, 1996 **A**; Franchignoni et al., 1997 **C**). Weight bearing on the paretic right side affords Mrs LM proprioceptive and tactile stimulation.
- Pelvic lifting, in itself an important function, together with contraction of abdominal muscles, provides dynamic stability of the lower trunk and contains elements of movement for walking. To achieve this we need, amongst other things, active movement of both legs, to attain and retain crook lying, adaptation of the soles of both feet to the surface, range of movement of dorsiflexion of the ankles, extension of the hips, muscular power to lift the hips and maintain the position and normal sensation – all while preventing compensations or the appearance of ARs (Bobath, 1990 **C**). It is worth remembering that pelvic lifting can be made easier by placing a pillow below the buttocks thus reducing external torque.
- Abdominal muscles can be facilitated by lifting the head and shoulders from the pillow towards the paretic side, while the therapist places her hands on the lower ribs. Mrs LM is asked to 'pull her tummy in' in order to activate her transverse abdominus muscle.
- Every function demands active and selective movements – between different areas of the trunk, between the trunk and the limbs, between different parts of the limbs themselves (Davies, 1985, 1990 **C**). We have to check that all the passive ranges are full and, if not, treat passively following with placing, holding and active control. Mrs LM had a weak trunk, which inhibited effective function of her extremities. Rotation is important for all daily tasks, enhancing movement and reducing

spasticity. Extension of the trunk is important for many functions, for example when raising the arms (Crawford and Jull, 1993 **A**).

- We need to check whether the weakness is symmetrical or asymmetrical and strengthen the muscles accordingly. Asymmetrically weak muscles should be strengthened asymmetrically. In order to strengthen a specifically weak muscle, it should be placed in a shortened position while elongating all the compensatory muscles, for example, sitting with the weak buttock raised and exercising the abdominal muscles on the same side. The trunk can be strengthened in all starting positions, taking care to prevent fixations or ARs appearing on the right side. While sitting – with the therapist giving, if needed, external support from behind or supporting the arms from the front – general and selective movements in all directions are performed. If Mrs LM's trunk shows signs of collapsing when sitting, extension should be encouraged first – either in mid-position or with the trunk in rotation, always paying attention that hip flexion does not exceed 89° – in order to avoid total extension. Raising the good left hand will also facilitate active extension. I would now follow with selective movements, which will also activate the abdominal muscles and those around the hip joints.
- If Mrs LM pushes on the floor with her feet, in addition to raising the height of the bed slightly, so that her feet are not in contact with the floor, passive movements of the joints and soft tissues of the foot will improve range and proprioceptive awareness, and reduce the pushing.
- The presence of unilateral visual neglect demands that the therapist address herself especially, but not only, to the patient's right side. Owing to Mrs LM's difficulties with the midline, exercises should be performed after she has been brought towards the end range of rotation and side flexion. Mrs LM should be encouraged to follow her movements with her head and eyes (Rothwell, 1994 **C**). Karnath (1994 **B**) suggested that facilitating proprioception in the cervical area will improve awareness of the midline. He recommended vibrating the cervical erector spine muscles on the neglected side. This should be performed gradually and with caution, noting whether Mrs LM suffers from, or complains of, nausea during or following the treatment. Proprioceptive stimulation – while lying and sitting – can also be given with the whole body rotating against the cervical spine (Wiart et al., 1997 **A**).
- When appropriate, balance reactions (BR) may be introduced to the treatment. If necessary, to keep her upright against gravity, I would choose treatment in a standing position to encourage normal extension of the whole body (Davies, 1990 **C**; Edwards, 1996 **C**), and when lying supine to encourage selective hip movements. While sitting, together

with treatment of the trunk, active movements of the limbs should be encouraged while practising partial weight bearing on the paretic hand (CKC) and maintaining range of movement of the right upper extremity. This should be performed while giving manual support to the upper trunk and axilla. CKC movements, away from pathological patterns, reduce spasticity and facilitate normal movement (Davies, 1985 **C**; Bobath, 1990 **C**).

Why is Mrs LM's left side overactive? Explanations may include: compensation for the motor, proprioceptive involvement and neglect of the right side; lack of knowledge of the midline; searching for information because of perceptual difficulties or slight involvement of the left side with abnormal recruitment of motor units (Desrosiers et al., 1996 **C**). Performing placing of Mrs LM's left upper and lower extremities, different passive and guided movements of the left hand and foot and partial weight bearing on a supporting surface of various textures may all help. Environmental references should be given, such as sitting or standing with a table in front, or in a corner (Affolter, 1987 **C**; Davies, 1994 **C**). Mrs LM has partial active movements in the right leg, which should be encouraged with OKC and CKC movements, and by placing in many different starting positions. These movements must all be performed without fixations or ARs.

Mrs LM has no active movements in the right upper extremity, which is spastic, has developed shortening of various muscle groups and ARs appear on effort (Dvir and Panturin, 1993 **A**; Dvir et al., 1996 **A**). This shortening can have many causes (Gardiner, 1996 **C**) and should be avoided and treated. Treatment possibilities, holistic and specific, are many, in both lying and sitting:

- movements of the trunk (an integral part of the shoulder complex) affecting the tonus of the extremities (Tokizane et al., 1951 **B**; Wyke, 1979 **C**; Dewald, 1987 **C**; Bobath, 1990 **C**);
- passive, and, if possible, active movements of the scapula (Bagg and Forrest, 1988 **B**), followed by movements of the whole upper extremity (CKC and OKC);
- sitting with partial weight bearing on the hand while moving the trunk. This will affect tonus and encourage active selected movement (Brouwer and Ambury, 1994 **B**). Weight bearing is always partial and the therapist's hand must always support the patient's armpit. Weight bearing should be performed with the hand in different positions: (a) flat, though never with a completely flaccid hand, in position of use which means maintaining the arches of the hand, and with clenched fist;

or (b) with elbows supported on a table, moving the trunk (CKC) and encouraging active movement of the right arm (Davies, 1985 **C**; Ryerson and Levit, 1997 **C**). If possible, all these activities should be performed in relation to appropriate specific functions, such as eating, dressing and holding the baby. Using self-assisted pulleys to gain range in the glenohumeral joint is not recommended (Kumar et al., 1990 **C**);
- passive movements using neurodynamic principles (Davies, 1994 **C**; Panturin, 1998 **C**).

The Passive Components of Treatment

The causes of restriction of movements which Mrs LM developed in the trunk, in both ankle joints and feet, shoulders, right elbow, right palm and the pain in her right shoulder should all be investigated. Are they caused by spasticity, shortening of soft tissues or both? Routinely, the range of joints, soft tissues, muscles and the peripheral nervous system must be treated and maintained. If the limitations are due purely to a problem within the joint, the joint should be treated using manual therapy techniques. If the limitation is caused by changes in the muscle or soft tissues (Gardiner, 1996 **C**), these tissues need to be elongated and mobilized in different ways:

- elongating the muscle by moving another part of the body, for example the latissimus dorsi muscle, by moving the pelvis in different starting positions;
- elongating a localized muscle by kneading the muscle while gently moving the trunk or extremity;
- fascial restrictions can be released by soft tissue mobilization and elongation (Jackson, 1998 **C**);
- very specific trunk and cervical mobilizations;
- as the nervous system is a continuum, to approach the limitation and pain in Mrs LM's shoulder I would try to see if side flexion of the neck to either side or straight leg raising (SLR) of the right or left leg relieves, or worsens, symptoms. To attain good movement around the hip joint, I would try either using SLR to improve hip extension, or passive knee bending (PKB) while side lying to improve SLR (Panturin, 1998 **C**). After achieving a range of movements in the distal parts with the whole extremity in neutral position, I would attempt to achieve them again with the extremity in different tension positions. For example: elongating the Achilles tendon and mobilizing the foot with the leg in different angles of SLR (and similarly with the upper extremity). Neurodynamic techniques should be used in different lying, sitting and standing positions (Davies, 1994 **C**; Panturin, 1998 **C**). Any passive range of movement achieved should be complemented with active control.

The causes of the painful shoulder should be established and treated accordingly. The pain is frequently due to poor co-ordination of muscle contractions, leading to malalignment of the shoulder complex, causing impingement and, therefore, pain. Improving the activity of all the muscles of the shoulder complex usually helps (Laynt, 1992 **C**). When sitting, resting the hands on a tray or table in front can also relieve pain.

Very often, people with hemiparesis present with palpable anterior and/or inferior subluxation (Prevost et al., 1987 **B**). The causes of inferior subluxation are many (Culham et al., 1995 **C**). Treatment may include: facilitating activity of all muscles of the shoulder complex and, as suggested by Faghri (Faghri et al., 1994 **A**; Pouran et al., 1994 **A**), giving electrical stimulation to the supraspinatus and posterior deltoid muscles. The upper extremity should be continually supported in an anatomical position. This can be attained in many different ways, for example: using a Bobath sling (using Neophrem), or sitting with the elbows resting on a table (Moodie et al., 1986 **A**) or specific taping.

Standing

Before each attempt to stand and later walk, I would treat Mrs LM with selective movements of trunk, upper and lower extremities (Winter, 1991 **C**), passive and active ranges of extension of the hip while side lying and dorsiflexion and movement of the feet. Treatment should be carried out with and without shoes. The position of the foot on the floor is of great importance and, when treating barefoot, and before deciding on suitable foot supports or orthoses, a towel can be placed under Mrs LM's right foot to help position it correctly. Sometimes a toe spreader can be used (DeSaca et al., 1994 **A**). The instability of Mrs LM's ankle joint may be helped by taping. Associated reactions in the upper extremity should be avoided in all stages of standing, and Mrs LM's left arm should not be allowed to push against the table in front of her. I would treat her with and without back splints (to right, left or both legs), using a waist-high table to support the hands, legs apart with weight transfer, step standing (for Mrs LM it will be easier to start with the left leg in front), standing on tiptoe and, while standing, raise the good arm diagonally to encourage extension of the hip (Davies, 1990 **C**; Edwards, 1996 **C**). My handling and support would always be according to Mrs LM's ability, for example: using my hands to give external support below the axillary area, or resting her arms on my shoulders. In this position I can also relieve some of Mrs LM's body weight and facilitate her performance (Barbeau et al., 1987 **C**). Because of weakness of gluteus medius and maximus, I would stand in close proximity to Mrs LM's body, keeping the hip joint in normal alignment and enabling the muscles to function better. Standing and walking are made up of many different components of movement (Winstein et al., 1989 **A**), therefore, when practising the stance phase, in order to imitate this component of gait, inertia must be taken into account by bringing the trunk and the swinging leg forward.

Following treatment in the stance phase I would now, using all these starting positions, introduce components of movement in the swing phase. The healthy side is also affected and frequently there is difficulty in transferring weight to this side (Yi-Chung Pai et al., 1994 **A**). As Mrs LM pushed with her left hand and foot it had an adverse effect on her ability to swing the right leg, and this should be treated. After attaining the ability to perform anterior and posterior pelvic tilt when sitting, she should practise this in various standing positions, with knees slightly bent.

Walking

When Mrs LM began walking, using a figure-of-eight bandage to maintain dorsiflexion of the foot and supported by two therapists, all the components of her walking needed to be analysed and the deficiencies treated (Moore et al., 1993 **C**; Mosely, 1993 **C**).

Treatment of Balance

To improve balance when sitting and standing, I would consider the following points:

- Movements should be performed under different conditions, in different surroundings and lighting (Horak, 1997 **C**; Hines and Mercer, 1997 **C**).
- I would advise Mrs LM to practise proactive and reactive balance responses separately (Ragnarsdottis, 1996 **C**).
- Sensory interaction in balance, such as exercising with eyes closed, or while standing on a mattress or both, should be encouraged (Shumway-Cook and Horak, 1986 **C**).
- Ankle, hip and step strategies should be exercised (Horak et al., 1990 **C**; Shumway-Cook and Woollacott, 1995 **C**). According to Maki (Maki and McIlroy, 1997 **C**), 'Change in support strategies (step strategies) are not strategies of last resort, but are often initiated well before the centre of mass is near the stability limits of the base of support'. Jeka (1997 **A**) claimed that in addition to tactile and proprioceptive stimulation of the feet, fingers touching a surface reduces sway considerably. I would use this strategy while treating Mrs LM when sitting and standing.

Mrs LM did not, apparently, display vestibular problems requiring treatment.

Sensory Treatment

Mrs LM has sensory loss in her right arm and leg and quite possibly in the right side of her face, head and trunk. Sensory treatment is very important, to improve not only sensation but also movement (Magnusson et al., 1994 **C**). Sensory treatment can be specific, demanding both attention and concentration (Yekutiel and Guttman, 1993 **A**) and can be introduced as an integral part of motor treatment such as using both hands to drink from a glass or while putting shoes on with the left hand – the patient's right hand, guided by the therapist, will slide gently down the right leg, trouser or sock. Throughout treatment care should be taken to prevent secondary loss and learned non-use (Wolf et al., 1989 **A**; Taub et al., 1993 **A**, 1994).

Implications

The treatment described here is only a beginning of the whole rehabilitation process, which continues in the rehabilitation centre and in the patient's home, with follow up through life. Of course, many questions remain; most importantly, is the treatment described here effective? More research is required before we can answer this question clearly. We also need to know what the effect of treatment is immediately following the event, and whether an early start to treatment produces significant gains. In a recent systematic review, Langhorne et al. (1996 **R**) concluded that more physiotherapy is better than less. If so, how much more and when do we reach maximum effectiveness?

References

Affolter FD (1987) Perception, Interaction and Language. Berlin: Springer Verlag.

Annoni J, Ackerman D, Kesselring J (1990) Respiratory function in chronic hemiplegia. International Disability Studies May: 78–80.

Arsenault AB, Winter AD, Marteniuk RG (1987) Characteristics of muscular function and adaptation in gait. Physiotherapy Canada 39: 1.

Bach-y-Rita P (1987) Recovery from stroke. In Duncan PW, Badke MB (Eds) Stroke Rehabilitation. Year Book Medical Publishers, Ch.3: 79–108.

Bagg SD, Forrest WJ (1988) A biomechanical analysis of scapular rotation during arm abduction in the scapular plane. American Journal of Physical Medicine & Rehabilitation 67: 238–45.

Barbeau H, Weinberg M, Finch L (1987) Description and Application of a System for Locomotor Rehabilitation. Medical and Biological Engineering and Computers 25: 341–4.

Bernstein N (1967) The Co-ordination and Regulation of Movements, 1st edn. London, New York: Pergamon Press.

Bobath B (1990) Adult Hemiplegia: Evaluation and Treatment, 3rd edn. Oxford: Heinemann Medical.

Brimioulle S, Moraine JJ, Norrenberg D, Kahn RJ (1997) Effects of positioning and exercise on intercranial pressure in a neurological intensive care unit. Physical Therapy 77(12): 1682–9.

Brouwer BJ, Ambury P (1994) Upper extremity weight bearing effect on cortical spinal excitability following stroke. Archives of Physical Medicine and Rehabilitation 75: 861–6.

Carr JH, Shepherd RB (1987) A motor learning model for rehabilitation. In Carr JH, Shepherd RB, Gordon J, Gentile AM, Held JM. Movement Science. Aspen Publications, pp 35–92.

Conine T, Sullivan T, Mackie T, Goodman M (1990) Effects of serial casting for the prevention of equinus in patients with acute head injury. Archives of Physical Medicine and Rehabilitation 71(5): 310–21.

Crawford HJ, Jull GA (1993) The influence of thoracic posture and movement on range of arm elevation. Physiotherapy Theory and Practice 9: 143–8.

Culham EG, Noce RR, Bagg SD (1995) Shoulder complex position and glenohumeral subluxation in hemiplegia. Archives of Physical Medicine and Rehabilitation 76: 857–63.

Davies PM (1985) Steps to Follow. Berlin, Heidelberg: Springer-Verlag.

Davies PM (1990) Right in the Middle. Berlin, Heidelberg: Springer-Verlag.

Davies PM (1994) Starting Again. Berlin, Heidelberg: Springer-Verlag.

Dean E (1997) Oxygen transport deficits in systemic disease and implications for physical therapy. Physical Therapy 77(2): 187–202.

Dean E, Frewnfelter D (1996) Clinical Case Study Guide to Accompany Principles and Practice of Cardiopulmonary Physical Therapy, 3rd edn. St Louis, Mo: Mosby, 222–31.

DeSaca LR, Catlin PA, Segal RL (1994) Immediate effects of the toe spreader on the tonic toe flexion reflex. Physical Therapy 74(6): 561–70.

Desrosiers J, Bourbonnais DJ, Bravo G, Roy PM, Guay M (1996) Performance of the unaffected upper extremity of elderly stroke patients. Stroke 27: 1564–70.

Dewald JPA (1987) Sensorimotor and the basis of neurofacilitation therapeutic techniques. In Murray E, Brandstater JV, Basmaijan JV (Eds) Stroke Rehabilitation. Baltimore, MD: Williams & Wilkins, 5: 109–83.

Dunn V, Brown C, McGuigan A (1994) The ecology of human performance: a framework for considering the effect of context. American Journal of Occupational Therapy 48: 595–607.

Dvir Z, Panturin E (1993) Measurement of spasticity and associated reactions in stroke patients before and after physiotherapeutic intervention. Clinical Rehabilitation 7: 15–21.

Dvir Z, Panturin E, Prop I (1996) The effect of graded effort on the severity of associated reactions in hemiplegic patients. Clinical Rehabilitation 10: 95–8.

Edwards S (Ed) (1996) Neurological Rehabilitation. Edinburgh: Churchill Livingstone.

Faghri PD, Rodgers MM, Glaser RM, Bors JG, Ho C, Akuthota P (1994) The effects of FES on shoulder subluxation. Archives of Physical Medicine 75(6): 73–9.

Fisher CM (1992) Concerning the mechanism of recovery in stroke hemiplegia. Canadian Journal of Neurological Science 19(1): 57–63.

Franchignoni FP, Tesio L, Ricupero C, Martino MT (1997) Trunk control test as an early predictor of stroke rehabilitation outcome. Stroke 28(7): 382–5.

Gardiner R (1996) The pathophysiology and clinical implications of neuro-muscular changes following cerebro-vascular accident. Australian Physiotherapy 42(2): 139–47.

Gentile AM (1987) Skill Acquisition: action, movement and neuromotor processes. In Carr JH, Shepherd RB, Gordon J, Gentile AM, Held JM. Movement Science. Aspen Publications, pp 93–117.

Haley SM, Caster WJ, Binda-Sundberg K (1994) Measuring physical disablement: the contextual challenge. Physical Therapy 74: 443–51.

Held JM (1987) Recovery of function after brain damage: theoretical implications for therapeutic intervention. In Carr JH, Shepherd RB, Gordon J, Gentile AM, Held JM. Movement Science. Aspen Publications, pp 157–73.

Herdman SJ (1997) Advances in the treatment of vestibular disorders. Physical Therapy 77(6): 602–18.

Herman WM (1992) Spatial neglect: new issues and their implications for occupational therapy pactice. American Journal of Occupational Therapy 46(3): 207–15.

Higgins S (1991) Motor skill acquisitions. Physical Therapy 71(2): 123–39.

Hines C, Mercer V (1997) Anticipatory postural adjustments: an update. Neurology Report, Neurology Section, American Physical Therapy Association 21(1): 17–21.

Hodges P, Richardson C, Jull G (1996) Evaluation of the relationship between laboratory and clinical tests of transversus abdominis function. Physiotherapy Research International 1(1): 30–40.

Hodges P, Richardson C (1997) Contraction of the abdominal muscles associated with movement of the lower limb. Physical Therapy 77(2): 132–43.

Horak FB (1997) Postural pertubations: new insights for treatment of balance disorder. Physical Therapy 77(5): 517–33.

Horak FB, Nashner LM, Dener HC (1990) Postural strategies associated with somatosensory and vestibular loss. Experimental Brain Research 82: 167–77.

Jackson J (1998) Specific treatment techniques. In Stokes M (Ed) Neurological Physiotherapy. London: Mosby, 24: 299–311.

Jeka JJ (1997) Light touch contact as a balance aid. Physical Therapy 77(5): 476–87.

Karnath HD, Sievering D, Fetter M (1994) The interactive contribution of neck muscle proprioception and vestibular stimulation to subjective straight ahead orientation in man. Experimental Brain Research 101: 140–6.

Kidd G, Lawes N, Musa I (1992). Understanding Neuromuscular Plasticity. London: Edward Arnold (Hodder & Stoughton).

Kumar R, Metter EJ, Mehta AJ, Chow T (1990) Shoulder pain in hemiplegia (the role of exercise). American Journal of Physical Medicine and Rehabilitation 69(4): 205–8.

Langhorne P, Wagenaar R, Partridge C (1996) Physiotherapy after stroke: more is better? Physiotherapy Research International 2: 75–88.

Laynt RL (1992) The source of shoulder pain in hemiplegia. Archives of Physical Medicine and Rehabilitation 73: 409–13.

Lee RG, Van Donkelaar P (1995) Mechanisms underlying functional recovery following stroke. Canadian Journal of Neurological Sciences 22(4): 257–63.

Le Vere TE (1980) Recovery of function after brain damage: a theory of the behavioral deficit. Journal of Physiology & Psychology 8: 297–308.

Magnusson M, Johannson K, Johannson BB (1994) Sensory stimulation promotes normalization of postural control after stroke. Stroke 25: 1176–80.

Maki BE, McIlroy WE (1997) The role of limb movements in maintaining upright stance: the change-in-support strategy. Physical Therapy 77(5): 487–507.

Miltner WHR, Bauder H, Sommer M, Dettmer SC, Taub E (1999) Effects of constraint induced movement therapy on patients with chronic motor deficits after stroke. Stroke 30: 586–92.

Moodie NB, Brisbin J, Morgan AMG (1986) Subluxation of the glenohumeral joint in hemiplegia: evaluation of supportive devices. Physiotherapy Canada 38(3): 155–7.

Moore S, Schurr K, Wales A, Mosely A, Herbert R (1993) Observation and analysis of hemiplegic gait: swing phase. Australian Physiotherapy 39(4): 270–8.

Moseley AM (1993) The effect of a regimen of casting and prolonged stretching on passive ankle dorsiflexion in traumatic head-injured adults. Physiotherapy Theory & Practice 9(4): 215–21.

Mulder T (1991) Process-oriented model of human motor behavior: toward a theory-based rehabilitation approach. Physical Therapy 71(2): 157–64.

Panturin E (1998) Adverse neural tension. In: Stokes M (Ed) Neurological Physiotherapy. St Louis, Mo: Mosby, pp 287–91.

Park S, Fisher AG, Velozo CA (1994) Using the assessment of motor and process skills to compare occupational performance between clinic and home setting. American Journal of Occupational Therapy 48(8): 697–709.

Perry SB (1998) Clinical implications of a dynamic system theory. Neurology Report, Neurology Section, American Physical Therapy Association 22(1): 4–10.

Pillar T, Dickstein R, Smolinski Z (1991) Walking reeducation with partial relief of body weight in rehabilitation of patients with locomotor disabilities. Journal of Rehabilitation Research and Development 28(4): 47–52.

Pobl PS, Dunn W (1998) Ecology of human performance: application to physical therapy. Neurology Report, Neurology Section, American Physical Therapy Association 22(1): 11–15.

Pouran D, Faghri PD, Roders MM, Glaser RM, Bors JG, Ho C, Akufhota P (1994) The effects of functional electrical stimulation on shoulder subluxation, arm function recovery and shoulder pain in hemiplegic stroke patients. Archives of Physical Medicine and Rehabilitation 75: 73–9.

Prevost R et al. (1987) Shoulder subluxation in hemiplegia: a radiological correlation study. Archives of Physical Medicine and Rehabilitation 68: 782–5.

Ragnarsdottis M (1996) The concept of balance. Physiotherapy 82(6): 368–75.

Richardson DLA (1991) The use of the tilt table to effect passive tendo-Achilles stretch in a patient with head injury. Physiotherapy Theory and Practice 7: 45–50.

Riddoch MJ, Humphreys GW, Bateman A (1995) Cognitive deficits following stroke. Physiotherapy 81(8): 465–73.

Rothwell J (1994) Control of Human Voluntary Movement. London: Chapman & Hall.

Ryerson S, Levit K (1997) Functional Movement Re-education. Edinburgh: Churchill Livingstone, Ch 7, pp 218–26, Ch 9, pp 306–7.

Schmidt RA (1975) A schema theory of discrete motor skill learning. Psychology Review 82: 225–60.

Schenkman M, Shipp KM, Chandler J, Studenski SA, Kuchibhalta M (1996) Relationships between mobility of axial structures and physical performance. Physical Therapy 76(3): 272–85.

Shumway-Cook A, Horak FB (1986) Assessing the influence of sensory interaction on balance. Physical Therapy 10: 1548–50.

Shumway-Cook A, Woollacott M (1995) Motor Control. London: Williams & Wilkins, pp 402–3.

Taub E, Crago JE, Burgio LD, Groomes TE, Cook EW, Deluca SC, Miller NE (1993) An operant approach to rehabilitation medicine: overcoming learned non-use by shaping. Journal of Neurology, Neurosurgery & Psychiatry 53: 208–14.

Taub E, Miller NE, Novack TA, Cook EW, Fleming WC, Nepomuceno CS, Connell JC, Crago JE (1994) Technique to improve chronic motor deficit after stroke. Archives of Physical Medicine & Rehabilitation 74: 347–54.

Thilman AF, Fellows SJ, Garms E (1990) Pathological stretch reflexes on the 'good' side of hemiparetic patients. Journal of Neurology, Neurosurgery & Psychiatry 53: 208–14.

Tokizane T, Murac M, Ogata T, Kendo T (1951) Electromyographic studies on tonic neck, lumbar and labyrinthine reflexes in normal persons. Japanese Journal of Physiology 2: 130–146.

Vliet P et al. (1995) The influence of functional goals in the kinematics of reaching following stroke. Neurology Report, Neurology Section, American Physical Therapy Association 19(1): 11–16.

Wiart L, Bon Saint Come A, Debelleix X, Petit H, Joseph PA, Mazaux JM, Barat M (1997) Unilateral neglect syndrome rehabilitation by trunk rotation and scanning training. Archives of Physical Medicine and Rehabilitation 78(4): 424–9.

Wilson VJ, Schor RH, Suzuki I, Park BR (1986) Spatial organization of neck and vestibular reflexes acting on the forelimbs of the decerebrate cat. Journal of Neurophysiology 55(3): 514–26.

Winstein CJ (1987) Motor learning considerations in stroke rehabilitation. In Duncan PW, Badke MB (Eds) Stroke Rehabilitation. Year Book Medical Publishers.

Winstein CJ (1991) Knowledge of results and motor learning implications for physical therapy. Physical Therapy 71(2): 140–9.

Winstein CJ, Gardner ER, McNeal DR, Barto PS, Nicholson DE (1989) Standing balance training: effect on balance and locomotion in hemiparetic adults. Archives of Physical Medicine & Rehabilitation 70: 755–62.

Winstein CJ, Pohl PS, Cardinale C, Green A, Scholtz L, Waters CS (1996) Learning a partial-weight-bearing skill: effectiveness of two forms of feedback. Physical Therapy 76: 985–93.

Winter SL (1991) The Biomechanics and Motor Control of Human Gait. University of Waterloo Press.

Wolf SL, Lecraw DE, Barton LA, Jann BB (1989) Forced use of hemiplegic upper extremities to reverse the effect of learned nonuse among chronic stroke and head-injured patients. Experimental Neurology 104: 125–32.

Wyke B (1979) Neurology of the cervical spinal joints. Physiotherapy 65(3): 72–6.

Yekutiel M, Guttman E (1993) A controlled trial of the retraining of the sensory function of the hand in stroke patients. Journal of Neurology, Neurosurgery & Psychiatry 56(3): 241–4.

Yi-Chung Pai, Rogers MW, Hedman LD, Hanke TA (1994) Alterations in weight transfer capabilities in adults with Hemiplegia. Physical Therapy 74(7): 647–60.

Later Rehabilitation of a Stroke Patient

FIONA JONES

Introduction

There are several factors to be taken into consideration about the history of Mrs LM's present condition that may affect her long-term outcome and the potential for further improvement. It is now five months post-incident, and there is some level of agreement that most recovery takes place within the first three months (Wade and Wood, 1985 **A**; Lindmark, 1988 **A**; Taub et al., 1994 **A**). This is by no means absolute and Dam (Dam et al., 1993 **A**) suggests that prolonged rehabilitation can produce significant gains in gait and activities of daily living (ADL) up to one year post-incident. A number of key factors have nonetheless been recognized as providing predictive information about likely level of recovery (Jongbloed, 1986 **A**; Alexander, 1994 **A**). These may help to influence decisions about treatment.

The level of motor activity Mrs LM had at 33 weeks was minimal, with presumably no measurable function in the upper limb; this is a poor prognostic indicator for regaining function of the arm at a later stage (Parker et al., 1986 **A**; Heller et al., 1987 **A**). However, Mrs LM is only 29 years old, and although age on its own cannot be viewed as a simple predictor, there is a reduced likelihood of pre-existing disease and disability affecting the starting conditions for recovery (Benbow et al., 1994 **A**; Nakayama et al., 1994 **A**; Ashburn, 1997 **C**). Therefore she may be able to tolerate more intensive therapy and adapt to different environments and positions.

General Principles

It appears that Mrs LM has had an extensive haemorrhage and subsequent infarction affecting the area surrounding the basal ganglia; the site of the lesion can be critical in determining adaptive recovery and functional potential (Shah et al., 1990 **A**). In addition, Mrs LM also had a period of raised intracranial pressure (ICP), which could have potentially led to areas of infarction. There is no detailed scan report available, and this would be essential information to determine level of damage accurately (WHO, 1989 **A**). The diversity of problems described in the early weeks post-haemorrhage would suggest problems in the frontal, parietal and possibly occipital areas, together with the confirmed damage to the basal ganglia. This might lead one to envisage problems with the association areas of the brain, problems with automaticity of movement, and integration of postural responses and motor patterns (Cohen, 1993 **C**).

A factor that will have to be taken into account is the additional emotional distress Mrs LM will be suffering at not being able to interact with her baby and assume her previous social, family and leisure roles; this will no doubt have a tremendous effect on her self-esteem and motivation. These may all influence adherence to more therapy (Henley et al., 1985 **A**).

Five months post-incident Mrs LM was discharged home with some severe problems remaining. The length of time in a hospital setting, with loss of normal interactions and routine, will have meant deprivation at an environmental, behavioural and emotional level. The possible long-term psychological and social effects can in themselves be more disabling than the physical effects (Greveson et al., 1991 **A**); it is therefore essential to have an acute awareness of, and sensitivity to, these issues.

Mrs LM has many functional difficulties, others must care for her baby, she is dependent for personal care and all domestic tasks, and she wishes to be more independent; these may all be used as motivational factors in her physiotherapy programme of treatment. The World Health Organization (1989) recommends that the true purpose of rehabilitation is the integration of the patient into their family, work and social environment. The community phase of Mrs LM's rehabilitation is therefore well placed to address these objectives.

Factors such as mood state, self-esteem, compliance with treatment regimens, length of time in hospital, and significant changes to her previous role within the home may all be influential in determining potential for regaining functional level (Partridge et al., 1993 **A**). I would wish to establish which of these areas are priorities for this woman. A belief in a greater degree of personal control over recovery has been shown to be beneficial (Partridge and Johnston, 1989 **A**) and this would be important to consider. A starting point of treatment, therefore, would be a joint goal-setting session with Mrs LM and her family. If therapy is to be successful it needs to fit with the goals and values of the patient being treated (Haas, 1993 **A**). Reid and Chesson (1998 **A**) reviewed the use of goal attainment scaling (GAS) and suggested that it may result in treatment being more focused, and enable enhanced decision-making skills in the light of treatment priorities. McGrath and Davis (1992 **C**) suggest that a vital part of successful rehabilitation is the moving together of the client's and the professional's goals. Careful identification of Mrs LM's expectations and the desires and factors which motivate her to persevere is essential. This may not be achieved within the initial few sessions but I would envisage a continued reviewing and discussion of the appropriateness of her chosen goals.

At what levels will the treatment be focused? Clinical Consensus (1998 **C**) suggests that physiotherapists frequently mix the treatment of both disability and impairment, at whatever stage post-stroke. Lennon (Lennon and Hastings, 1997 **C**) suggests that most physiotherapists recognize two stages in stroke care. The initial phase focuses on impairment, and the second phase on disability and handicap. This information may help to influence the nature of goals set, and information discussed with Mrs LM and her family about likely changes at a functional level.

Langhorne et al. (1996 **A**) undertook a systematic review of randomized controlled trials (RCT) of physiotherapy and found that a reduction in impairment and disability was possible with more intensive physiotherapy, but this change was transient and of a limited scale. Bethune (1994 **C**) cites Back-y-Rita when suggesting that recovery of comprehensive long-term goals may be achieved as late as five years post-onset. This evidence seems to support the possibility of improvement in disability at a later stage, but not specific improvement in impairment.

Recovery of function may occur, however, in periods of acquisition alternating with periods of consolidation (Bethune, 1994 **C**). This raises the question of the timing of intervention: the acute phase may be the time for Mrs LM's spontaneous recovery but would intervention in the later stages aid reacquisition and consolidation over a longer time period?

Baseline measurement, at the levels of impairment, disability and handicap using valid, reliable, sensitive outcome measurements (Wade, 1988 **C**) will help inform overall management of Mrs LM. The Rivermead Motor Assessment Scale has been tested more vigorously than most other published assessments of motor function (Adams et al., 1997), and would be one of my preferred clinical measurements. It does not, however, address such issues as successful activities of daily living (ADL) and quality of life that may be more important at this stage. As Mrs LM is still involved in active rehabilitation, I would include it as part of an assessment battery. Turner-Stokes (Turner-Stokes and Turner-Stokes, 1997 **C**) advocated the need for a 'basket of measures' to be available, accepting that no one instrument is suitable across all services and settings. The interpretation of assessment findings, and the quest for the reasons behind patterns of motor dysfunction, will help to guide where treatment begins.

Functional movement could be dependent on biomechanical factors such as joint range and adaptive shortening (Carr and Shepherd, 1998 **C**). Nonetheless, upper limb function would be dependent on developing both strength and dexterity (Ada et al., 1996 **A**), both of which would require normal relationship between joints and musculature. I would therefore envisage using some form of stretching, and positioning to prevent adaptive shortening. The history suggests a persistent tightness in the tendo-calcaneus and triceps surae – why? Is it due to the alteration in tonal responses due to the initial neural component because of reduced supraspinal control, or has the hypertonicity resolved and is she left with intrinsic changes to the muscle which have led to stiffness and contracture? Either way, one or a combination of both may affect the ability to facilitate normal ankle movement that is necessary for postural responses such as sway (Scrutton et al., 1996 **A** – single case study). The relationship between involuntary muscle behaviour and functional disability remains largely hypothetical. It may therefore be of questionable value to give priority to reducing tone at this stage as it would not necessarily lead to greater function (Ada et al., 1998 **A**).

Dvir and Panturin (1993 **A**) examined methods of measuring spasticity and associated reactions before and after treatment according to the 'Bobath' approach, in a controlled non-randomized trial of 33 hemiplegic patients. Their findings suggested not only a significant reduction in 'associated reactions' but also an improvement in the level of ADL following treatment. The Bobath approach places much emphasis on the inhibition of pathological patterns and compensations (Bobath, 1990 **C**). Measurement of tone reduction may go some way to confirming the effectiveness of the Bobath approach, especially in view of the paucity of evidence supporting its efficacy as a treatment choice. Treating spasticity *per se* may have no functional relevance to Mrs LM. There is also an increasing body of evidence to support the use of specific strength training, and the notion that this may have a detrimental effect on spasticity is now being questioned (Sharp and Brouwer, 1997 **A**). If there is merit in trying to reduce the spasticity, and if this is important to Mrs LM, then a method of evaluating change may be useful to use as part of the assessment battery in order to evaluate change. However, Haas et al. (1996 **A**), found that the Ashworth Scale – one of the few available, in both the original and modified versions – was unreliable for measuring spasticity in the ankle.

From the previous history it appears that Mrs LM has a significant problem of visuo-spatial processing and difficulty with integration of sensory information. Prognosis is suggested to be poorer with patients suffering right hemisphere damage when associated with attentional dysfunction or proprioceptive loss (Riddoch et al., 1995 **C**). Consideration must be given to factors such as arousal, attention and memory for successful rehabilitation. It seems implausible that the earlier perceptual and cognitive dysfunctions have completely resolved by five months and it would therefore seem inappropriate to focus solely on the physical problems. This raises other issues such as compartmentalization of treatment and the need to work jointly with other rehabilitation professionals such as psychologists, speech and language therapists and occupational therapists.

The question of how much Mrs LM should be purposefully trying to guide and control her movements will be paramount in her management whichever treatment approach is followed. If one is working at the level of integration and facilitation of automatic responses, such as the Bobath approach, then the level of involvement, particularly cognitive, may be discouraged. However, it is questionable whether an alternative approach such as the motor learning model of Carr and Shepherd (1998 **C**) demonstrates sufficient evidence. Both approaches are concerned with the re-education of normal movement but as yet there have been no sound trials to compare the effectiveness of these widely accepted therapeutic methods. Some attempts have been made to examine neurodevelopmental or neurophysiological methods against 'traditional' treatment (Logigian et al., 1983 **A**; Dickstein et al., 1986 **A**; Brunham and Snow, 1992 **A** – single case study). However, most of these studies fail to define specific parameters of the treatment techniques and should therefore be interpreted with caution.

There is a degree of volition in most normal movement and the level at which that volition and specific training can be incorporated into the treatment programme has yet to be evaluated. I am sure that in practice the level of active participation is an individualistic and dynamic state dependent on individual responses and skill of the physiotherapist (Clinical Consensus, 1998 **C**). My own personal view, having had some experience of using different approaches, would be to use whichever method elicited the most positive reaction during therapy sessions, and the techniques Mrs LM sensed were being most effective. I would therefore adopt an eclectic approach.

The effects of disempowerment and the feeling of lack of involvement in therapy should not be underestimated if the ultimate aim is the ability to transfer changes made to the home setting and daily routines.

Treatment and Management

Assessment prior to treatment would not only include undertaking a range of measurements already mentioned, but also paying particular attention to the environment and social set-up. Issues such as height of chairs and bed, access to such things as the garden, and bathing could be jointly assessed with the occupational therapist. I would consider it part of my responsibility to inform others or refer for help regarding other important issues such as ongoing medical support, home care and financial advice. There would also be a unique opportunity to assess interaction with her family and her specific difficulties of coping with a new disability at home, together with levels of help provided.

One starting point may be the use of a position which is not too demanding but one in which there is some facilitation of her postural responses, such as equilibrium reactions. This may then provide the greater postural stability required for using her arm (Davies, 1990 **C**; Edwards, 1996 **C**). There will not be access to variable height plinths and tables, and rehabilitation will relate directly to her home environment. The kitchen may be one place to start as it is an environment where Mrs LM may wish to gain some feeling of independence and control, and practise using positions of standing and perched sitting. Using variability in handling and making demands of postural responses is suggested to be necessary in order to avoid her being inactive and passive during treatment. The prudent and skilful use of handling techniques is encouraged in the Bobath concept in order to promote normal afferent input and postural tone, resulting in experience of normal movement patterns (Plant, 1998 **C**). If trunk and shoulder girdle activity can be achieved through careful facilitation it might be possible to guide the right arm through a functional task such as reaching for a cup or wiping the kitchen worksurface. 'Guiding' is a concept specifically described by Affolter, in which there is always a meaningful goal for the patient (Neilson, 1995 **C**). The practice of a motor task in its entirety, explanation and demonstration are also key components of motor relearning (Carr and Shepherd, 1998 **C**). In this way, specific named approaches tend to merge together, and continuation and development of a technique will largely depend on the responses achieved.

I would use a functional goal to aim for during treatment, such as using Mrs LM's affected arm to stabilize her body whilst reaching with the left arm, and I would relate to her desired functions. There may also be some benefit in providing bilateral practice of functional tasks as opposed to unilateral (Mudie and Matyas, 1996 **A**), for example drinking from a cup holding it with two hands. I would ideally have addressed important prerequisites of function such as length of soft tissues, joint range, alignment and relationship with any observable movement patterns prior to beginning functional practice. However, I could find no clear evidence of efficacy of the commonly used methods of preparation such as 'specific inhibitory mobilizations'(SIMS) prior to active participation and functional practice. The notion of spending the whole session passively mobilizing musculature would surely not provide Mrs LM with a sense of successful function, which would ideally be relevant to her own individual goals.

Mrs LM's arm may have no real 'purpose' for the rest of her body. To use aspects of a sensorimotor programme with the upper limb, as described by Bleton and Odier (1994 **C**), involving feeling and touching a variety of textures and objects, may help to provide some proprioceptive input and feedback to the cerebellum and brainstem. On the basis of the literature it may never be possible to regain functional use of the arm; however, none of us can discount the possibility that change may occur and to disregard the arm in treatment would seem inappropriate (Clinical Consensus, 1998 **C**). Sensory mapping and sensory integrative methods, particularly for face, hands and feet, may well be useful to leave as ideas for practice at home; for example, holding a variety of objects in the hand, and passively guiding the hand to feel, along with specific application of sensory techniques to the face, hand and foot. These areas will no doubt have been deprived of the usual wealth of sensory input, and in order for the CNS to begin to recognize input and integrate a response, it may be beneficial to give this aspect particular priority.

There may be many tasks that require analysis and treatment intervention to encourage more active involvement and integration of postural responses in movement. Is each task analysed and dealt with separately, or is the treatment a continuum of handling and moving which will allow for an automatic translation into many different situations? Experience and clinical consensus (Clinical Consensus, 1998; Plant, 1998 **C**) confirms the use of an eclectic approach that suits the individual problems and needs of the patient. It may be that working at a cognitive level, and 'learning' the sequences of a movement, for example getting out of bed, will reap greater changes (Carr and Shepherd, 1998 **C**; Carr, 1998 **C**). In a sequence of movement such as moving in bed, which involves a variety of postural and motor demands, I would initially envisage a fairly low level of active involvement from Mrs LM. This may be one of the first times her problem has been addressed on a normal mattress and in a known environment. Facilitating movement from supine to side lying and through into sitting, and returning, with minimal effort may help to provide the experience of normal postural responses. It may then be possible, once a pattern or technique of movement is established, that one could progress to reducing handling input, and encouraging more active participation. Eventually it may be possible to achieve a degree of independence, with or without the use of key handling or cueing.

The effects on the abnormal posturing of Mrs LM's foot whilst moving between positions may be a cause for separate consideration. At five months there is still what appears to be a positive support reaction (Bobath, 1990 **C**), with a tendency for tightness in the triceps surae muscles. If there is an additional scenario of hypertonicity that is compounded by effort, struggle and subsequent 'associated reactions', then a reduction in effort when moving between positions may improve matters. If Mrs LM's abnormal posturing flexion has become a habitual response and is causing concern, I would request assessment by a neurophysiologist. This would be to determine whether there was abnormally high activity in the triceps surae muscles, especially during walking, as identified by EMG. In that event she may be helped by a Botulinum toxin injection (Bti). Scrutton et al. (1996 **A** – single case study) described good short-term results with Bti in a case study of a 26-year-old man with an established positive support reaction. Further research in this area is ongoing in the form of an RCT, but its use is becoming more widely available and requested as an adjunct to treatment by neurological physiotherapists (Clinical Consensus, 1998 **C**). Mrs LM will no doubt want to achieve a high level of mobility both in and outdoors, and ideally be able to walk on a variety of surfaces. The demands that this will place on her balance would make this an avenue well worth pursuing.

Changes in the treatment environment may work in different ways. If an approach has been chosen where the aim is for transference of normal responses, it would be applicable to practise in different rooms of the house, and to look more closely at her daily routine, particularly interaction with her children. How could this be facilitated to be beneficial to both mother and children? By spending time working down on the floor, perhaps playing with her baby, or helping her older child to draw or read. Potentially this may require greater use of so-called 'abnormal compensatory strategies' but it will need to be addressed if she is to gain confidence in handling and moving not only herself but her children.

Reassessment at the End of Therapy

It may well be appropriate to change the goals during the intervention period, and a record of achievement of goals may be helpful to encourage adherence to the treatment regimen and continued motivation towards co-operating with therapy. I would also choose to reassess at all the levels mentioned, that is impairment, disability and handicap. It may also be worth considering use of quality of life measures such as the Dartmouth COOP (Nelson et al., 1987), particularly looking at areas such as social interaction, intellectual stimulation and work and leisure.

Following reassessment and a period of re-evaluation of the interventions, joint planning with Mrs LM, her family and others significantly involved in her care would be useful to outline the issues to be tackled during the next phase of treatment.

The following questions may be considered after the first phase of treatment:

- What did Mrs LM find most useful? What is unchanged or has the potential to deteriorate?
- What level should she should try to work for during the non-intervention period?
- Does the family wish for instructions and advice? This could lead to discussion of a level of possible activity to aim for during each day.
- Are specific tasks given to practise? There may well be a difference of opinion amongst therapists as to whether as soon as Mrs LM is asked 'to practise' a task the basis for normal movement is being changed, that is, the movement then becomes purely volitional. In this case I would be guided by (a) what Mrs LM feels motivated to practise; (b) how this could be guided to provide maximum therapeutic benefit; and (c) how it can be integrated into her daily routine. In this way a suitable home programme could be devised and updated as appropriate.

Esmonde and McGinley (1997 **A**) studied patients on a stroke ward and found an association between level of motor ability and the observation of motor activity in unstructured time. This suggests that general activity levels are important, not simply what is practised in physiotherapy – which is only for a limited time. This may support the use of home as the most appropriate environment for rehabilitation as there would be greater opportunity for activity and involvement in daily tasks. It would also endorse the notion that therapy is not just what happens when the physiotherapist is present.

Delivery and Timing of Intervention

There may be consensus amongst professionals that it is possible to make some small change at impairment or disability level in almost every patient. A change in function such as walking can in some cases be achieved even at a later stage (Collen and Wade, 1991 **A**) and the potential for further improvement should not be discounted. The validity of treatment approaches, the individualistic nature of a stroke and the therapist's own personal skill mean that quantifying and justifying choice of treatment approaches is extremely difficult. If we consider the scenario that, following some intervention, Mrs LM has achieved a visible change in activity in shoulder girdle musculature, she is able to move further out of her base of support in sitting and some postural responses are beginning to show in her trunk, what use does this have long term? In order to progress, the treatment must not stand still, with demands on the CNS constantly needed. The motivational element of working towards the patient's chosen task, together with involvement in active problem-solving (Thorsteinsdottir, 1995 **C**), may help to afford some carry-over so that these changes are incorporated. However, the evidence is unclear as to the stage during a treatment when the patient may have to use abnormal compensatory movement. Five months post-stroke may be the time for use of compensation. Theories such as ipsilateral innervation and somatotrophic reorganization suggest that potential for functional recovery is present in all patients but will depend largely on the amount of damage incurred. Lee and Van Donkelaar (1995 **B**) argue, however, that more work is required to establish approaches that provide a more significant influence on these processes. This emphasis on the neurophysiological basis for recovery could be considered a narrow view, and one needs to consider the effect that the injury has on the wider context of life, for example the patient's role within the family and the ability to make a positive contribution to relationships with her family members. The idea of facilitating a level of function that allows for continued improvement and, possibly more importantly, avoids deterioration in functional level, is not to be underestimated, and if a functional goal is achieved ways can be found to enable further progression and improvement. The idea of incorporating Mrs LM's affected upper limb could be carried into every situation, even if it is a passive participant.

The amount of treatment is a contentious issue. Enhanced therapy has been shown to give a small but statistically significant advantage in recovery of arm function (Sunderland et al., 1992 **A**). However, this trial excluded over 60% of stroke patients admitted and its results should therefore be viewed cautiously. The ideal situation is often considered to be the opportunity to deliver therapy intensively. In reality it may well impose on the dynamics of family life. It is for this reason that it may be beneficial to discuss with Mrs LM what method will suit her own routine and aspirations, and through this work towards a compromise that also fits with the realistic workload of the therapist. I am assuming for this reason that the treatment will be arranged to be carried out through an 'intensive burst' delivery. Clear short-term goals will be set at the beginning of each period of treatment, for example perhaps daily for four weeks, and then four weeks off treatment to work on the changes that have been made during the treatment time. These ideas are purely arbitrary, and may well not be suitable for Mrs LM. However, this method of delivery may allow for a balance between the demands for therapy and the need for her to integrate it into some form of role within the family. Very little work has been carried out looking at the timing and continuation of physiotherapy intervention long term. These suggestions are being made on the basis of my own experience of managing a community neurological caseload long term, feedback I have had from neurological clients, available evidence and Clinical Consensus (1998 **C**). I am also assuming that there will be the opportunity for some form of supervision of functional tasks, by the family and the therapy helper, and occupational therapy input to address some of the particular domestic and social problems described.

At some stage it may be appropriate to move the emphasis away from physiotherapy as the only 'therapy' and move towards reintegration into some of her previous roles. The use of general exercise may be appropriate. There is a body of evidence to link inactivity with cardiovascular disease (Blair, 1996 **A**), and it might be worth assessing general levels of activity and fitness. Despite the unsuitability of some gym equipment, it may be possible to arrange a joint visit to a gym to assess whether there are any appropriate activities that can incorporate graded strength training and a rise in heart rate beneficial to general fitness. It may well be possible to incorporate use of equipment such as a treadmill. Evidence has suggested that this may help to improve such parameters as single-limb stance loading (Hassid et al., 1997 **A**) and may facilitate the automatic postural adjustments necessary for walking. It would be worth pursuing this only if Mrs LM is well motivated to comply, and rates it as a priority in terms of her own and her family's time.

One other issue to consider would be the provision of an ankle–foot orthosis (AFO), particularly if the problem of plantar flexion is not resolving. Advocates of orthotics would argue that they should not be used as a last resort but as an important adjunct to treatment at all stages. Advantages and disadvantages of different orthoses are well documented (Edwards, 1996 **C**). Hesse et al. (1996 **A** – single case studies) investigated the use of a frequently prescribed AFO on functional gait parameters in a small group of hemiplegic patients. A significant improvement was found in walking velocity, cadence, stride length and gait line of the affected and non-affected foot. The potential benefits should, however, be considered alongside the compliance and wishes of Mrs LM. Use of a temporary AFO and full orthotic assessment may be indicated.

The evidence is inconclusive as to whether physiotherapy *is* effective in stroke rehabilitation over and above factors such as spontaneous recovery (Riddoch et al., 1995 **C**). The choice of treatment approach is largely superseded here by a need to respond to the stage of recovery and the individual needs of Mrs LM.

The general prognosis may be relatively unknown but the knowledge from a number of studies helps to give a range of prognostic indicators, and it is useful to use them alongside individual needs and performance.

It can often be the long-term emotional, psychological and social effects of stroke that are more disabling, and there is a prevalence of unrecognized depression and feelings of social isolation (Greveson et al., 1991 **A**). This confirms the need for ongoing care and support to be available, and not only in the form of physical management. Angeleri et al. (1993 **C**) suggest that results considered by the physiotherapist to be satisfactory do not necessarily parallel the satisfaction of the stroke patient and their family. As Mrs LM's physiotherapist I would need to be aware of what help and support could be provided by other members of the team, together with other agencies such as the Stroke Association and volunteer groups.

The final question, and possibly the most difficult one, would be when to discharge. This again would, it is hoped, be a question addressed jointly between therapist and patient. In my experience it is the initial assessment and planning that is one determinant of successful discharge. A situation whereby Mrs LM does not feel she is ever free of therapy, on the one hand, or a feeling of being abandoned by therapy services, on the other, is clearly to be avoided. One solution may be the offer of ongoing follow-up assessments over time to discuss working towards clearly defined goals and to monitor any change and evolving difficulties.

References

Ada L, Vanttanasilp W, O'Dwyer NJ, Crosbie J (1998) Does spasticity contribute to walking dysfunction after stroke? Journal of Neurology Neurosurgery Psychiatry 64: 628–35.

Ada L, O'Dwyer N, Green J, Yeo W, Neilson P (1996) The nature of the loss of strength and dexterity in the upper limb following stroke. Human Movement Science 15: 671–87.

Adams SA, Pickering RM, Ashburn A, Lincoln NB (1997) The scalability of the Rivermead motor assessment in non-acute stroke patients. Clinical Rehabilitation 11: 52–9.

Alexander MP (1994) Stroke rehabilitation outcome: a potential use of predictive variables to establish levels of care. Stroke 25: 128–34.

Angeleri F, Angeleri V, Foschi N (1993) The influence of depression, social activity, and family stress on functional outcome after stroke. Stroke 24(10): 1478–83.

Ashburn A (1997) Physical recovery following stroke. Physiotherapy 83(9): 480–90.

Baskett J, Broad J, Reekie G (1999) Shared responsibility for ongoing rehabilitation: a new approach to home-based therapy. Clinical Rehabilitation 13: 23–33.

Benbow SJ, Watkins C, Sangster G, Ellul J, Barer D (1994) The availability and reliability of information on the premorbid functional status of stroke patients in hospital. Clinical Rehabilitation 8: 281–5.

Bethune D (1994) Another look at neurological rehabilitation. Australian Journal of Physiotherapy 40(4): 255–62.

Blair SN (1994) Physical activity and cardiovascular disease risk in women. Medicine and Science in Sports and Exercise 28(1): 9–10.

Bleton JP, Odier F (1994) A cognitive approach in the rehabilitation of the upper extremity in hemiplegic stroke patients. In Harrison MA (Ed) Physiotherapy in Stroke Management. New York: Churchill Livingstone, pp 39–48.

Bobath B (1990) Adult Hemiplegia: Evaluation and Treatment, 3rd edn. London: Heinemann Medical Books.

Brunham S, Snow CJ (1992) The effectiveness of neurodevelopmental treatment in adults with neurological conditions: a single subject study. Physiotherapy Theory and Practice 8: 215–22.

Carr JH (1998) Neurological Rehabilitation: Optimising Motor Performance. Oxford: Butterworth-Heinemann.

Carr JH, Shepherd RB (1998) A motor learning model for stroke rehabilitation. Physiotherapy 75: 372–80.

Clinical Consensus (1998) Focus group: senior neurological physiotherapists, Harrowlands Rehabilitation Centre.

Cohen H (1993) Neuroscience for Rehabilitation. Philadelphia: JB Lippincott.

Collen FM, Wade DT (1991) Residual mobility problems after a stroke. International Disability Studies 13(1): 12–15.

Dam M, Tonin P, Casson S, Ermani M, Pizzolato G, Iaia V, Battistin L (1993) The effects of long-term rehabilitation therapy on post-stroke patients. Stroke 24: 1186–91.

Davies PM (1990) Right in the Middle: Selective Trunk Activity in the Treatment of Adult Hemiplegia. Berlin: Springer-Verlag.

Dickstein R, Hocherman S, Pillar T, Shaham R (1986) Stroke rehabilitation: three exercise therapy approaches. Physical Therapy 66: 1233–8.

Dvir Z, Panturin E (1993) Measurement of spasticity and associated reactions in stroke patients before and after physiotherapeutic intervention. Clinical Rehabilitation 7: 15–21.

Edwards S (1996) Neurological Physiotherapy: A Problem Solving Approach. London: Churchill Livingstone.

Esmonde T, McGinley J, Wittwe J, Goldie P, Martin C (1997) Stroke rehabilitation: patient activity during non-therapy time. Australian Journal of Physiotherapy 43(1): 43–51.

Granger CV, Hamilton BB, Fiedler RC (1992) Discharge outcome after stroke rehabilitation. Stroke 23: 978–82.

Greveson CG, Gray CS, French JM, James OFW (1991) Long-term outcome for patients and carers following hospital admission for stroke. Age and Aging 20: 337–44.

Haas BM, Bergstrom E, Jamous A, Bennie A. (1996) The interrater reliability of the original and of the modified Ashworth scale for the assessment of spasticity in patients with spinal cord injury. Spinal Cord 34: S60–S64.

Haas J (1993) Ethical considerations of goal setting for patient care in rehabilitation medicine. American Journal of Physical Medicine and Rehabilitation 74(1): S16–S20.

Harrison MA (Ed) (1995) Physiotherapy in Stroke Management. London: Churchill Livingstone.

Hassid E, Rose D, Commisarow J, Guttry M, Dobkin BH (1997) Improved gait symmetry in hemiparetic patients during body weight-supported treadmill stepping. Journal of Neurological Rehabilitation 11: 21–6.

Heller A, Wade D, Wood VA, Sunderland A, Langton-Hewer R, Ward E (1987) Arm function after stroke: measurement and recovery over the first three months. Journal of Neurology, Neurosurgery and Psychiatry 50: 714–19.

Henley S, Pettit S, Todd-Pokropek A, Tupper AM (1985) Who goes home? Predictive factors in stroke recovery. Journal of Neurology, Neurosurgery and Psychiatry 48: 1–6.

Hesse S, Lueke D, Jahnke MT, Mauritz KH (1996) Gait function in spastic hemiparetic patients walking barefoot, with firm shoes, and with ankle-foot orthosis. International Journal of Rehabilitation Research 19: 133–41.

Jongbloed L (1986) Prediction of function after stroke: a critical review. Stroke 17(4): 765–76.

Langhorne P, Wagenaar R, Partridge C (1996) Physiotherapy after stroke: more is better? Physiotherapy Research International 1: 75–88.

Lee RG, Van Donkelaar P (1995) Mechanisms underlying functional recovery following strokes. Canadian Journal of Neurological Science 5(22): 257–63.

Lennon S, Hastings M (1997) Key physiotherapy indicators for quality of stroke care. Physiotherapy 82(12): 655–64.

Lindmark B (1988) The improvement of different motor functions after stroke. Clinical Rehabilitation 2: 275–83.

Logigian MK, Samuels MA, Falconer J (1983) Clinical exercise trial for stroke patients. Archives of Physical Medicine Rehabilitation 64: 364–7.

Macko RF, DeSouza CA, Tretter LD, Silver KH, Smith GV, Anderson PA, Tomoyasu N, Gorman P, Dengel DR (1997) Treadmill aerobic exercise training reduces the energy expenditure and cardiovascular demands of hemiparetic gait in chronic stroke patients. Stroke 28: 326–30.

McGrath JR, Davis AM (1992) Rehabilitation: where are we going and how do we get there? Clinical Rehabilitation 6: 225–35.

Mudie MH, Matyas TA (1996) Upper extremity retraining following stroke: effects of bilateral practice. Journal of Neurological Rehabilitation 10: 167–84.

Musa I (1986) The role of afferent input in the reduction of spasticity – an hypothesis. Physiotherapy 72(4): 179–82.

Nakayama H, Jorgenson HS, Raaschou HO, Olsen TS (1994) The influence of age on stroke outcome. Stroke 25: 808–13.

Neilsen K (1995) The recollection of my whole body in my brain: physiotherapy based on the Affolter concept. In Harrison MA (Ed) Physiotherapy in Stroke Management. New York: Churchill Livingstone, pp 71–6.

Nelson E, Wasson J, Kirk J, Keller A, Clark D, Dietrich A, Stewart A, Zubkoff M (1987) Assessment of function in routine clinical practice: a description of the COOP chart method and preliminary findings. Journal of Chronic Disease 40: 53s–63s.

Parker VM, Wade D, Langton-Hewer R (1986) Loss of arm function after stroke: measurement, frequency and recovery. International Rehabilitation Medicine 8: 69–73.

Partridge C, Johnston M (1989) Perceived control of recovery from physical disability: measurement and prediction. British Journal of Clinical Psychology 28: 53–9.

Partridge C, Morris LW, Edwards MS (1993) Recovery from physical disability after stroke: profiles for different levels of starting severity. Clinical Rehabilitation 7: 210–17.

Potempa K, Braun LT, Tinknell T, Popovitch J (1996) Benefits of aerobic exercise after stroke. Sports Medicine 5: 337–46.

Reid A, Chesson R (1998) Goal attainment scaling: is it appropriate for stroke patients and their physiotherapists? Physiotherapy 84(3): 136–44.

Riddoch MJ, Humphreys GW, Bateman A (1995) Stroke: issues in recovery and rehabilitation. Physiotherapy 81(11): 689–94.

Scrutton J, Edwards S, Sheean G, Thompson A (1996) A little bit of toxin does you good? Physiotherapy Research International 1(3): 141–7.

Shah S, Vanclay F, Cooper B (1990) Efficiency, effectiveness and duration of stroke rehabilitation. Stroke 21: 241–6.

Sharp SA, Brouwer BJ (1997) Isokinetic strength training of the hemiparetic knee: effects on function and spasticity. Archives of Physical Medicine Rehabilitation 78: 1231–6.

Stokes M (Ed) (1998) Neurological Physiotherapy. London: Mosby.

Sunderland A, Tinson DJ, Bradley EL, Fletcher D, Langton-Hewer R, Wade DT (1992) Enhanced physical therapy improves recovery of arm function after stroke: a randomised controlled trial. Journal of Neurology, Neurosurgery and Psychiatry 55: 530–5.

Taub N, Wolf C, Richardson E, Burney P (1994) Predicting the disability of first time stroke sufferers at one year. Stroke 25: 352–7.

Thorsteinsdottir M (1995) The motor relearning programme: In Harrison MA (Ed) Physiotherapy in Stroke Management. New York: Churchill Livingstone, pp 77–86.

Turner-Stokes L, Turner-Stokes T (1997) The use of standardised outcome measures in rehabilitation centres in the UK. Clinical Rehabilitation 11: 306–13.

Wade D, Wood V, Langton-Hewer R (1985) Recovery after stroke: the first three months. Journal of Neurology, Neurosurgery and Psychiatry 48: 7–13.

Wade D (1988) Measurement in rehabilitation. Age and Aging 17: 289–92.

Wade DT, Collen FM, Robb GF, Warlow CP (1992) Physiotherapy intervention late after stroke and mobility. British Medical Journal 304: 610–13.

World Health Organization (1989) Recommendations on stroke prevention, diagnosis and therapy. Stroke 20(10): 1407–31.

Traumatic head injury

Case report – Mr ND

Background

Mr ND was an 18-year-old man who had run away from Scotland to London and was living in a hostel for young homeless people. He was unemployed, and had not been in contact with his family for at least a year. He was very talented with computers, and loved music. There were no known health problems. Mr ND was hit by a minibus whilst crossing the road.

On Admission to Hospital

- Glasgow Coma Scale was 3/15.
- He was transferred to the intensive care unit where he was intubated, sedated, ventilated.
- Patient reviewed by the neurosurgical team and his prognosis was considered to be poor.
- A right frontal external ventricular drain was inserted to help control the rising intracranial pressure (ICP), which was in the region of 30 mm Hg.
- A nasogastric tube was inserted for nutritional needs.

Mr ND remained relatively unstable with fluctuating vital signs.

Main Diagnoses

Head injury (closed) resulting in a subarachnoid haemorrhage with widespread blood extending into the ventricles, cerebrum and corpus callosum and hydrocephalus. Fractured mandible. Third nerve palsy right. Possible fracture of right clavicle.

Main Incidents

Intensive Care Unit (days 1–8)

Respiratory status:

- Progressed from full ventilation to synchronized intermittent mandatory ventilation, continuous positive airways pressure with T-piece.
- On day 6 a tracheostomy and wiring of the mandible were undertaken.
- His chest was productive of very foul-smelling sputum throughout this period, requiring oxygen therapy (28–35%) to maintain satisfactory saturation levels.

Neurological status: Unable to assess for approximately four days as a result of sedation and paralysis. ICP levels remained > 20 mm for most of the time. As sedation levels were decreased, signs of marked agitation and fluctuating flexion and extension tone in all limbs and extensor tone in the trunk became apparent. A small soft tissue injury of the right malleolus was noted, which was thought to have occurred at the time of injury. Full range of motion could be maintained.

The prognosis remained poor. Contact was made with Mr ND's parents who agreed to organ donation and he was transferred to a neurosurgical ward within the hospital.

Neurosurgical Ward (days 9–20)

Day 9:
Respiratory status:

- High respiratory rate (> 40) and tachycardic (> 150) especially on stimulus.
- Oxygen saturation level of approximately 97%, on 28% oxygen.
- Pyrexia 40°. Secretions thick and bloodstained with an offensive odour.

Neurological status:

- No eye opening, fitting, and extending in response to any stimulus.
- Decision taken by medical team that Mr ND was not appropriate for active management.

Days 10 and 11
Respiratory status:

- Coughing spontaneously. Chest continued to be productive but on ausculation air entry present throughout.
- Blood pressure and pulse stable during treatment.

Neurological status:

- Tone in the lower limbs and trunk now constantly increased and in extension. The upper limbs continued to fluctuate between flexion and extension, although the right showed more sustained flexion.

Days 12–20:
There was a dichotomy of views between therapists and medical staff. Doctors continued to feel very pessimistic with regard to prognosis. Therapists considered a more proactive approach was necessary as the patient's physical status was being compromised.

Summary of Neurological Status (in supine)

- *Head*: tendency to pull into right-side flexion with rotation. Right eye remained shut but with minimal left eye opening to command.
- *Trunk*: over-extension throughout with additional right-side flexion.
- *Pelvis*: tilted anteriorly with obliquity to the left. Right anterior superior iliac spine higher than left.
- *Left arm*: beginning to move spontaneously at all joints. Movement gross and dominated by flexor activity.
- *Right arm*: tendency to be held in internal rotation and adduction at the shoulder. Shoulder girdle elevated and protracted, complicated by a 'sprung' acromion. Elbow, wrist and fingers all dominated by marked flexor tone. No voluntary movement evident.
- *Left leg*: moderate increase in extensor tone throughout. Some evidence of gross flexor movements. Tendo Achilles noted to be –15° to plantargrade, with considerable muscle stiffness on handling.
- *Right leg*: moderate to severe increase in extensor tone with mild adduction at the hip. A loss of –20° to plantargrade at tendo Achilles noted. There was poor carry-over between treatment sessions. No voluntary movement was evident. The sore was still present over right malleolus but much reduced in size.

Mr ND was now stable enough to be stood for short periods of two to three minutes. Five therapists are required to stand him with good alignment. Tendo Achilles became contracted over the weekend because of periods of sustained posturing.

Therapists observed that Mr ND seemed to be attempting to communicate and appeared to be reliable in squeezing a hand for yes and no to simple questions.

Respiratory status: Mr ND now apyrexial, and chest improving, rarely requiring suction.

General Surgical Ward (3 weeks post-injury)

Jaw wire removed, programme of oral desensitization begun and swallow assessment carried out by speech and language therapist. Mr ND makes some attempts at vocalization.

Referral to two different rehabilitation units considered, one in Scotland (parents undecided on their desired level of involvement) and one in London close to his friends.

Respiratory status: Weaning process commenced. Mr ND was extubated on day 31 post-injury.

Neurological Summary

Mr ND continues to require three therapists to enable him to stand. He only tolerates periods of up to five minutes before becoming pale and sweaty, and is unable to sit unsupported.

- *Trunk*: selective lumbar trunk extension achieved for short periods. Tone remains generally low in trunk and pelvis. Pelvis remains 'stiff' into end of range of anterior and posterior tilt. Right-side flexion in trunk is compounded by shortening of muscles, especially latissimus dorsi.
- *Head*: control much improved, but Mr ND continues to show a preference to right side flexion and rotation; his right eye remains closed.
- *Left arm*: full range active movement but with no co-ordination.
- *Right arm*: mild weakness. Movement present at all joints, although the propensity towards flexor activity persists, especially at the elbow. Poor alignment at shoulder girdle, especially at the acromio-clavicular joint. Muscle tightness in the upper fibres of trapezius, pectoralis major and minor, latissimus dorsi and teres major.
- *Left leg*: full range active movement but Mr ND lacks hip stability and there is minimal co-ordination. Tendo Achilles remains slightly short but his heel touches the floor during standing.
- *Right leg*: mild weakness. Voluntary movement throughout range. Mixed tone, but mostly low proximally. Persistent shortening of approximately $-10°$ at the tendo Achilles.

Mr ND's first word spoken – therapist's name! Speech dysarthric.

Memory problems becoming apparent.

Day 40
Mr ND now attending the neurology gym daily for continued rehabilitation from the therapy team. Parents have visited and both he and his parents have expressed a wish for him to return to Scotland for the immediate future.

Transfer to Rehabilitation Unit (2 ½ months post-injury)

Impairments, restriction of activity and participation:

- Mild weakness in right upper limb with altered shoulder girdle alignment.
- Right pelvic instability.
- Decreased balance reactions.
- Persistently tight TAs: left plantargrade, right –5° plantargrade.
- Dysarthric speech.
- Mild memory problems.
- Decreased concentration.
- Partial ptosis right eye.
- Independent in all transfers.
- Able to walk with the minimal assistance of one person.
- Independent with dressing except for buttons and zips.

Respiratory Management of Patient with Traumatic Head Injury

Suzanne Roberts

General Principles

The primary aims of management in closed head injury are the avoidance of secondary insults to the traumatized brain and the stabilization and management of extra-cranial injuries (Andrews et al., 1990 **A**). That is, the avoidance of hypoxaemia (PaO_2 < 8 kPa), hypotension (systolic BP < 90 mmHg) and intracranial hypertension (intracranial pressure > 20 mmHg) and, in addition, the avoidance of hypercapnia ($PaCO_2$ > 6 kPa) (Wilden, 1993 **C**). This is in order to maintain cerebral perfusion and oxygenation in the face of raised intracranial pressure (ICP), which occurs in about 70% of severe head injuries (Bullock and Teasdale, 1990 **C**). In the presence of raised ICP and reduced systemic blood pressure (BP), cerebral perfusion pressure (CPP) will fall below 60 mmHg, resulting in cerebral ischaemia. In the uninjured state the brain regulates its own blood supply and maintains constant perfusion over a wide range of systemic blood pressure but the injured brain is extremely vulnerable to permanent damage resultant from hypotension and hypoxia. Mean arterial blood pressure (MAP) needs to be maintained over 70–80 mmHg, as cerebral perfusion pressure is a product of this minus intracranial pressure:

$$CPP = MAP - ICP$$

Hypercapnia results in cerebral vasodilation, and subsequent increase in cerebral blood volume adversely affects ICP where cerebral oedema is at critical levels. When intracranial pressure rises, cerebrospinal fluid is driven out of the intracranial compartment and if pressure continues to rise brain shift occurs, leading to 'coning'. As compensation fails, the signs of impaired consciousness level-fixed dilated pupils, cardiovascular and respiratory abnormalities – develop and ultimately, if unchecked, death occurs (Bullock and Teasdale, 1990 **C**; Miller, 1991 **C**). Coning can cause third cranial nerve compression, which may have been an issue in this particular patient's case (Bullock and Teasdale, 1990 **C**).

Other medical issues relate to the prevention of seizures, use of full paralysis, elective hyperventilation and hyperosmolar diuretics (Bullock and Teasdale, 1990. C). The extent to which hyperventilation is employed has been the issue of much debate but the consensus in recent literature is that less than 3.3 kPa should be avoided as it may contribute to cerebral ischaemia (Jeevaratnam, 1996 **C**; Matta and Menon, 1996 **C**).

The arrival of a young, previously fit, head-injured man in the intensive care unit will demand that the physiotherapist assessing the patient reviews the events leading up to arrival on the unit and overall medical management to date, then, using a sound grasp of pathophysiology and general management principles, identifies a problem list and coherent treatment plan highlighting indications and contra-indications for physiotherapy.

Leaving aside the issues of passive movements and early rehabilitation, and addressing respiratory physiotherapy for patients in the first 72 hours – the time period over which cerebral oedema peaks – it must be aimed at ensuring adequate oxygenation whilst not precipitating any sustained rise in ICP or fall in MAP. Inference from research suggesting stable patient parameters for intrahospital transfer (Andrews et al., 1990 **A**) might be a good point to start when looking to assess safety for physiotherapy intervention.

These parameters are given as:

- Systolic BP 90–160 with MAP >70 mmHg/60–80 mmHg.
- HR 60–120 sinus rhythm.
- ICP <20 mmHg.
- ccp >60 mmHg.
- PaO_2 >8 kPa, SaO_2 >90%.

Initial assessment of this patient showed he was:

- paralysed, sedated;
- ICP ~ 30 mmHg with external ventricular drain;
- reported as relatively unstable with fluctuating vital signs.

We do not know what this means in terms of:

- MAP, and therefore ccp;
- HR and rhythm;
- or what PaO_2 was achieved with how much PEEP.

We do know he was 'producing very foul smelling sputum' but can also wonder what his temperature was, were there any chest X-ray (CXR) changes or verbal reports indicative of vomiting and aspiration, was there a history of heavy smoking or recent respiratory tract infection or history of asthma?

Overall we can see that in the face of higher than ideal ICP we have a patient who also has sputum which may be a contributing factor to his abnormal oxygenation such that treatment should be planned that assists in the clearance of the latter without exacerbating the former.

Considering respiratory physiotherapy let us examine what evidence can readily be found.

Timing of Intervention

Pre-planning should occur to allow treatment time to be kept smooth and unhurried but as brief as possible. Cumulative procedures without adequate rest periods have been shown to lead to cumulative and sustained rises in ICP (Hough, 1996 **C**; Innocenti, 1986 **C**). Clinical consensus also suggests that many patients in the initial 48–72 hours are best managed when respiratory physiotherapy input is aimed at team discussion to establish appropriate position changes and suction as opposed to hands-on intervention. This is particularly so in the patient who has no respiratory compromise, and intubation and ventilation is for management of ICP and protection of the airway.

Paralysis

Clinical consensus suggests that patients with ICP uncontrolled by sedation alone are fully paralysed to reduce metabolic demand, prevent cough reflex and control $PaCO_2$. However, routine use of paralysis has been shown to lead to higher levels of pneumonia (Hsiang et al., 1994 **A**). During physiotherapy treatment ICP has been shown to rise as soon as manual hyperinflation (MHI) and vibrations were initiated in the unparalysed patient and continued to rise steadily as treatment progressed over a 17-minute time period. The same treatment protocol initiated in paralysed patients showed an initial fall in ICP with baseline ICP being exceeded only after 10 minutes, a steady rise in ICP occurring from 13 minutes onwards (Garrod and Bullock, 1986 **A**).

Positioning

Turning patients increases ICP but this effect is largely negated if head alignment is kept in neutral to minimize obstruction of venous drainage from the brain (Chudley, 1994 **C**). Head-down positioning increases ICP (Lee, 1989 **A**). Common practice suggests the patient's head should be elevated

15–30 degrees to improve venous drainage as was recommended by Feldman et al. (1992 **A**). Rosner and Colley (1986 **A**) however, showed that whilst keeping the neck in neutral maximized CPP, head elevation was not recommended as a fall in MAP led to reduced CPP.

Horiuchi et al. (1997 **A**) looked at the effects on oxygen consumption of patients during chest physiotherapy following cardiac surgery and showed a 50% increase in oxygen requirements following turn to side lying, which was suppressed by the use of sedative and paralysing agents. Gentilello et al. (1988 **A**) looked at the use of continuous lateral rotation therapy, carried out on beds that rotate to up to 40 degrees in side lying, in 65 patients with trauma leading to head injuries or requiring traction. They showed a reduced incidence of atelectasis and pneumonia but its use was contraindicated in the presence of raised ICP.

Manual Hyperinflation (MHI)

Garrod and Bullock (1986 **A**) looked at non-paralysed severely head-injured patients and suggested that periods of hyperinflation should be kept brief, < 3.5 minutes. However, the technique used reports a flow rate of only 8 litres per minute and it is possible that the patients were being underventilated.

A multidisciplinary audit of MHI in a Neurosurgical ITU set as standard:

- a flow rate of 15 litres of 100% oxygen to a two-litre bag;
- a tidal volume 1.5 times the ventilator volume up to 1000 ml (where patients were receiving tidal volumes of 700 ml or more);
- a peak inflation pressure less than or equal to 40 mmHg, or 50 mmHg (where airway pressures were 30mmHg or greater on the ventilator).

When auditing nursing and physiotherapy staff as to whether these standards were met, patients were left undisturbed for 15 minutes prior to MHI. Sedation and paralysis were optimum with no visual or physiological signs of respiratory effort or stress. In 81% of cases ICP fell even when starting pressures were above 30 or 40 mmHg. When increases in ICP did occur the largest were in association with periods of under-ventilation delivered in the baseline audit. At re-audit, after two practice sessions using flow, volume and pressure manometers in circuit and with these standards explicitly set out, 96% of patients were ventilated as a minimum to ventilator settings, that is not underventilated, and in 77% of cases appropriate volume sigh breaths were achieved. We are not told for how long MHI was carried out (Clapham et al., 1995 **A**).

Enright (1992 **A**) looked at the addition of MHI to the treatment of positioning with manual shaking and vibrations and showed a reduction in mean treatment time from 30 minutes to seven minutes in a mixed population of ITU patients as compared with treatment without MHI as reported by Mackenzie and Shin (1985 **A**) in a group of patients with post-traumatic respiratory failure. Of particular interest to us is that Enright (1992 **A**) showed minimal variation in MAP during or after treatment.

Rothen et al. (1993 **A**) looked at inflation pressures generated during MHI aimed at re-expansion of atelectasis in anaesthetized adults with healthy lungs, and suggested that airway pressures of 40 cm H_2O and a double tidal volume needed to be reached to achieve re-expansion.

Robb (1997 **A**) reports that MHI may impede venous return to the thorax leading to relative venous stasis to the head and an increase in ICP, and that a fall in venous return may lead to a reduced cardiac output and MAP. High levels of positive end expiratory pressure (PEEP) are usually avoided because of these same effects, although McGuire et al. (1997 **A**) showed that detrimental effects of increased PEEP on ICP are by no means certain.

Traditionally it has been suggested that MHI and shaking be carried out for five or six breaths, followed by short periods of 'bag-squeezing' maintaining ventilator tidal volumes and repeated as necessary until secretions are loosened (Innocenti, 1986 **C**).

Suction

In severe head injury, suction via endotracheal tube is uniformly reported to cause a rise in ICP; it is also considered a necessary procedure. Additional sedation or assessment of sedation level prior to suction is usually recommended. Wood (1998 **C**) gives an excellent literature review of endotracheal suction (ETS) with a comprehensive and well-referenced set of guidelines, of which some are of particular relevance in severe head injury.

To minimize hypoxia:

- Duration of catheter insertion 10–15 seconds.
- Hyper-oxygenate pre- and/or post-suction using 100% oxygen or 20% increase above baseline. The American Association of Respiratory Care (AARC) states that the patient should receive 100% oxygen for 1 minute following suction.

Frequency of ETS – to avoid complications of inadequate suction:

- unknown, but AARC guidelines suggest, without specifying, 'a minimum frequency is necessary to maintain patency of artificial airway'. Other authors are reported as advocating 4–6 hourly or hourly.

In a single case study report by Kerr and Brucia (1993 **A**), when pre-treatment arterial CO_2 was 4 kPa, CPP was maintained within normal limits during a regimen of four hyperinflations, one 10-second suction, 4–8 hyperinflations, one 10-second suction and 4 hyperinflations, whereas a starting $PaCO_2$ of 4.5 kPa gave a lower starting CPP that fell to 42mmHg during treatment, changes in CPP being mainly due to a rise in ICP; in both cases the patient was sedated but not paralysed.

Effectiveness of suction has also been linked to adequate patient hydration, humidification and warming of inspired gases. Heat and moisture exchange filters (HMEs) are generally reported as adequate in the well-hydrated patient without thick inspissated secretions or for short-term use (24–48 hours), conventional heated humidification being indicated when a patient falls outside these parameters (Joynt and Lipman, 1994 **B**; Judson and Sahn, 1994 **C**). By inference, the practice of fluid restriction and the use of hyperosmolar and renal diuretics to produce a degree of therapeutic dehydration to manage cerebral oedema in severe head injury, coupled with the caution with which all techniques to clear pulmonary secretions must be employed, suggests the use of heated humidification should be more rapidly instituted than may otherwise be the case.

Much debate surrounds the instillation of 0.9% saline prior to suction. Reported harmful effects are decrease in oxygen saturation, increased rate of respiratory infection and increased intracranial pressure. These findings have not been uniformly reported and other authors cite enhanced secretion clearance (Raymond, 1995 **C**). The claim that normal saline enhances removal of secretions through stimulation of cough reflex (probably undesirable in severe head injury) or by decreasing adherence of the secretions to the ETT (possibly desirable in the presence of tenacious secretions and danger associated with repeated suction) remains unproved. Clinical practice suggests that the instillation of 5 ml of normal saline, slowly and with rigorous attention to sterile technique, is an acceptable practice. Some clinicians also suggest it be warmed by holding the unopened ampoule under a running hot tap to prevent bronchospasm.

Manual Shaking, Vibrations and Percussion

It is known that in the spontaneously breathing patient with copious secretions, active cycle of breathing in gravity-assisted postural drainage positions can be only minimally enhanced by the addition of these techniques with respect to sputum clearance (Sutton et al., 1985 **A**). The possible benefit where postural drainage or active cycle of breathing is precluded and in the intubated ventilated patient is less well studied. Judson and Steven (1994 **C**) stated that because of impaired mucociliary transport in intubated patients, suctioning needs to be coupled with chest physiotherapy (CPT), by which was meant postural drainage, shaking or vibrations and assisted coughs. Their review of the literature suggests CPT to be of most benefit in treatment of atelectasis and acute lung collapse, and in particular more effective than MHI and suction alone, and that it should be trialled to assess increased efficiency over position changes and suction for effects on sputum clearance. Enright (1992) reports that a regimen of lateral positioning, MHI and manual shaking and vibrations initiated at peak inflation to achieve a maximum expiratory flow is beneficial, as demonstrated by an immediate and sustained decrease in intrapulmonary shunt.

Garrod and Bullock (1986 **A**) found that percussion applied for up to seven minutes in sedated patients whilst they remain on the ventilator resulted in a drop in ICP and in paralysed patients the drop was slightly greater. Vibrations, as an individual technique and therefore presumably applied during exhalation from ventilator breaths, showed no effect on ICP. Shaking on expiration from MHI was shown to increase ICP, as did MHI alone, but as has been seen above, there is some suggestion that the patients may have been under-ventilated. Guidelines at the end of their paper suggest extreme caution in starting physiotherapy when ICP exceeds 15 mmHg, and that MHI and shaking be kept to 3.5 minutes. This is in contrast with Clapham et al. (1995 **A**), as seen above, who documented falls in ICP with manual hyperinflation even when starting pressures were above 30 and 40 mmHg.

In their review of practice and implications for management, Matta and Menon (1996 **C**) find physiotherapy to be routine in 80% of UK and Irish units managing severe head injuries but no policy for administration of any specific medication pre-treatment. They comment that fear of increase in ICP should not prevent effective pulmonary toilet with frequent change in position and suction but that sedation should be increased pre-physiotherapy and pre-suction.

Clinical Practice

The First 72 Hours

The decision to intervene or let well alone is often a difficult one with regard to respiratory physiotherapy in the unstable ITU patient. However, I would take the following thoughts into account:

- Does poor respiratory status contribute to the unstable condition?
- Is the respiratory picture amenable to physiotherapy treatment?
- How does the patient tolerate procedures such as pressure area care (position change)?
- Are conditions for physiotherapy intervention as optimal as possible?

To optimize Mr ND's condition one would look to minimize bronchospasm, if present, with nebulized bronchodilators, look at the need for additional humidification where secretions are tenacious and ensure effective sedation, with full paralysis where needed, prior to intervention. A rest period of 15 minutes before and again after respiratory physiotherapy techniques should be instituted. I would then introduce techniques stepwise to assess the effect on ICP, sputum clearance and oxygenation.

For Mr ND, with documented foul sputum and whose ICP is persistently greater than 20 mmHg, I would recommend additional humidification, regular (two to four hourly) change in position through lying to alternate side, lying with neck in neutral, and suction, with pre and post increased oxygenation through the ventilator, as first-line treatment. If stable, particularly with respect to ICP and MAP, the patient may remain side lying for a period of drainage and ventilation with altered line of resistance ultimately followed by further suction.

Intervention would need to be progressed if examination suggested this was insufficient to maintain oxygenation without raising inspired oxygen or PEEP. Progression of Mr ND's treatment would then be to add in either percussion or manual hyperinflation (or both) if indicated to improve sputum clearance and reverse atelectasis respectively. To achieve an effect on atelectasis we have seen it suggested that an airway pressure of 40 cmH_2O is needed during MHI. In practice this might be sufficient in Mr ND to cause a fall in MAP. Hypotension is particularly likely if a respiratory swing in BP is evident with the phases of inspiration and expiration whilst ventilated. I would be cautious in instituting MHI with a MAP of less than 80 mmHg, and when used would ensure that the expiratory phase is longer than the inspiratory phase and that it is carried out as deep-breathing exercises, interspersed with periods of 'bagging' to mimic ventilator breaths. If Mr ND is being nursed head up, a decision, depending on his ICP and MAP response, would be made as to whether to lower the bed head to flat for physiotherapy or to maintain the head-up position .

Where tenacious secretions are audible in the endotracheal tube (ETT) or palpable through the anterior chest wall but not clearing with suction I would instil a 5 ml bolus of normal saline followed by two or three manual hyperinflations. This is often sufficient, even without a cough reflex, to send sputum shooting out of the ETT like a rabbit out of a hole! I use sterile 0.9% saline drawn up in a sterile syringe kept inside the syringe packet on an appropriate tray, with its vial for identification. When instilled, care is taken to avoid contact with the outside of the ETT with its likely load of oral and skin pathogens.

Frequency of physiotherapy intervention at this stage and involvement of nursing staff in a co-operative approach to interventions to maximize pulmonary toilet and function will depend on assessment of the effect of treatment.

Clinical Practice

Days 5–8

Once paralysis has been withdrawn, sedation reduced and Mr ND is being ventilated on any of the modes that allow a degree of spontaneous ventilation, I am unaware of any body of research to suggest the way forward in relation to chest physiotherapy. Mr ND's own drive to breathe will increasingly determine levels of $PaCO_2$ and positioning will be determined by patient activity and therapeutic efforts to normalize tone. It is still, however, reasonable to say that periods of intervention for whatever purpose should be interspersed with periods of rest. Respiratory physiotherapy goals will be driven by auscultatory findings, chest X-ray changes and ease of sputum clearance. For Mr ND, once sedation was withdrawn at four days and in view of the continued production of foul sputum, I would expect him to require at least twice-daily respiratory physiotherapy. My plan would be to minimize atelectasis and ensure clearance of pulmonary secretions by:

- Nursing in alternate side lying, whilst in bed.
- Facilitation of increased depth of breathing by some or all of the following: positioning, manual stimulation, upper limb and shoulder girdle rhythmic movements (with care in respect of effects on tone) and possibly the techniques of neurophysiological facilitation of respiration as described by Bethune (1975 **C**), although I have no experience of these.
- Once stable, in conjunction with his neurological rehabilitation, periods of positioning out of bed in supported sitting and standing for the prevention of or management of basal collapse. If unable to achieve increase in tidal volumes by these means, then employment of MHI in synchrony with the patient's own respiratory pattern (to prevent blowing off of CO_2 and reduction in drive to breathe).

- Effective humidification and suction, with or without normal saline instillation.
- The use of shaking on expiration to clear sputum if more sputum was cleared by its use than with the above measures alone.

Sputum remains 'very foul' but inspired oxygen levels are low, therefore with the above measures it is unlikely that significant ventilation perfusion mismatch by way of collapse or consolidation would be a major issue.

As a last comment on this period, although the prognosis undoubtedly remained poor on the information available from the Case Report we have the comment 'Contact made with Mr ND's parents who agreed to organ donation', which cannot be allowed to stand without further consideration. Using the organ donation code I am familiar with, at no point did Mr ND fulfil the criteria for organ donation. The code of practice lays down that the *diagnosis*, prognosis and concept *of brainstem death needs to be made* and discussed with the relatives *before the discussion of organ donation takes place*. Even if it were expected that Mr ND might deteriorate following his discharge to the ward, the code of practice then states: 'artificial ventilation as part of resuscitation is only justified if it is of potential benefit to the patient'. He therefore either would not end up re-ventilated or if re-ventilated it would be with active therapeutic intervention towards his recovery and he would therefore again not, at that point, be a candidate for donation. To avoid mixed messages being given to the family at such times of vulnerability it is my opinion that all staff, including physiotherapists, working in the intensive care setting be conversant and fully understanding of the meaning of brainstem death and its implications for organ donation.

Clinical Practice (day 9 to discharge)

Following discharge from ITU to a ward environment the requirements for respiratory physiotherapy assessment and intervention usually increase. The team member primarily concerned with maintenance of respiratory functioning, including assessment for patency of tracheostomy, is often the physiotherapist. Respiratory physiotherapy at this stage will involve some or all of the following:

- Assessment for provision of prescribed level of oxygen with working humidification.
- Provision of working suction with all necessary equipment for safe, sterile suction.

- Liaison regarding the nature of tracheostomy, for example cuffed, uncuffed, single or double lumen, fenestrated or not and indications for care.
- Liaison with nursing team regarding positioning for optimum respiratory function, bearing in mind the effect of position on altered tone.
- Frequency of suction required so far.
- Teaching of suction technique particularly with a view to effectiveness and minimizing of tracheal trauma.
- Teaching regarding alteration in baseline findings suggestive of partially or imminently occluded tracheostomy, and appropriate action.

Mr ND's observations on day 9 may be accounted for by a number of different scenarios requiring different action.

Pyrexia of 40°C could be:

- due to infection, most likely respiratory, requiring among other things chest physiotherapy to clear sputum and maintain alveolar ventilation although the possibility of other sources of infection should be remembered; or
- of central origin requiring antipyretics.

The most likely causes of the tachypnoea would be:

- as a result of raised metabolic rate, given the pyrexia and requiring appropriate management of the pyrexia; or
- as a result of partially occluded tracheostomy leading to increased work of breathing requiring attention to sputum clearance and tracheostomy hygiene; or
- as a result of impending respiratory failure, possibly due to poorly regulating brainstem function, requiring full team assessment, including ABGs to show $PaCO_2$ level, followed by measures to reduce work of breathing, for example, attention to positioning and need for ventilatory support if deemed appropriate.

The tachycardia would be a partner to tachypnoea in each of these scenarios but also may be a sign of dehydration or pain needing medical review and appropriate action.

Respiratory physiotherapy would continue as planned for the period following discontinuation of sedation on intensive care. However, once the patient was coughing effectively, with nursing staff suctioning to clear the tracheostomy and a regular pattern of position changes established, respiratory monitoring could be taken over, following liaison, by the neurological physiotherapy team and integrated with continuing rehabilitation, which would be the prime physiotherapy input.

During the process of cuff deflation and weaning from tracheostomy cannulation to normal ventilation via the upper airways, further specific respiratory physiotherapy assessment, in association with speech and language therapy assessment and intervention, would be looking for signs of aspiration, the ability to clear sputum if present and to manage the increased work of breathing given the increased dead space. This may require the return to daily respiratory physiotherapy input for a period of time.

Implications

Given the reasonable body of evidence supporting respiratory intervention by physiotherapists in patients with head injury, it is important that all intensive care-based physiotherapists are conversant with the appropriate interventions and that we look to underpin our treatments with further specific physiotherapy research, particularly into the indications for using or withholding treatment techniques over and above positioning and suction and into the frequency of intervention. It is interesting to note that many patients in the UK with similar injuries to those in this case study are currently managed in general intensive care units without intracranial pressure monitoring and are then transferred to busy general surgical wards with non-specialist care. A recent report on the management of patients with head injuries (RCS England, 1999 **C**) has called for all such patients to be managed in specialist neurosurgical units before transferring directly to rehabilitation units. Were this to be achieved, it would present a far better structure for investigating and following through outcomes of different treatment pathways.

References

Andrews PJ, Piper IR, Dearden NM, Miller JD (1990) Secondary insults during intra-hospital transport of head-injured patients. Lancet 335(8685): 327–30.

Bethune D (1975) Neurophysiological facilitation of respiration in the unconscious adult patient. Physiotherapy Canada 27(5): 241–5.

Bullock R, Teasdale G (1990) Head injuries – ABC of major trauma. British Medical Journal 300(6738): 1515–58.

Chudley S (1994) The effect of nursing activities on intra-cranial pressure. British Journal of Nursing 3(9): 454–5.

Clapham L, Harrison J, Raybould T (1995) A multi-disciplinary audit of manual hyperinflation technique (sigh breathing) in a neurosurgical intensive care unit. Intensive & Critical Care Nursing 11(5): 265–71.

Code of Practice, England and Wales: Diagnosis of brain stem death. March 1998.

Enright S (1992) Cardio-respiratory Effects of Chest Physiotherapy. Intensive Care, Britain, Greycoat 1, Harley St, London, pp 118–23.

Feldman Z, Kanter MJ, Robertson CS, Contant CF, Hayes C, Sheinberg MA, Villareal CA, Narayan RK, Grossman RG (1992) Effects of head elevation on intra-cranial pressure, cerebral perfusion pressure and cerebral blood flow in head injured patients. Journal of Neurosurgery 76(2): 207–11.

Garrod J, Bullock M (1986) The effect of respiratory therapy on intra cranial pressure in ventilated neurosurgical patients. Australian Journal of Physiotherapy 32(2): 107–11.

Gentilello L, Thompson DA, Tonneen AS, Hernandez D, Kapadia AS, Allen SJ, Houtchens BA, Miner ME (1988) Effects of a rotating bed on the incidence of pulmonary complications in critically ill patients. Critical Care Medicine 16(8): 783–6.

Horiuchi K, Jordan D, Cohen D, Kemper MC, Weisman C (1997) Insights into the increased oxygen demand during chest physiotherapy. Critical Care Medicine 25(8): 1347–51.

Hough A (1996) Physiotherapy in Respiratory Care, A Problem Solving Approach, 2nd edn.

Hsiang JK, Chenut KM, Crisp CB, Klauber MR, Blunt BA, Marshall LF (1994) Early routine paralysis for ICP control in severe head injury, is it really necessary? Critical Care Medicine 22(9): 1471–6.

Innocenti D (1986) Handling the critically ill patient. Physiotherapy 72(3): 125–8.

Jeevaratnam DR (1996) Survey of intensive care of severely head injured patients in the UK. British Medical Journal 312(7036): 944–7.

Joyntt GM, Lipman J (1994) The use of heat and moisture exchangers in critically ill patients. Care of Critically Ill 10(6): 271–4.

Judson MA, Steven SA (1994) Mobilisation of secretions in ICU patients. Respiratory Care 39(3): 213–23.

Kerr ME, Brucia J (1993) Hyperventilation in the head injured patient: an effective treatment modality? Heart and Lung 22(6): 516–22.

Lee ST (1989) Intra-cranial pressure changes during positioning of patients with severe head injury. Heart and Lung 18(4): 411–14.

Mackenzie CF, Shin B (1985) Cardio-respiratory function before and after chest physiotherapy in mechanically ventilated patients with post-traumatic respiratory failure. Critical Care Medicine 13(6): 483–6.

Matta B, Menon D (1996) Severe head injury in the UK and Ireland – a survey of practise and implication for management. Critical Care Medicine 24(10): 1743–8.

McGuire G, Crossley D, Richards J, Wong D (1997) Effects of varying levels of positive end expiratory pressure on intra-cranial pressure and cerebral perfusion pressure. Critical Care Medicine 25(6): 1059–62.

Miller JD (1991) Changing patterns in acute management of head injury. Journal of Neurological Science 103(Suppl): 533–7.

Raymond SJ (1995) Normal saline instillation before suction: Helpful or harmful? A review of the literature. American Journal of Critical Care 4(4): 267–71.

Robb J (1997) Physiological changes occurring with positive pressure ventilation: Part one. Intensive and Critical Care Nursing 13: 293–307.

Rosner MJ, Colley IB (1986) Cerebral perfusion pressure, intra cranial pressure and head elevation. Journal of Neurosurgery 65(5): 636–41.

Rothen HU, Sporee B, Engberg G, Wegenius G, Hedenstierna G (1993) Re-expansion of atelectasis during general anaesthesia: a computed tomography study. British Journal of Anaesthesiology 71(6): 788–95.
Royal College of Surgeons of England (1999) Report of the Working Party on the Management of Patients with Head Injuries. London: RCS, June.
Sutton PP, Lopez-Vidriero MT, Pavia D, Newman SP, Clay MM, Webber B, Parker RA, Clarke SW (1985) European Journal of Respiratory Disease 66: 147–52.
Wilden JN (1993) Rapid resuscitation in severe head injury. Lancet 342(8884): 1378.
Wood CJ (1998) Endotracheal suctioning: a literature review. Intensive Care and Critical Care Nursing 14: 124–36.

Physical Management and Rehabilitation of Patients with Traumatic Head Injury (1)

MAGGIE CAMPBELL

Introduction

I have chosen to approach the discussion of intervention for physical management and rehabilitation in this case study in two stages. The first stage is in the form of a commentary on the facts and events described in the case study, addressing both the immediate issues raised by the information given and the secondary issues implied by the narrative. I shall then project forward into the sub-acute period to introduce a longitudinal perspective. However, in advance of discussion of this specific case I shall briefly introduce the essence of the approach used as a basis to guide management decisions at all stages of the process.

General Principles

In brief, the basis of the approach adopted throughout the rest of this chapter reflects the application of three main strands of knowledge, refined by clinical experience. The first strand is the pathophysiology of traumatic brain injury (TBI) encompassing injury mechanisms and known patterns of primary and secondary cerebral damage. The second is the descriptive literature that details deficit profiles following TBI and their functional impact, including the impact on family units and wider social relationships. The final strand of knowledge is drawn from the basic biomedical sciences, for example biomechanics, neurophysiology and muscle physiology.

This approach acknowledges from the outset the paucity of clinical trials and documented single-case experiments concerning physical interventions after traumatic brain injury and the need to derive (and test) treatment hypotheses from transferable evidence. However, knowledge of the pathophysiological effects of TBI is well founded, and many of the immediate and longer-term deficits (other than sensorimotor) and their functional impact have been well described and replicated over many studies. In summary, there is probably sufficient guidance to define with some confidence the overall approach within which physiotherapeutic practice should be based (Burke, 1987 **C**; Eames and Wood, 1989 **C**; Oddy et al., 1989 **C**; Greenwood and McMillan, 1993 **C**; NIH, 1998 **C**), but only limited evidence to defend the choice of physiotherapeutic interventions.

Evidence

Pockets of literature related to physical management have begun to develop. However, this is mainly at the level of defining the problem; for example, highlighting the complexity and difficulty in documenting the descriptions of early motor recovery (Mayo et al., 1991 **A**; Swaine and Sullivan, 1996a **A**; Swaine and Sullivan, 1996b **A**, 1999 **A**) or documenting the incidence and to some extent the categories of residual deficit (Brooks et al., 1987 **A**; Newton, 1995 **A**; Ponsford et al., 1995 **A**; Hillier and Metzer, 1997 **A**; Hillier et al., 1997 **A**; Hibbard et al., 1998 **A**; Koskinen, 1998 **A**). Similarly, attention has been drawn to the lack of clear evidence of effective physical intervention (Edwards, 1996 **C**; Watson, 1997 **A**) and the need for systematic documentation and research (McMillan and Greenwood, 1993 **C**; Butler et al., 1997 **C**; Watson, 1997 **C**; Campbell, 2000d **C**).

Reports of successful rehabilitative intervention focused on physical domains remain largely restricted to anecdotal case studies. However, evidence from the wider literature indicates that the overall approach to rehabilitation needs to take into account the complex mixture of deficits that results from the typically diffuse brain injury and that the often lifelong nature of residual deficits following significant injury necessitates active consideration of family and social issues (see Campbell, 2000 **B**) for a full review.

Commentary on Case Study Information

Pre-injury History

Although Mr ND is reported to have had no significant pre-injury medical history, there are other potentially influencing pre-injury factors that require consideration in the course of assessment and in trying to identify rehabilitation goals and intervention strategies. For example, his lifestyle may have affected his nutritional or general health status at the time of the injury. Similarly, the social or personal issues that caused him to leave the parental home, or even the fact that there had been a breakdown in his relationship with his parents, are likely to complicate any attempts to effectively involve family in the rehabilitation process. On a more positive note, knowledge of Mr ND's interest in, and aptitude for, music and information technology may be used in efforts to make the rehabilitation process relevant to him.

Pathophysiology

A summated Glasgow Coma Scale (GCS) of 3/15 indicates no eye opening, communication or motor response, suggesting a very severe injury. This is confirmed by the presence of a traumatic subarachnoid haemorrhage, hydrocephalus, significantly raised intracranial pressure, a third nerve palsy and unstable vital signs. It is worthy of note that while the increased respiratory rate, tachycardia and pyrexia may be related to infection they may also relate to brainstem damage, especially in the presence of decerebrate posturing. The importance of acknowledging the presence of significant brainstem injury relates to the observation that these types of lesions may be associated with delayed physical recovery (Eames and Wood, 1989 **C**). This has obvious import for decisions regarding timing and type of intervention.

Management Decisions and Intervention Choices

The differing views concerning active treatment reflect a still common dichotomy between medical and therapeutic staff. The primary issue is the recognition of the need to act to prevent negative secondary changes when there is *any* chance of survival. There is no question that tissue viability is compromised in the face of extended periods of pressure or when circulation is restricted, and nursing care is informed by this accepted fact. Similarly, muscles and other soft tissues change in response to changes in the internal or external environment (Goldspink and Williams, 1990 **B**). The immediate and secondary negative effects of soft tissue changes following TBI are, however, not just a theoretical possibility but a well-documented occurrence (for example Rusk et al., 1966 **A**; Moseley, 1997 **A**). Restricting proactive management when survival is in doubt can have lasting negative effects on later rehabilitation programmes and subsequent functional outcome (Campbell, 2000c).

Use of Removable Splints

In the case of Mr ND, I would have argued for the application of lightweight, removable, full-cylinder below-knee splints while he remained sedated, on the basis of his being at high risk for loss of tissue extensibility and joint range. While sedated he would be unable to counter the force of gravity (risking excess plantarflexion) and on withdrawal of sedation he would be at high risk of developing decerebrate or decorticate posturing (again risking excess plantarflexion) because of his initial low GCS and evidence of brainstem damage. Clinical experience has illustrated the speed with which loss of range into dorsiflexion can and frequently does occur and also the strong negative impact of loss of ankle range on intervention sessions, positioning and long-term physical status. Other authors have observed similar pathological progression and promote proactive casting (Conine et al., 1990 **A**; Edwards and Charlton, 1996 **C**). Other published articles describing methods of intervening to limit the development of hypertonicity and soft tissue adaptation (Bernard et al., 1984 **A**; Sullivan et al., 1988 **A**) or the process of corrective splinting (Booth et al., 1983 **A**; Mills, 1984 **A**; Cornall, 1992 **C**; Moseley, 1997 **A**) confirm the universal incidence of this problem.

In post-acute care I have observed a particular link between limited dynamic tissue extensibility in the posterior tibials and excess extensor activity in the upper trunk and head. I would therefore expect that in addition to minimizing loss of range and extensibility at the ankle joints, proactive application of the splints would also lessen the problem of overextension noted later in Mr ND's case description.

I would apply the splints based on local guidelines (Directorate of Professional Services, 1999 **C**) developed from the ACPIN (Association of Chartered Physiotherapists in Neurology) UK national guidelines (Association of Chartered Physiotherapists in Neurology, 1998 **C**). I would not interpret the documented soft tissue injury as a contraindication to splinting but would add special observations to the routine (two-hourly) inspection regime. The rationale for using removable (rather than permanent) splints is that they hold the feet in the functionally important plantargrade position but allow frequent access for inspection, skin care and periods of active intervention including intermittent stretch, which is thought to be the most beneficial form of stretch for inactive muscle (Goldspink and Williams, 1990 **B**).

The Influence of Pain and Abnormal Joint Mechanics

I would want to consider the impact of the right shoulder girdle derangement on the development of flexion and retraction around the shoulder, the flexion in the arm and the side-flexion in the trunk. I would also consider the impact of the abnormal posturing on the disorganized joints. I would seek a review of pain relief and ask for advice from specialist musculoskeletal colleagues concerning the management of this issue. Within the confines of advice given regarding the promotion of joint integrity I would wish to proactively manage the potential shortening of soft tissues caused by the imbalance in muscle activity. I would address this by periods of positioning, and where possible activity, that achieve length in the trunk, with protraction (without elevation) of the shoulder girdle and external rotation of the humerus. The exact positions, means of achievement and how nearly the positional ideal could be accomplished would be highly dependent on Mr ND's individual tonal and behavioural presentation. The objective would be to gain the best compromise in a variety of positions and activities across the daily management regime and this would require the co-operation of, and contributions by, all members of the professional team in addition to that which could be achieved during periods of direct physiotherapy contact.

Barriers to Standing

If the problems noted in progressing standing were related to poor regulation of blood pressure, the use of blood pressure monitoring as an objective measure within sessions (and in assessing response to graded elevation via, for example, a tilt table) would assist decisions on progression of treatment. I would also consider other reasons for the apparent autonomic response, such as pain, fear or dizziness from vestibular or other sensory dysfunction. Subsequent management would depend on the outcome of these considerations.

Pelvic Stiffness

I would guess that the pelvic stiffness noted in the presence of low muscular tone reflects the limited excursion through range that has occurred during the period of gross extensor posturing and would strive to include the experience of movement through full range as part of the overall management regime. I would want, however, to check for any evidence of heterotopic ossification (HO). Mr ND carries an increased risk of developing HO because of his youth but the absence of multiple fractures may lessen this risk (Hurvitz snd Mandac, 1992 **A**). If HO was present, I would still wish to pursue activity. Although anecdotally HO after TBI is said to be associated with 'aggressive' passive movements, there is no real evidence of this link. Similarly, while surgical intervention has been thought to be equally ill advised and likely to produce further HO, there have been recent reports of bony excision (around elbows and knees) followed by continuous passive movement with improved pain-free range and low levels of reccurrence (Ippolito et al., 1999a **A**, 1999b **A**). For me this raises the question as to whether inactivity is actually a primary influencing factor.

Abnormal Head Position

Mr ND's head position may be being influenced by a number of factors such as the imbalance of muscle activity around the shoulder girdle. This imbalance may in turn result from CNS damage, pain or mechanical factors or any combination of these. Equally it may reflect Mr ND's need to centralize his left eye to achieve an optimal visual field or it may be part of a balance reaction in response to a perception of a threat to stability. It is likely that many of these components are combining to contribute to the preferred head position. Again, the choice of direct intervention and management would be informed by evaluation of the underlying factors and would be likely to involve an innovative combination of measures to drive resolution of each identified problem or to manage its effect. Whatever the underlying factors, their immediate and secondary effects will continue to form a significant focus of intervention throughout Mr ND's rehabilitation.

Throughout the whole period of early rehabilitation I would attempt to include as much task-oriented movement as possible. As well as applying knowledge of how to achieve skilled motor control (Rosenbaum, 1991 **B**) this would also help to make therapy sessions contextually relevant and so more easily understandable to a potentially confused and disoriented individual. Task relevance would also aid communication of what is being asked of Mr ND at a time when communication via language is limited. I would regard this as an important facet of a wider strategy of delivering reassurance to minimize anxiety, and limit the possibilities for conflict within treatment sessions and therefore the need for, or likelihood of, behavioural outbursts or dyscontrol.

Family and Related Issues

How friends and family members respond to TBI and how they subsequently deal with the longitudinal effects on their loved one and on themselves is an individual and complex process (Douglas, 1990 **B**; Ponsford, 1995 **B**). Professionals have a responsibility to take carers' personal trauma into account, to make sure that they give appropriate information in a timely fashion and that they do not make unreasonable demands on individuals (Campbell, 2000c).

In this case there are a number of additional issues adding to an already emotionally complex situation. We do not have any real information about Mr ND's parents' reaction to the news of their son's predicament. We do not know what the pre-existing relationship issues were. What is clear is the number and extent of complex emotional issues that they have to deal with in a short period of time. I would expect that even if they apparently coped with these issues at the time, the effects of having to do so would become obvious at some time further along the rehabilitation process.

There is no mention in the case study of Mr ND's current friends or associates. It may be that he was essentially alone, but there may well be people around his London life who cared for him. It would be important that any such people were not disenfranchised with the reappearance of his parents. In addition, they may have much to offer the rehabilitation professional in terms of their up-to-date knowledge of Mr ND; for example, in identifying motivating issues to include in the goal-setting process.

Sub-acute Management

The case description ends with a summary of Mr ND's impairments, disabilities and handicaps at the point of transfer to a rehabilitation unit, some two and a half months post-injury. While eleven bullet points are listed, much of the detail required to help define the approach and content of a physical programme is missing. In addition, there are a number of important issues raised in the foregoing narrative that are not covered in the list, for example, Mr ND's communication status. Therefore, in projecting forward into the period of sub-acute management I shall also raise questions related to missing information.

The Rehabilitation and Adjustment Process

As a background to developing a meaningful rehabilitation programme, it is useful to understand the process through which Mr ND and his family are travelling and where they are in that process. Tyerman suggests that, following TBI, individuals need to progress through a four-stage process of acute care, rehabilitation, resettlement and long-term adjustment (Tyerman, 1991 **C**). Within this model Mr ND remains very near the beginning of the process. This is important to acknowledge and to take into account in the design and implementation of the physical programme. The extent to which this is possible will be influenced to some degree by the scope of services potentially available, and in reality it may be necessary to set intervention goals in line with the limited resources available. It is, however, important to note that discharge from a primary hospital, or indeed from a follow-up in-patient rehabilitation unit, does not equate to an end point in recovery. Moreover, whether formal service beyond in-patient care exists or not, treatment planning needs to be informed by the individual's need for a period of resettlement and by an awareness of an extended process of longer-term adjustment. In terms of friends and family members, Douglas describes a flexible five-stage model of shock, expectancy, reality, mourning and adjustment (Douglas, 1990 **B**). Ponsford (1995 **C**), in highlighting the usefulness of Douglas's model, also emphasizes how individuals may move backwards and forwards between stages as they attempt to come to terms with the changes brought about by the TBI. It should also be evident that, in considering both models, not all individuals achieve progression to full adjustment.

Approach to Intervention

Ideally Mr ND's ongoing rehabilitation should be delivered within a specialist TBI service (Burke, 1987 **C**; Greenwood and McMillan, 1993 **C**) following a cognitive-behavioural model (Greenwood and McMillan, 1993 **C**; NIH, 1998 **C**). Physiotherapy provision should be set within the context of an interdisciplinary team to help ensure comprehensive, efficient assessment (Body et al., 1996), prevent the occurrence of conflicting or irrelevant treatment goals (Powell et al., 1994 **C**) and provide an appropriate working environment for effective communication (Campbell, 2000 **C**). The ethos of the service should be positive and forward-looking (Eames and Wood, 1989 **C**) and collaborative, involving both Mr ND and his family and friends as appropriate (Eames and Wood, 1989 **C**; NIH, 1998 **C**; Campbell, 2000 **C**).

Projected Programme

As we have only limited information about Mr ND's overall status (see below) it is impossible to discuss issues such as the prioritization of intervention goals or prognostic indicators with any certainty. I shall therefore discuss these factors in only general terms but stress the importance of this aspect of programme decision-making. Physical goals should not be pursued in a vacuum and should always be consciously linked to a realistic projection of the longer-term functional outcome. Decisions concerning the precise design and content of any intervention would first require further enquiry to establish the factors underlying diminished function and also to ascertain the extent of co-existing non-physical deficits and preserved abilities.

Physical Influences

Right Upper Limb

We know that Mr ND has a 'mild weakness in the right upper limb with altered shoulder girdle alignment'. We do not know what constitutes the weakness. Is it a functional weakness caused by poor shoulder girdle biomechanics or pain? Is it difficulty in initiating movement? Can movement be initiated but not sustained; is there a disuse component? Is the term 'mild weakness' being used to describe a co-ordination problem, slowness of movement or some difficulty in manipulating objects? What about the quality of the soft tissues – have structural changes occurred that could impact on muscle function?

Pelvis

Similarly, Mr ND is said to have 'pelvic instability' on the right. Is this due to an imbalance of muscle activity or an inability to recruit the appropriate muscles or in an appropriate synergy? Are the problems of the upper limb and pelvis linked? Is there still a problem of trunk side-flexion?

Balance

Are the 'decreased balance reactions' secondary to the above motor performance issues or the continuing limitations of range distally in the lower limbs? What 'balance reaction' components are diminished? Is it anticipatory postural activity, mode of response or simply reaction time? Is there a similar problem in all starting positions or, if not, how does it vary?

Gait

What form does the 'minimal assistance' to walk take and why is it required? Does this ambulatory status apply in all circumstances or only to the hospital environment?

Summary

These are just some of the questions requiring attention in order to identify the appropriate intervention strategy from a physical point of view. For each of these problems, whether linked or not, it is essential to be as precise as possible about the musculoskeletal and neuromuscular basis for the motor performance problem in order to design intervention programmes that target faulty components and demand the type of motor output required to enable optimum performance of various functional tasks. I have already referred to the use of task-specific therapy in relation to the application of motor learning theory but specificity of interventions can also be supported from a neurobiological point of view (Dobkin, 1998a **B**, 1998b **B**) and from knowledge of the plastic interaction between functional use, structural composition and performance in skeletal muscle (Vrbova et al., 1978 **B**; Pette and Vrbova, 1985 **B**).

Beyond achieving more clarity around the problem areas identified, I would also want to establish baselines regarding Mr ND's level of stamina and fatigue for general and specific physical activities and to include work for stamina and fitness within the wider programme. This would be to help reverse expected changes in exercise tolerance (Bateman et al., 1999 **A**) and possibly to contribute to improved cognitive performance (Rosenfeld, 1998 **A**; Grealy et al., 1999 **A**). I would want to screen Mr ND's sensory status within the clinical setting and obtain additional specialist assessment as indicated by the findings. I would certainly seek an ophthalmology or orthoptic opinion with the aim of incorporating any appropriate exercise or visual management strategies into the overall programme.

Cognitive Influences

From my experience and knowledge of common brain injury patterns I would be very surprised if the 'mild memory problems' and 'decreased concentration' noted in Mr ND's problems list were the sum total of cognitive dysfunction resulting from such a severe initial injury. There is no reference to the length of Mr ND's post-traumatic amnesia, which remains the single best predictor of long-term functional outcome (Wilson et al., 1993 **C**; Ellenberg et al., 1996 **A**). However, the substantial bleed, raised ICP and the third nerve damage suggest diffuse injury. I would therefore wish to have knowledge of the results of a full cognitive assessment and access to advice from, and the opportunity for discussion with, neuropsychology, speech and language therapy and occupational therapy colleagues as appropriate to the assessment findings. Brazzelli and Della Sala (1997 **B**) highlight the tremendous potential of proactive collaboration between neuro-psychologists and physiotherapists for more effective delivery of rehabilitation programmes in the presence of brain damage. The implications for physiotherapeutic practice and some practical suggestions for the management of cognitive and behavioural dysfunction are addressed by Campbell (Campbell, 2000a) and set in the context of an interdisciplinary approach to TBI rehabilitation.

Factors Affecting Functional Outcome

Cognition and Behaviour

There is substantial evidence that cognitive and behavioural factors have more influence on the long-term functional outcome for survivors of TBI than do physical factors, particularly when good outcome is defined as return to gainful employment (Lezak, 1978 **A**; Oddy et al., 1978 **A**; Brooks and Aughton, 1979 **A**; Levin et al., 1979 **A**; Brooks and McKinlay, 1983 **A**). It is difficult without knowing Mr ND's full cognitive profile to anticipate or discuss specific barriers that he may face. Memory problems limit independence and without management place demands on others. They can be addressed via the development of appropriate compensatory strategies including the use of structure, routine and personalized memory management systems and be applied and consolidated across the rehabilitation programme.

The other specific issue highlighted in the case summary was a problem of concentration but again we do not know the detail. This might represent, among many other things, a primary problem of attending to task, limitations in sustaining attention or it may indicate resistance to attempting particular tasks because they do not appear relevant. Success within treatment sessions and the achievement of optimum functional outcome would be dependent on knowing as much information as possible relating to Mr ND's cognitive and communicative abilities in order to ensure appropriate design and pacing of the physical programme from a cognitive point of view.

Physical

Whatever the levels of Mr ND's physical recovery, optimum functional outcome will be dependent on his being able to routinely use his physical skills at home and in the community. Because of the likely co-existing cognitive limitations, especially the difficulties in what is commonly termed executive functions (for example, planning, organizing, pacing, self-monitoring) this will require guided practice. Lack of generalization may mean addressing each activity area in turn, for example at home, at leisure or at work. The establishment of some form of physical leisure, especially in the presence of continuing physical deficits, would be important to help reverse the unavoidable deconditioning and to establish an exercise habit to promote cardiovascular fitness and possibly to aid cognitive ability.

Social and Community Factors

Clinical experience suggests that the presence of a healthy support network for TBI survivors is a major factor in achieving and maintaining good outcomes. There is some evidence to suggest that this is also an important factor for carers of those who survive TBI, even in the presence of significant residual deficits (Douglas, 1996 **A**). Referring back to the recovery and adjustment models of Tyerman (1991 **B**) and Douglas (1990 **B**) and in the face of limited information about Mr ND's home circumstances, it seems appropriate simply to highlight the desirability of access to longer-term support and specialist advice (Burke, 1987 **C**; McMillan et al., 1989 **C**; Oddy et al., 1989 **C**; NIH, 1998 **C**) and to emphasize the need for physiotherapeutic intervention to be influenced by individual lifestyle factors, family and cultural issues and be informed by a comprehensive assessment of post-injury limitations and abilities.

References

Association of Chartered Physiotherapists in Neurology [ACPIN] (1998) Clinical Practice Guidelines on Splinting Adults with Neurological Dysfunction.

Bateman AJ et al. (1999) Exercise tolerance in patients who have suffered recent brain injury. Journal of Sports Sciences 17(1): 27–8.

Bernard PH, Dill H, Held JM, Judd DL, Nalette E (1984) Reduction of hypertonicity by early casting in a comatose head injured individual: a case report. Physical Therapy 64: 1540–2.

Body R, Herbert C, Campbell M, Parker M, Usher A (1996) An integrated approach to team assessment in head injury. Brain Injury 10(4): 311–18.

Booth BJ, Doyle M, Montgomery J (1983) Serial casting for the management of spasticity in the head injured patient. Physical Therapy 63: 1960–6.

Brazzelli M, Della Sala S (1997) Physiotherapy and neuropsychology: an interaction that could ease the remedy of brain disease. Physiotherapy Theory and Practice 13: 243–6.

Brooks D, Campsie L, Symington C, Beattie A, McKinlay W (1987) The effects of severe head injury on patient and relative within seven years of injury. Journal of Head Trauma Rehabilitation 2(3): 1–13.

Burke D (1987) Planning a system of care for head injuries. Brain Injury 1(2): 189–98.

Butler P, Farmer E, Major R (1997) Improvement in gait parameters following late intervention in traumatic brain injury: a long term follow-up report of a single case. Clinical Rehabilitation 11: 220–6.

Campbell M (2000a) Cognitive, behavioural and individual influences in programme design. In Campbell M Rehabilitation for Traumatic Brain Injury: Physical Therapy Practice in Context. Edinburgh: Churchill Livingstone.

Campbell M (2000b) Defining goals for intervention. In Campbell M Rehabilitation for Traumatic Brain Injury: Physical Therapy Practice in Context. Edinburgh: Churchill Livingstone.

Campbell M (2000c) Initial considerations in the process of assessment. In Campbell M (Ed) Rehabilitation for Traumatic Brain Injury: Physical Therapy Practice in Context. Edinburgh: Churchill Livingstone.

Campbell M (2000e) Understanding the impact of the traumatic event and the influence of life context. In Campbell M Rehabilitation for Traumatic Brain Injury: Physical Therapy Practice in Context. Edinburgh: Churchill Livingstone.

Campbell M (2000f) Understanding traumatic brain injury. In Campbell M Rehabilitation for Traumatic Brain Injury: Physical Therapy Practice in Context. Edinburgh: Churchill Livingstone.

Conine T, Sullivan T, Mackie T, Goodmann M (1990) Effect of serial casting for the prevention of equinus in patients with acute head injury. Archives of Physical Medicine and Rehabilitation 71: 310–12.

Cornall C (1992) Splinting and contractures. Synapse April: 50–4.

Directorate of Professional Services (1999) Clinical Practice Guidelines for the Application and Management of Removable Splints for Adults with Neurological Dysfunction within Central Sheffield University Hospitals NHS Trust. Sheffield: Central Sheffield University Hospitals NHS Trust.

Dobkin B (1998a) Activity-dependent recovery contributes to motor recovery. Annals of Neurology 44(2): 158–60.

Dobkin B (1998b) Driving cognitive and motor gains with rehabilitation after brain and spinal cord injury. Current Opinion in Neurology 11: 639–41.

Douglas J (1996) Indicators of long-term family functioning following severe traumatic brain injury in adults. Brain Injury 10(11): 819–39.

Douglas MJ (1990) Traumatic brain injury and the family. Making Headway, NZSTA Biennial Conference, Christchurch, NZ.

Eames P, Wood R (1989) The structure and content of a head injury rehabilitation service. In Wood RL, Eames P (Eds) Models of Brain Injury Rehabilitation. London: Chapman & Hall, pp 31–58.

Edwards S (1996) Abnormal tone and movement as a result of neurological impairment. In Edwards S (Ed) Neurological Physiotherapy: A Problem Solving Approach. Edinburgh: Churchill Livingstone, pp 63–86.

Edwards S, Charlton P. (1996) Splinting and the use of orthoses in the management of patients with neurological disorders. In Edwards S (Ed) Neurological Physiotherapy: A Problem Solving Approach. Edinburgh: Churchill Livingstone, pp 161–88.

Ellenberg J, Levin S, Saydjari C (1996) Post-traumatic amnesia as a predictor of outcome after severe closed injury. Archives of Neurology 53: 782–91.

Goldspink G, Williams P (1990) Muscle fibre changes and connective tissue changes associated with use and disuse. In Ada L, Canning C (Eds) Key Issues in Neurological Physiotherapy. London: Butterworth Heinemann, pp 197–218.

Greenwood R, McMillan TM (1993) Models of rehabilitation programmes for the brain-injured adult, I: Current provision, efficacy and good practice. Clinical Rehabilitation 7: 248–55.

Hibbard M, Uysal S, Sliwinski M, Gordon W (1998) Undiagnosed health issues in individuals with traumatic brain injury living in the community. Journal of Head Trauma Rehabilitation 13(4): 47–57.

Hillier S, Metzer J (1997) Awareness and perceptions of outcomes after traumatic brain injury. Brain Injury 11(7): 525–36.

Hillier S, Sharpe M, Metzer J (1997) Outcomes 5 years post-traumatic brain injury with further reference to neurophysical impairment and disability. Brain Injury 11(9): 661–75.

Hurvitz E, Mandac R (1992) Risk factors for heterotopic ossification in children and adolescents with severe traumatic brain injury. Archives of Physical Medicine and Rehabilitation 73: 459–62.

Ippolito E, Formisano R, Farsetti P, Caterini R, Renta F (1999a) Resection of elbow ossification and continuous passive motion in post comatose patients. Journal of Hand Surgery (American Volume) 24(3): 546–53.

Ippolito E, Formisano R, Farsetti P, Caterini R, Renata F (1999b) Excision for the treatment of periarticular ossification of the knee in patients who have had traumatic brain injury. Journal of Bone and Joint Surgery (American Volume) 81(6): 783–9.

Koskinen S (1998) Quality of life 10 years after a very severe traumatic brain injury (TBI): the perspective of the injured and the closest relative. Brain Injury 12(8): 631–48.

Lezak M (1978) Subtle sequelae of brain damage: perplexity, distractibility and fatigue. American Journal of Physical Medicine 57: 9–15.

Mayo NE, Sullivan SJ et al. (1991) Observer variation in assessing neurophysical signs among patients with head injuries. American Journal of Physical Medicine and Rehabilitation 70(3): 118–23.

McMillan T, Bonham A, Oddy M, Stroud A, Rickard R (1989) A comprehensive service for the rehabilitation and long-term care of head injury survivors. Clinical Rehabilitation 3: 253–9.

McMillan T, Greenwood R (1993) Head injury. In Greenwood R, Barnes MP, McMillan TM, Ward CD (Eds) Neurological Rehabilitation. Edinburgh: Churchill Livingstone, pp 437–50.

Mills V (1984) Electromyographic results of inhibitory splinting. Physical Therapy 64: 190–207.

Moseley AM (1997) The effect of casting combined with stretching on passive ankle dorsiflexion in adults with traumatic brain injury. Physical Therapy 77: 240–7.

Newton R (1995) Balance abilities in individuals with moderate and severe traumatic brain injury. Brain Injury 9(5): 445–51.

NIH (1998) Consensus Statement: Rehabilitation of Persons with Traumatic Brain Injury. National Institutes of Health Consensus Development Conference.

Oddy M, Bonham E, McMillan T, Stroud A, Rickard S (1989) A comprehensive service for the rehabilitation and long-term care of head injury survivors. Clinical Rehabilitation 3: 253–9.

Pette D, Vrbova G (1985) Neural control of phenotype expression in mammalian muscle fibres. Muscle and Nerve 8: 676–89.

Ponsford J (1995) Working with families. In Ponsford J, Sloan S, Snow P (Eds) Traumatic Brain Injury: Rehabilitation for Everyday Adaptive Living. Hove: Lawrence Erlbaum, pp 265–94.

Ponsford J, Olver J, Curran C (1995) A profile of outcome: 2 years after traumatic brain injury. Brain Injury 9(1): 1–10.

Powell T, Partridge T, Nickolls T, Wright L, Mould H, Cook C, Anderson A, Blakey L, Boyer M, Davis L, Grimshaw A, Johnsen E, Lambert L, Pearce D, Smith A, Sturman S, Searle Y, Tatter S (1994) An interdisciplinary approach to the rehabilitation of people with brain injury. British Journal of Therapy and Rehabilitation 1(1): 8–13.

Rosenbaum DA (1991) Human Motor Control, 1st edn. San Diego: Academic Press.

Rusk H, Loman W, Block JM (1966) Rehabilitation of the patient with head injury. Clinical Neurosurgery 12: 312–23.

Sullivan T, Conine TA, Goodman M, Mackie T (1988) Serial casting to prevent equinus in acute traumatic head injury. Physiotherapy Canada 40: 346–50.

Swaine BR, Sullivan SJ (1996a) Reliability of early motor function testing in persons following severe traumatic brain injury. Brain Injury 10(4): 263–76.

Swaine BR, Sullivan SJ (1996b) Longitudinal profile of early motor recovery following severe traumatic brain injury. Brain Injury 10(5): 347–66.

Swaine BR, Sullivan SJ (1999) Interpreting reliability of early motor function measurement following head injury. Physiotherapy Theory and Practice 15: 155–64.

Tyerman A (1991) Counselling in head injury. In Davis H, Falklowfield L (Eds) Counselling and Communication in Health Care. Chichester: Wiley, pp 115–28.

Vrbova G, Gordon T, Jones R (1997) Nerve–Muscle Interaction. London: Chapman & Hall.

Watson M (1997) Evidence for 'significant' late stage motor recovery in patients with severe traumatic brain injury: a literature review with relevance to neurological physiotherapy. Physical Therapy Review 2: 93–106.

Wilson JTL, Teasdale GM, Hadley DM, Weidmann KD, Lang D (1993) Post-traumatic amnesia: still a valuable yardstick. Journal of Neurology, Neurosurgery, and Psychiatry 56: 198–201.

Physical Management and Rehabilitation of Patients with Traumatic Head Injury (2)

ANNE MOSELEY

Background

The evidence for physiotherapy practice for the case history of Mr ND, an 18-year-old man with a severe traumatic head injury (THI), will be organized using the five steps outlined by Sackett et al. (2000, pp 3–4). The first step involves asking a clinical question in a form that can be answered. The second, searching for the best external evidence. The third, critically appraising the evidence for its validity and importance. The fourth, applying the evidence to clinical practice; and lastly, evaluating performance.

A four-part formula (Richardson et al., 1995) will be used for the first step of the evidence-based practice process, that is, asking a clinical question in a form that can be answered. Each question will contain the following elements:

- patient (a person with a severe THI);
- outcome(s) of interest;
- therapy of interest;
- alternative or comparison therapy.

All questions will relate to the efficacy of therapy. Searches for the best external evidence (step two, above) will be limited to study designs with the least amount of bias for questions of efficacy. Based on the hierarchy of evidence for assessing the effectiveness of healthcare interventions (Fisher, 1989) the strongest evidence is provided by a systematic review of all relevant randomized controlled trials (level I), and at least one properly designed randomized controlled trial (level II). Searches will, therefore, be restricted to systematic reviews (or meta-analyses) and randomized controlled trials (or quasi-randomized controlled trials) because these provide the strongest evidence for the efficacy of physiotherapy interventions. Where these levels of evidence are unavailable for THI, searches will be broadened to other patient populations that exhibit some impairments comparable with THI rather than accepting lower levels of evidence. In these cases I shall use my clinical experience to adjust the effect sizes reported for other patient populations in order to decide which treatments may produce more good than harm for Mr ND. Where this approach is not possible, treatment decisions will be based on clinical experience and a biological rationale.

The information sources used for searches (step two, above) will include the Physiotherapy Evidence Database (PEDro) (Herbert et al., 1998–99), Medline, Cumulated Index to Nursing and Allied Health Literature (CINAHL), and the Cochrane Library (which includes the Database of Abstracts of Reviews of Effectiveness, or DARE), depending on the nature of the question. The PEDro database is freely available on the Internet (http://ptwww.cchs.usyd.edu.au/pedro). It contains bibliographic details and author abstracts of systematic reviews and randomized controlled trials in physiotherapy. The majority of randomized controlled trials have been rated for methodological quality. The other computer databases are described elsewhere (Booth and Madge, 1998).

All searches were conducted in January 2000 and included terms to define the patient, outcome and therapy of interest. Medline and CINAHL searches also included method search terms in order to target randomized controlled trials and systematic reviews [(rand$.tw) or (systematic review.pt)] and, when relevant, search terms to confine the search to the area of physiotherapy [(physiotherap$.tw) or (exp physical therapy/) or (physical therapy.tw)]. Hard copies of relevant randomized controlled trials and systematic reviews were obtained for each search.

A series of methodological filters was used to critically appraise the external evidence (step three, above). The filters for randomized controlled trials were those features known to influence the results if not included in the research design (Guyatt et al., 1993). They were:

- subjects randomly allocated to groups;
- concealed allocation to groups;
- blinding of assessors, therapists and subjects;
- adequate follow-up (a dropout rate of less than 15% was used as the criterion).

The methodological filters applied to systematic reviews (Oxman et al., 1994) were:

- use of a comprehensive search strategy;
- rating of trial quality undertaken and considered in the subsequent analysis of results.

To complete the critical appraisal process (step three, above), the size of the treatment effect was determined. This involved some additional calculations when the authors did not report mean difference and confidence intervals for continuous data, or the number-needed-to-treat and confidence intervals for dichotomous data. The formulae provided by Sackett et al. (2000, pp 233–43) were used for all calculations.

General Principles

The remainder of this review will focus on the evidence for four questions related to the physiotherapy management of Mr ND. The first two questions relate to complications that are relatively common after severe THI: contracture and decubitus ulcers. The last two questions concern physiotherapy intervention aimed at improving motor function.

Question 1: After THI, are prolonged stretches more effective than passive movements in preventing and treating contractures?

Contractures are a relatively common problem after THI (Yarkony and Sahgal, 1987 **A**). Mr ND was assessed as having bilateral plantarflexion contractures during his stay in the neurosurgical ward (–15 degrees for the left ankle and –20 degrees for the right). If they are not already present, Mr ND is at risk of developing contractures at other joints because of his pattern of muscle weakness and overactivity (these include the right neck lateral flexors and rotators, right shoulder internal rotators and adductors).

Clinically, two broad types of stretching intervention are used to prevent and treat contracture. The first involves placing the 'at risk' muscle(s) in a position of stretch for lengthy periods of time. Prolonged low-load stretching, positioning, splinting and serial casting are examples of long duration stretches. The second involves stretching 'at risk' muscles(s) for short periods of time. High-load brief stretches, passive physiological movements and proprioceptive neuromuscular facilitation (PNF) exercises are examples of short-duration stretches. To determine the relative efficacy of these two types of stretching for Mr ND, I have posed the question: 'After THI, are prolonged stretches more effective than passive movements in preventing and treating contractures?'

A search of the PEDro database using 'stretching, mobilization, manipulation, massage' in the therapy field and 'neurology' in the subdiscipline field produced one systematic review and 24 randomized controlled trials (searches of Medline, CINAHL and DARE did not yield any additional trials or reviews). Three of the randomized controlled trials were relevant to the question but all investigated the remediation rather than the prevention of contracture (see Table 1). One trial of moderate quality (Moseley, 1997 **A**) was specifically in the area of THI and investigated the effect of serial casting versus no passive stretching to remediate plantarflexion contractures. Two low-quality randomized controlled trials compared prolonged low-load stretching with PNF exercises plus passive movements to remediate knee flexion contractures (Light et al., 1984 **A**; Steffen and Mollinger, 1995 **A**). Because the trials did not pass the four methodological filters for randomized controlled trials, their results are likely to overestimate the true effect of stretching treatment.

From the Moseley (1997 **A**) trial, a serial cast applied for one week increased passive ankle dorsiflexion by an average of 15.4 degrees more than one week of no passive stretching, with a 95% confidence interval of 5.6 to 25.2 degrees (effect size calculated by the author of this chapter). The subjects in this trial had all sustained severe THIs, so the results are directly relevant to the treatment of Mr ND.

The trials comparing long-duration stretching with short-duration stretching produced conflicting results. Light et al. (1984 **A**) report that one hour of stretching per day, five days per week for a period of one month increased passive knee extension by an average of 16.3 degrees more than 15 minutes of PNF exercises and passive movements at the same frequency, with a 95% confidence interval of 7.8 to 24.8 degrees (effect size calculated by the author of this chapter). In comparison, the between-group results from Steffen and Mollinger (1995 **A**) were not significant (see 95% confidence intervals in Table 1). Subjects in both studies were elderly nursing home residents with knee flexion contractures produced by a combination of disease processes (including stroke, osteoarthritis, hip fracture) who, for the Light et al. (1984 **A**) trial only, were unable to ambulate. Based on clinical experience I would expect the effect size to be larger for people with THI because of their younger age and lack of concomitant disease processes.

The available evidence would support the use of serial casting to remediate Mr ND's plantarflexion contractures (Moseley, 1997 **A**). Based on the lower limit of the 95% confidence interval (5.6 degrees, from Table 1), it is expected that a series of three casts would need to be applied to achieve at least a plantargrade position. However, the pressure area on

Table 1: Critical appraisal of randomized controlled trials examining the effects of stretching

Trial	Random allocation	Concealed allocation	Blinding			Adequate follow up	Size of effect
			Assessor	Therapists	Subjects		
Moseley (1997 A)	yes	no	no	no	no	yes	15.4 degrees (5.6 to 25.2)*
Steffen et al. (1995 A)	no	no	yes	no	no	no	0.8 degrees (–6.8 to 8.4)*
Light et al. (1984 A)	yes	no	no	no	no	no	16.3 degrees (7.8 to 24.8)*

Note: * mean between-group difference and 95% confidence intervals.

Mr ND's right lateral malleolus is a contra-indication for casting. Based on clinical experience, it may be possible to apply a cast with a window cut to expose the pressure area, but this would have to be trialled under close supervision. Alternatively, it may not be possible to cast the right ankle until the pressure area heals.

While no randomized controlled trials appear to have investigated stretching to prevent contracture, clinical experience indicates that it is likely that treatment would be similar to that required for contracture remediation. The trial by Steffen and Mollinger (1995 **A**) showed no evidence for effect for either long- or short-duration stretches. In contrast, Light et al. (1984 **A**) report that prolonged stretches are superior to PNF exercises and passive movements combined. Until further trials are undertaken in this area, clinical experience suggests that prolonged low-load stretches may prevent contracture. When Mr ND's ankle plantarflexion contractures have been remediated using serial casting, ankle flexibility could possibly be maintained using a regimen of tilt-table standing with a wedge placed under the feet (Bohannon and Larkin, 1985 **B**). A positioning programme could also be implemented to prevent contracture in other joints. For example, Mr ND's right shoulder internal rotators and adductors could be stretched by positioning his arm in abduction and external rotation during the day (see Figure 9.5b from Ada and Canning, 1990 **C**, p 230).

The treating physiotherapist could monitor how effective the stretching treatment is from two perspectives. First, she could check that Mr ND was actually receiving his planned prolonged low-load stretches. Second, she could measure passive range of motion of the joints being targeted to confirm that flexibility was being maintained or was increasing at the expected rate. If taken regularly (weekly or fortnightly), these joint measurements could be used to adjust the dose of stretching being implemented.

Question 2: After THI, does the use of a pressure-relieving mattress or cushion prevent the development of pressure areas compared with a regular foam mattress or cushion?

When admitted to the intensive care unit (ICU), Mr ND had an area of skin breakdown on his right lateral malleolus that is thought to have occurred at the time of injury. Until he is able to move enough to change his body position regularly, Mr ND is at risk of developing decubitus ulcers.

Treatments used to prevent decubitus ulcers include regular repositioning (two-hourly turns) or using pressure-relieving support surfaces (mattresses and cushions). To determine the efficacy of pressure-relieving mattresses, I have posed the question: 'After THI, does the use of a pressure-relieving mattress or cushion prevent the development of pressure areas compared with a regular foam mattress or cushion?'

I selected the Cochrane Library as the information source for this question because it is not physiotherapy specific. A search of the Cochrane Library using the terms 'pressure' and 'sore' produced three complete systematic reviews. Screening the titles of these reviews revealed that one was directly relevant to my question (Cullum et al., 1999 **A**). This review was further evaluated.

The Cullum et al. (1999 **A**) systematic review passed both methodological filters. It used a very comprehensive search strategy of computer databases, hand searching, citation tracking and contacting researchers in the area to identify 29 randomized controlled trials in a range of patient groups (none specifically after THI). All trials identified were rated for quality (they were generally of low quality), and these ratings were used in the narrative interpretation.

The main finding was that high-specification foam mattresses, constant low-pressure mattresses and alternating pressure mattresses were superior to standard foam mattresses in terms of pressure-area prevention. For example, one trial compared low-air-loss beds to 'standard ICU beds' (Inman et al., 1993 **A**). From this trial, three patients would need to use a low-air-loss bed in order to prevent one patient from developing pressure areas, with a 95% confidence interval of two to five (effect size calculated by the author of this chapter). The relative merits of the three alternatives for pressure-relieving mattresses, however, are unclear. Only two randomized controlled trials compared different types of seat cushions for preventing decubitus ulcers. There was no difference between slab and contoured-foam cushions (Lim et al., 1988 **A**), and a trend for gel cushions to be superior to foam cushions (Conine et al., 1994 **A**). In the latter trial, seven patients would need to use a gel cushion in order to prevent one patient from developing pressure areas, with a 95% confidence interval of three to 100.

The available evidence would support Mr ND's use of a pressure relieving mattress and a gel cushion while he is physically dependent. The health professionals involved in Mr ND's care would need to monitor his skin regularly for early signs of breakdown. For example, when repositioning Mr ND the physiotherapist could check for skin or tissue discoloration or damage that persists after the removal of pressure. Mr ND already has skin breakdown over his right malleolus that may require special attention. The health professionals responsible for wound healing could search the Cochrane Library to determine the current best intervention to heal an existing wound.

Question 3: After THI, does task-specific training of sitting balance improve functional outcomes more than neurophysiological treatments?

In the general surgical ward it was noted that Mr ND could not sit unsupported and, based on clinical experience, would still be likely to have impaired sitting balance when transferred to the rehabilitation unit at 2.5 months post THI. Broadly speaking, physiotherapists have trained sitting balance using one of two methods: by training of self-initiated movements in sitting (such as reaching to grasp a glass) or by having the patient respond to physiotherapist-induced movement. The former is advocated under the movement science or task-specific framework for physiotherapy intervention (Carr and Shepherd, 1998 **B**), while the latter is used in neurophysiological approaches (Bobath therapy) to treatment (Bobath, 1990 **C**). To determine the relative efficacy of these two forms of treatment I have posed the question: 'After THI, does task-specific training of sitting balance improve functional outcomes more than neurophysiological treatments?'

A search of the PEDro database using the terms 'sitting' and 'balance' in the abstract field and 'neurology' in the subdiscipline field produced two randomized controlled trials. Only one of these trials was relevant to the question, but provided an incomplete answer. Searching Medline, CINAHL and DARE did not yield any additional trials or reviews. Dean and Shepherd (1997 **A**) compared two weeks of task-specific sitting balance training to sham intervention in a small group of stroke patients. The trial was of high quality, fulfilling the methodological filters for random allocation, concealed allocation, assessor blinding and adequate follow-up.

Some of the variables used for between-group comparisons by Dean and Shepherd (1997 **A**) were the maximum reaching distance as well as time to reach and grasp a glass placed at 140% of arm's length away and the peak force through the affected leg during this reach. All reaches were performed with the unaffected arm in three directions: 45 degrees across the body towards the affected side, straight forward and 45 degrees away from the affected side. I have calculated the effect size for each of the reaching test variables that had a statistically significant between-group difference (see Table 2).

Task-specific sitting balance training had a clinically significant improvement for most of the variables reported in Table 2. For example, I projected that the smallest difference in maximum reaching distance that would make

TOURO COLLEGE LIBRARY

Table 2: Effect size of task-specific compared with sham sitting balance training (Dean and Shepherd, 1997 **A**)

Variable	Mean effect	95 % CI*
Increased distance reached towards the affected side (mm)	120	30 to 210
Increased distance reached forward (mm)	100	10 to 190
Increased distance reached towards the unaffected side (mm)	80	34.7 to 125.3
Decreased hand movement time when reaching to 140% of arm's length towards the affected side (seconds)	1.5	0.3 to 2.7
Decreased hand movement time when reaching to 140% of arm's length towards the unaffected side (seconds)	1.2	0.3 to 2.1
Increased force through affected leg when reaching 140% of arm's length towards affected side (% body weight)	12.1	5.5 to 18.7
Increased force through affected leg when reaching 140% of arm's length forward (% body weight)	9.5	5.0 to 14.0

Note: * 95% confidence intervals.

implementation of the task-specific sitting balance training clinically worthwhile was 20 mm. The lower limit of the 95% confidence interval exceeded this value for reaching towards and away from the affected side, while the distance reached forward just included this value.

The subjects used in the Dean and Shepherd (1997 **A**) trial had all been discharged from rehabilitation, were at least one year post-stroke and did not have any obvious cognitive or perceptual problems. In comparison, Mr ND is significantly more acute and would be expected to have significant neuropsychological impairments as a result of his THI. Based on clinical experience, I would expect the effect size for task-specific sitting balance training for a two-week period to be smaller for Mr ND because of his concomitant neuropsychological impairments.

While there appear to be no systematic reviews or randomized controlled trials that compare task-specific training and neurophysiological treatments for sitting balance, one randomized controlled trial has demonstrated a clinically significant effect of task-specific training after stroke (Dean and Shepherd, 1997 **A**). Until more trials are conducted in this area, the best available external evidence would support the implementation of task-specific sitting balance training for Mr ND. Dean and Shepherd (1997 **A**) describe a training programme that could be adjusted and progressed in order to challenge Mr ND's motor performance. The programme involves training self-initiated reaching movements in sitting under varied conditions (distance and direction reached, seat height, movement speed, object weight and extent of thigh support on the seat).

Some of the variables reported by Dean and Shepherd (1997 **A**) could be used to monitor the change in Mr ND's performance with the training programme. For example, the physiotherapist could measure the maximum distance Mr ND could reach with his left arm as he attempts to reach in different directions using a tape measure. Alternatively, bathroom scales could be used to measure the amount of weight borne through Mr ND's right foot as he reaches a standardized distance forward or to the right.

Question 4: After THI, does more intensive physiotherapy intervention lead to better functional outcomes when compared with less intensive physiotherapy intervention?

As Mr ND emerges from coma and becomes more orientated in the general surgical ward and, later, in the rehabilitation unit, the physiotherapist will need to make a decision about the quantity of motor training to provide. To investigate this issue about the amount of training and functional outcomes, I have posed the question: 'After THI, does more intensive physiotherapy intervention lead to better functional outcomes when compared with less intensive physiotherapy intervention?'

A search of the PEDro database using the term 'intensity' in the abstract field and 'neurology' in the subdiscipline field produced 13 records. While none of the records related to THI, there were two systematic reviews directly addressing the question for the stroke population (Kwakkel et al., 1997 **A**; Langhorne et al., 1996 **A**), two relevant randomized controlled trials for the stroke population that were published after the systematic reviews (Kwakkel et al., 1999 **A**; Lincoln et al., 1999 **A**) and nine other randomized controlled trials. Searching Medline, CINAHL and DARE did not yield any additional trials or reviews. I decided to appraise the most recent systematic review (Kwakkel et al., 1997 **A**) as well as the two relevant and more recent randomized controlled trials. The latter was undertaken to confirm that the results were consistent with the review and to assist with establishing the clinical significance of the results.

The Kwakkel et al. (1997 **A**) review passed both of the methodological filters for systematic reviews and summarized the results of nine randomized controlled studies. On average, intensive physiotherapy (48.4 minutes per day) was about twice the quantity of regular physiotherapy

(18.5 minutes per day). Intensive therapy was associated with better outcomes for activities of daily living (mean effect of 0.28 standard units, with a 95% confidence interval of 0.16 to 0.40), higher neuromuscular scores (mean effect of 0.37 standard units, with a 95% confidence interval of 0.13 to 0.61) and a trend towards higher functional levels (mean effect of 0.10 standard units, with a 95% confidence interval of –0.11 to 0.31). Each of the effect sizes was calculated by Kwakkel et al. (1997 **A**). Because the results were expressed as standard units, it was not possible to determine the effect size using clinically meaningful units.

Both of the randomized controlled trials were of relatively high quality (Kwakkel et al., 1999 **A**; Lincoln et al., 1999 **A**) (see Table 3). Kwakkel et al. (1999 **A**) compared standard physiotherapy (30 minutes per day) plus airsplint immobilization of the arm and leg with standard physiotherapy plus 30 minutes per day extra arm training, and standard physiotherapy plus 30 minutes per day extra leg training after stroke. Interventions used in the extra training could be broadly classified as task specific. During the 20 weeks of intervention, the extra leg training group could walk significantly faster and had significantly better functional ambulation, dexterity and functional abilities compared with the control group. For example, at 20 weeks subjects in the extra leg training group could walk an average of 0.36 metres per second faster than the control group, with a 95% confidence interval of 0.02 to 0.70 metres per second (effect size calculated by the author of this chapter). Over the same period, the extra arm training group had significantly better dexterity than the control group. Six weeks after training the reported effects were reduced. These results are consistent with the previously published systematic review by Kwakkel et al. (1997 **A**).

In contrast with the Kwakkel et al. (1999 **A**) trial, the Lincoln et al. (1999 **A**) study produced non-significant results. Lincoln et al. (1999 **A**) investigated the intensity of Bobath therapy on arm function after stroke. The control group received 30 to 45 minutes per day of Bobath therapy for five weeks. The experimental groups received the control therapy plus two hours per week extra Bobath therapy from either a qualified physiotherapist or a physiotherapy assistant. There were no significant between-group differences for dexterity or functional abilities at any of the follow-up assessments.

There do not appear to be any systematic reviews and randomized controlled trials that evaluate the effect of therapy intensity after THI. Until this research is undertaken, estimates for the effect size of intensive therapy may be drawn from the stroke literature. It is difficult to adjust the effect sizes reported by Kwakkel et al. (1997 **A**, 1999 **A**) to the THI population. People with THI are younger and generally free from concomitant disease processes, which suggests that larger effect sizes should be expected clinically. In contrast, however, people with THI have global neuropsychological

Table 3: Critical appraisal of randomized controlled trials examining the effects of physiotherapy intensity

Trial	Random allocation	Concealed allocation	Blinding			Adequate follow up
			Assessor	Therapists	Subjects	
Kwakkel et al. (1999 **A**)	yes	yes	yes	no	no	yes
Lincoln et al. (1999 **A**)	yes	yes	yes	no	no	no

impairments and neurobehavioural sequelae associated with frontal lobe damage, which would reduce the expected effect size.

One challenge faced by the physiotherapist is how to implement more intensive therapy in the presence of Mr ND's neuropsychological impairments (including memory problems and decreased attention). Based on clinical experience, strategies which may increase the total amount of practice include practising tasks important to Mr ND, using strong cues to draw his attention to the task (such as using a limb-load monitor to provide feedback about the amount of weight being borne through the right leg), changing the task or exercise frequently and having frequent but shorter physiotherapy sessions in order to maximize the total amount of practice. These strategies require empirical validation.

Ada (1999 **C**) has highlighted that implementing intensive one-on-one physiotherapy may be difficult in the current economic climate. Physiotherapists may need to explore other models of service delivery in order to provide more intense therapy without increasing staffing levels. Some solutions could include group exercise (a circuit class), structuring practice the patient can complete independently or with the assistance of their family and friends, and setting up work stations. Again, these solutions still require empirical validation.

Implications

The five-step process of evidence-based practice described by Sackett et al. (2000) was used to review the current evidence for physiotherapy intervention for people with THI. Four questions (two about complications and two about motor training) were posed. Only one randomized controlled trial conducted with THI subjects was identified during the four searches. For each question, systematic reviews and randomized controlled trials from other patient populations (mainly stroke) were used to estimate the effects of different treatments for Mr ND, an 18-year-old man with a severe THI. The answers to the questions reflect the external evidence available in early 2000. Evidence-based practice is a dynamic process, so it will be very interesting to repeat these questions in five years' time to see how the treatment recommendations have changed.

The search results from the questions posed about Mr ND's physiotherapy treatment highlight some areas of need for clinical research. Future research could be directed toward establishing the optimum type and amount of stretching and therapy specifically for the THI population. This research would expand the external evidence available to physiotherapists to facilitate evidence-based clinical decision-making.

References

Ada L (1999) Commentary on intense lower limb training enhances lower limb function and intense upper limb training enhances upper limb function following stroke. Australian Journal of Physiotherapy 45(4): 319.

Ada L, Canning C (1990) Anticipating and avoiding muscle shortening. In Ada L, Canning C (Eds) Key Issues in Neurological Physiotherapy. Oxford: Heinemann Medical, pp 219–36.

Bobath B (1990) Adult Hemiplegia: Evaluation and Treatment, 3rd edn. London: Heinemann Medical.

Bohannon RW, Larkin PA (1985) Passive ankle dorsiflexion increases in patients after a regimen of tilt table-wedge board standing: a clinical report. Physical Therapy 65(11): 1676–8.

Booth A, Madge B (1998) Finding the evidence. In Bury T, Mead J (Eds) Evidence-based Healthcare: A Practical Guide for Therapists. Oxford: Butterworth-Heinemann, pp 107–35.

Carr JH, Shepherd RB (1998) Neurological Rehabilitation: Optimizing Motor Performance. Oxford: Butterworth-Heinemann.

Conine TA, Hershler C, Daechsel D, Peel C, Pearson A (1994) Pressure sore prophylaxis in elderly patients using polyurethane foam or Jay wheelchair cushions. International Journal of Rehabilitation Research 17(2): 123–37.

Cullum N, Deeks J, Sheldon TA, Song F, Fletcher AW (1999) Beds, mattresses and cushions for pressure sore prevention and treatment (Cochrane Review). The Cochrane Library, Issue 4: Oxford: Update Software.

Dean CM, Shepherd RB (1997) Task-related training improves performance of seated reaching tasks after stroke. A randomized controlled trial. Stroke 28(4): 722–8.

Fisher M (Ed) (1989) Guide to Clinical Preventive Services: An Assessment of the Effectiveness of 169 Interventions. Baltimore: Williams & Wilkins, ch. 1.

Guyatt GH, Sackett DL, Cook DJ (1993) Users' guides to the medical literature, II: How to use an article about therapy or prevention, A. Are the results of the study valid? JAMA 270(21): 2598–601.

Herbert RD, Moseley AM, Sherrington C (1998–99) PEDro: a database of randomised controlled trials in physiotherapy. Health Information Management 28(4): 186–8.

Inman KJ, Sibbald WJ, Rutledge FS, Clark BJ (1993) Clinical utility and cost-effectiveness of an air suspension bed in the prevention of pressure ulcers. JAMA 269(9): 1139–43.

Kwakkel G, Wagenaar RC, Koelman TW, Lankhorst GJ, Koetsier JC (1997) Effects of intensity of rehabilitation after stroke: a research synthesis. Stroke 28(8): 1550–6.

Kwakkel G, Wagenaar RC, Twisk JW, Lankhorst GJ, Koetsier JC (1999) Intensity of leg and arm training after primary middle-cerebral-artery stroke: a randomised trial. Lancet 354(9174): 191–6.

Langhorne P, Wagenaar R, Partridge C (1996) Physiotherapy after stroke: more is better? Physiotherapy Research International 1(2): 75–88.

Light KE, Nuzik S, Personius W, Barstrom A (1984) Low-load prolonged stretch vs. high-load brief stretch in treating knee contractures. Physical Therapy 64(3): 330–3.

Lim R, Sirett R, Conine TA, Daechsel D (1988) Clinical trial of foam cushions in the prevention of decubitis ulcers in elderly patients. Journal of Rehabilitation Research and Development 25(2): 19–26.

Lincoln NB, Parry RH, Vass CD (1999) Randomized, controlled trial to evaluate increased intensity of physiotherapy treatment of arm function after stroke. Stroke 30(3): 573–9.

Moseley AM (1997) The effect of casting combined with stretching on passive ankle dorsiflexion in adults with traumatic head injuries. Physical Therapy 77(3): 240–7.

Oxman AD, Cook DJ, Guyatt GH (1994) Users' guides to the medical literature, VI: How to use an overview. JAMA 272(17): 1367–71.

Richardson WS, Wilson MC, Nishikawa J, Hayward RS (1995) The well-built clinical question: a key to evidence-based decisions. ACP Journal Club 123(3): A12–A13.

Sackett DL, Straus SE, Richardson WS, Rosenberg W, Haynes RB (2000) Evidence-Based Medicine: How to Practise and Teach EBM, 2nd edn. Edinburgh: Churchill Livingstone.

Steffen TM, Mollinger LA (1995) Low-load, prolonged stretch in the treatment of knee flexion contractures in nursing home residents. Physical Therapy 75(10): 886–95.

Yarkony GM, Sahgal V (1987) Contractures: a major complication of craniocerebral trauma. Clinical Orthopaedics and Related Research 219: 93–6.

Complete spinal lesion C6

CASE REPORT – MR SP

Background

Mr SP was a 24-year-old single man who lived with his parents. He worked as a supervisor in a shipping company, and enjoyed football and socializing with friends. He had a diving accident while on holiday in Spain and was admitted to a local Spanish hospital and then to hospital in London four days post-injury. He was finally transferred to a specialized spinal injury centre (SIC) 11 days later.

Diagnosis

C6 spinal fracture resulting in a C6 complete spinal lesion with a zone of partial motor and sensory preservation in C7.

On Arrival at the SIC

- Nursed on turning bed.
- Two litres O_2 via mask.
- Bladder managed by catheterization.
- To have skull traction applied.

Summary of Main Events

Week 1: Uneventful
Week 2: Two episodes of left lung collapse/consolidation. Transferred to SIC.
Week 3: Swollen leg. DVT suspected, passive movements stopped.
Week 4: Passive movements restarted when prothrombin time within therapeutic range.
Week 5: Skull traction removed.

Week 7: Ready to get up (fracture healed and stable) but delayed due to sacral skin split.
Month 3: Up in wheelchair, functional independence measure (FIM) score 57. Recurring urinary tract problems interferes with the rehabilitation for the first three months of the rehabilitation period.
Month 10: Ready for discharge, but no suitable accommodation has been identified.
Month 15: Discharge to independent living with 24-hour live-in carer in own flat. FIM score 103.

On Initial Examination

- Full range of movements of all joints.
- Muscle power: Last normally innervated myotome is C6, some motor sparing in C7 (triceps and wrist flexors) and nothing below.
- Tone: increased in upper limbs.
- Sensation: full sensation to and including the C6 dermatome, impaired in the C7 dermatome and nothing below.
- Proprioception intact in the upper limbs.
- Pain in right shoulder due to subscapularis tendinitis.
- Skin: pressure area over right heel.

On Discharge

Mr SP achieved a high level of independent hand function, using a tenodesis grip. He is able to pick up large and small objects of varying weights and textures but does not have any form of power grip or individual finger control. He uses his mouth a great deal to assist his hands, especially for stabilizing objects.

There is increased tone in the trunk and lower limbs, mostly in a flexor pattern.

There are no postural problems at present. Mr SP has been given advice on maintenance of good midline posture and he is able to instruct others in any positioning he is not able to achieve independently.

Functional abilities:

- Feeding: uses palmar strap to hold utensils, can use knife for lighter tasks.
- Independent drinking using any mug with handle, or straight-sided container if not too heavy (both hands used); uses palmar strap for tooth cleaning.
- Minimal assistance needed with showering.

- Independent shaving using wet or dry razor; uses strap for both methods.
- Mostly independent in dressing and undressing, needs assistance with buttons, zips and shoe laces.Takes longer than normal.
- Bladder/bowel management: requires full assistance.

Mobility: Mr SP uses a manual wheelchair; he is independent on flat and moderately rough terrain as well as moderate slopes; he needs minimum assistance for kerbs.

Transfers: Mr SP can transfer sideways independently from bed, toilet and shower and needs minimum assistance to transfer to an easy chair. A hoist is used to get him into a bath. He needs the assistance of two people to transfer into the standing frame.

Communication: Mr SP is able to hold books, turn pages and write small amounts using an orthoplast writing splint; he is able to use a computer/typewriter with a trackerball style mouse, and to access a standard telephone.

Self-care/leisure: He manages light snacks and drinks and uses a microwave to heat meals, buts needs help with shopping and preparing main meals as well as cleaning tasks.

Mr SP has continued to socialize with friends and family during his time at the spinal centre and when staying with parents on weekend leave. He is very interested in sport and has become involved in archery, weight training, snooker and quadball and is hoping to obtain a Tracker bike for use in the future.

Driving: Mr SP is keen to return to driving, but is awaiting reissue of his amended licence.

Employment, housing and future arrangements: Mr SP plans to return to work once he has settled back into the community. He has been offered a two-bedroom flat to accommodate a 24-hour live-in carer. The long-term aim is to reduce this level of care as his own independence increases.

Treatment and Management of a Patient with Spinal Cord Injury (1)

EBBA BERGSTRÖM

Background

Mr SP has had his life changed in an instant from being a fit, healthy and independent young man into someone with a physical impairment that has robbed him of all independence in the short term, and for whom the long-term outlook is unknown. It is frightening to be unable to feel or move one's body and it feels degrading to require help with even the most intimate functions. Not knowing what the future holds is both frightening and unsettling.

The physical and psychological trauma the patient is experiencing has to be addressed by all members of the rehabilitation team. The value of the team approach in rehabilitation is now widely acknowledged (Bromley, 1998a **C**).

The overall aim of physical rehabilitation of the spinal cord injured person is to maximize the function within the potential of the individual and to educate the patient in how to prevent complications commonly occurring in spinal cord injury (SCI).

The primary role of a physiotherapist is to equip the patient with as many skills and techniques as possible, and to educate both him and those who will care for him about the injury and its consequences. The therapist will frequently demand of the patient difficult and often frightening tasks. He will also need to be encouraged into a certain amount of daring. Therefore it is important to win the trust of the patient. It is also important that all questions about the injury and its consequences are answered truthfully and sensitively. The patient needs to be allowed to take a full part in the decision-making and goal setting (Hammel, 1995 **C**).

Acute Phase

Assessment

As soon as Mr SP was admitted, a comprehensive assessment of all aspects of the SCI was undertaken. The information for the assessment is collected from a variety of sources, such as medical notes, the patient himself and other members of the team. This will enable each team member to set relevant short and long-term treatment goals.

The assessment of Mr SP's social history, especially family circumstances, housing and occupation, will usually take some time to complete and will have to be undertaken with great sensitivity. The information required by the therapist for future planning will not necessarily be appreciated by the patient and his relatives in the early stages. SP was living with his parents in a two-storey semi-detached house that was not suitable for the needs of a wheelchair-dependent tetraplegic.

The complete assessment of the acute patient includes the following.

Neurological Status

The level of the lesion is always referred to as the last intact neurological level, and the completeness of the injury is graded in accordance with the ASIA impairment scale (Maynard et al., 1997 **C**) which is a modified Frankel scale (Frankel et al., 1969 **C**). It is important to be aware of the neurological level in order to monitor any changes in the condition, especially in a cervical lesion where a rise of one or two levels may affect the respiratory function. On admission Mr SP was diagnosed as having a neurological lesion of C6 Frankel grade A with zone of partial preservation in C7. His lowest innervated key muscles were extensor carpi radialis and triceps at grade 3 and 2 respectively.

Mr SP had normal sensation in the C6 dermatome and impaired sensation in the C7 dermatome. He had no motor or sensory preservation below C7.

Muscle tone will be assessed according to the Ashworth scale (Ashworth, 1969). Mr SP had increased tone after the spinal shock had subsided.

Stability of the vertebral fracture as well as pain should be taken into consideration when assessing the patient and planning treatment. The assessment of muscle power and tone and range of movement (ROM) in all joints, both affected and unaffected, will be limited by the position Mr SP has to maintain in order not to disturb the fracture.

Respiratory Function

As Mr SP's injury occurred through diving, there is cause for concern as he may have inhaled potentially infected water. This increases the risk of a chest infection after a few days.

Chest movements and the ability to cough would be examined. In the case of tetraplegia at C6 the intercostal and abdominal muscles are not functioning. This will decrease the vital capacity considerably and the patient will not be able to cough independently. Results of investigations, such as X-rays and blood gases, are important for the planning of treatment.

Treatment

The main aims of the treatment at this stage for tetraplegia, Frankel grade A are to prevent respiratory complications, prevent circulatory complications, prevent loss of range of movement in all joints, to improve muscle strength in partially affected muscle groups and to maintain power in unaffected muscles.

Respiration

Because of the neurological level and history of Mr SP's injury the treatment needs to be implemented immediately. It includes deep breathing, postural drainage and assisted coughing. In addition, incentive spirometry and intermittent positive pressure breathing (IPPB) may be used prophylactically to help keep the airways clear (Jackson, 1983 **C**).

The treatment needs to be carried out several times each day and the respiratory function monitored by measuring the vital capacity daily. A sudden drop in vital capacity may signal a rise of the neurological level or a deterioration of the respiratory function. For someone with already diminished respiratory capacity swift action will have to be taken. At each treatment the respiratory function is assessed and the treatment readjusted accordingly.

Breathing exercises will consist of manually assisted exhalation during deep breathing. This improves the elastic recoil and promotes a deeper inspiration (Bromley et al., 1998 **C**).

Basic postural drainage is carried out with the regular turning that Mr SP undergoes in order to prevent skin problems. It is helpful if the patient is nursed on a turning bed as he then maintains the positions for longer, compared with other methods of turning, such as log rolling to inspect the skin. In the event of respiratory complications more specific drainage positions may have to be implemented. However, the patient should not be left unattended in these positions as there is a risk of choking if the mucus shifts and the patient cannot cough unaided.

The assisted cough is a very important part of the prophylactic chest treatment. It effectively clears the lungs of mucus. Several techniques are described by Bromley et al. (1998 **C**). The assisted cough consists of externally applied pressure over the diaphragm in a posterior and cranial direction to create the force needed to expel the air with sufficient speed to effectively remove secretions. In order to achieve an effective assisted cough, practice is required to establish the necessary timing between the therapist and the patient. When the cough sounds like a normal cough it is strong and efficient. This should always be practised, regardless of the status of the chest, in preparation for any acute situation such as getting food down the wrong way. It is also a useful method for blowing the nose.

Initially, during spinal shock when there is risk of developing paralytic ileus, and in the case of abdominal injury, the assisted coughing technique must be modified to exert the pressure more widely across the chest to avoid trauma to the abdomen.

Common problems are chest infections and collapse of the lung due to stagnant secretions. Mr SP suffered collapses and consolidation of the left lung within the first two weeks of sustaining his injury. During these episodes of collapsed lung the IPPB, BIRD ventilator can be used very effectively as a treatment to help clear the secretions and to prevent further incidences of lung collapse. After these two episodes Mr SP had no further respiratory complications.

Circulation and Joint Range of Motion

I would try to find out more about the history of the management of the injury up to the time Mr SP was admitted to our hospital. What we now do will depend on how the patient has been managed previously, particularly as regards the prophylactic anticoagulation treatment, which will determine when passive movements may be started.

If Mr SP has been treated from the beginning with passive movements to the legs, in such a way that it aids the circulation, for example with repeated rhythmical movements of the whole leg, then it should be continued. However, if he has not been substantially moved then it is prudent to wait until the level of anticoagulation is within therapeutic range.

The patient's current level of fitness, together with possible previous medical problems, such as ankylosing spondylitis, rheumatoid arthritis, chronic obstructive airways dicease, will affect our treatment and management plan. Mr SP is said to have had an acute subscapularis tendinitis at the time of his injury. However, the pain did not interfere with the range of movement. He had no other associated injuries and he was a fit young man.

A comprehensive and meticulous programme of passive movements will be implemented as soon as possible. This is done twice daily initially when the risk of developing deep vein thrombosis (DVT) and contractures is at its greatest. When the anticoagulation therapy is stabilized in therapeutic range, passive movements may be cut down to once daily as long as the joint range of movement is not compromised. Continuous reassessment of the joints will determine the treatment regimen.

Eighteen days post-injury Mr SP had a swollen leg; this was thought to be due to a DVT. Under these circumstances passive movements would be discontinued while the anticoagulation therapy was reassessed and the treatment amended accordingly. Joint range of movement may be checked after consultation with medical staff. Mr SP's passive movements were restarted at 26 days post-injury.

The rehabilitation outcome will depend on mobility and stability of the musculoskeletal system as well as the strength of the muscles that remain neurologically intact.

All joints are moved in their full anatomical range. Consideration also has to be given to muscles and tendons, particularly those muscles that span more than one joint. Awareness of the functional use that each of these joints and muscles is going to play in the future rehabilitation will lay the foundation for the precise nature of these movements (Bergström and Rose, 1992 **C**). In some muscles full range is imperative, as in elbow extension for lifting and transfer, and in others some tendon shortening is necessary to achieve the desired function, as in the tenodesis grip. Passive movements with particular reference to the SCI are described in detail in Bromley (1998b **C**).

Trick movements will allow function otherwise not possible with the neurological level of injury that Mr SP has, and they are of great functional benefit.

It is possible to extend the elbow when in the supine position despite lack of triceps muscle power and this should be taught after a few weeks. At that stage the movement required of the arm will not incur undue risk of movement to the neck. When this trick movement is mastered Mr SP will be able to take some responsibility and influence the outcome of his own treatment. He will be able to position the arms extended by his side independently, thus lessening the risk of shortened biceps tendons (Bergström and Rose, 1992 **C**). In order to achieve this the elbow needs to have full range of extension as well as pronation and supination without any tension of the biceps tendon.

However, the tenodesis grip requires some tension in the tendons of both finger flexor and extensor tendons as well as the stability of the metacarpophalangeal (MCP) and interphalangeal (IP) joint of the thumb. This will give strength to the grip and a release mechanism respectively but it is important to ensure that contractures of the joints do not occur.

A careful splinting regimen will be used to complement the passive range of movements of the hand. Particular care is taken to develop a good tenodesis grip as this is the only way someone with a complete C6 lesion can have a functional grip. Short paddle splints may be worn to maintain the arches of the hand. Taping of SP's fingers into 90° flexion of MCP and PIP joints may be used to aid shortening of the flexor tendon. More extensive splinting may be needed if the hands swell.

Elbow splints may be used to supplement the passive movements if some tension in the biceps tendon is experienced and there is risk of losing extension together with supination and pronation. Careful positioning of the arms and frequent changes of position are other ways to ensure that good movement is maintained, particularly of the shoulder. These positions are described in detail by Edwards (1998 **C**).

Passive stretches of the shoulder elevators should not be overlooked. Gravity will mostly elevate the shoulders when supine, particularly when the patient is on pillows to ensure optimal position of the spinal column and to prevent pressure. Future function, particularly lifting, will require good shoulder depression.

Later, reconstructive surgery to improve upper limb function (Moberg, 1978 **C**) may be considered. This can be undertaken only if the joints and muscles are maintained in optimal position.

Passive movements have to be carried out with great care when handling desensitized joints. A proportion of SCI patients develop para-articular ossification (PAO), most commonly round the large joints. It is thought to be caused by micro-trauma in the muscles (Bodley et al., 1993 **A**). This can be a devastating complication, particularly for a tetraplegic of Mr SP's level with potential to achieve high functional independence, but only if all biomechanical factors are stacked in his favour. It can therefore never be overstated how important this early part of the rehabilitation is for the later outcome.

Good range of movements of the lower limbs is imperative for future function as well as symmetrical and upright sitting posture. Stretching of the hamstring muscles should be limited to 70° as some tension may enhance the stability in long sitting.

Splinting of the lower limbs and feet can be a useful adjunct to passive movement, particularly in those who have participated actively in sport. They often have strong muscles with underlying high tone and are at greater risk of developing shortened muscles.

Mr SP will be taught to understand the necessary biomechanical principles in order to comply with the treatment regimen, particularly splinting, as the implications may not be obvious to the patient while still in bed.

Strengthening exercises can be started when the neck is deemed stable enough to withstand the strain that may be exerted upon it. This will be decided in liaison with the medical officer in charge of the patient. Great care has to be taken, particularly with unilateral movements that may cause rotation of the spinal column.

In preparation for getting up in a wheelchair, static neck exercises should be started during the last few weeks of bed rest. This will enhance the tolerance of the upright position, which can be very taxing on the neck muscles during the initial period and can cause pain. Mr SP did have sacral skin problems during this phase and the time for mobilization was delayed for one month as a result. During this extended time in bed rehabilitation can start with more active strengthening exercises within the constraints of his position, which is side lying to avoid the sacral area. He would now be allowed to work harder and unilaterally as the neck is stable. Weight training with the arm splinted in extension and weights attached or the use of an overhead gantry can be done with minimal help.

Shoulder Pain

Owing to the enforced bed rest period Mr SP's subscapularis tendinitis will have the opportunity to rest. The range of movement was not compromised so movement of the shoulder could continue. The shoulder did not cause any problems during the active rehabilitation phase.

The teaching process in terms of chest care, skin care and joint care also starts during this time as the rationale of management is explained to Mr SP.

The Wheelchair Rehabilitation Phase

The transition to upright position after a long period supine is difficult for some tetraplegic patients. To allow the blood pressure to adapt Mr SP will start to sit up in bed, or use a tilt table to gradually learn to tolerate the upright position. An abdominal binder and elastic stockings may help the venous return. The abdominal binder will also help the function of the diaphragm (Goldman et al., 1986 **B**). Some tetraplegic patients may require ephedrine.

As soon as the orthostatic problem has been overcome and Mr SP can tolerate a few hours sitting up, active physical rehabilitation starts. Usually a cervical collar is worn for a short period of about one month after getting out of bed. It can be discontinued when flexion and extension radiographs confirm stability of the fracture site. The collar is worn to protect the neck during the initial stage when the balance and stability of the patient are limited and sudden jerky movements may cause the head to tilt with some force. As long as Mr SP is wearing the collar he is restricted in his functional activities, and excessive flexion and any rotation is avoided.

Assessment

Reassessment is now undertaken to establish the functional implications of the impaired neurological level and the patient's biomechanics. The muscle and ROM charts should be redone with the patient in the correct positions. This will enable the therapist to set realistic short- and long-term goals.

Treatment

In order to accomplish complicated tasks such as transfers and dressing Mr SP needs a solid foundation of good posture, balance and strength. Without this the rehabilitation can become frustrating for both the patient and the therapist and be at risk of not being pitched high enough.

Posture and Seating

Good posture strives towards normal alignment of the spine. It will optimize the function of the shoulder girdle, thus allowing freedom of movement and function. It will also enhance the lung function, cardiovascular system, and renal and digestive systems. Good posture is essential to avoid skin and musculoskeletal problems.

Stability is the foundation upon which everybody builds the ability to relax, move, balance and eventually take the centre of gravity outside the base of support, thus accomplishing controlled function such as transfers. Even weight distribution is important for individuals with paralysis and desensitized skin. This will minimize the risk of pressure sores.

These aspects have to be given careful consideration when choosing the seating system, which consists of a wheelchair and a cushion. Another feature to consider is comfort. This is important, to allow Mr SP to lead a full life not limited by discomfort. The transfer technique may require a wheelchair with footplates that swing out of the way. The brakes have to be operated with limited hand function. Mr SP has the potential to be largely functionally independent but only if the biomechanics (of which the wheelchair is one aspect) are to his advantage; the chair and cushion have to be chosen with great care in all details. For long-distance pushing outdoors particularly, push handles of adequate height for an attendant may have to be considered. This assessment may take some time to complete.

The cushion is an integral part of the seating system. The primary requirement of the cushion is to offer good skin protection by weight distribution over as wide an area as possible. It must therefore conform to the shape of the body. It must also provide a stable base and promote good posture as previously described.

All these considerations are often not fully appreciated by the patient until some time after discharge when he has had the opportunity to settle back into a more normal life. As he consolidates his skills and becomes more confident, changes may be necessary.

Balance

Balance for the tetraplegic patient will largely be achieved through compensatory movements of the head, shoulders and upper limbs. Mr SP will have to learn to use visual cues as well as sensory input from neurologically intact parts of the body. The use of a mirror will help him to appreciate what happens when he moves and how he can compensate to counteract the movement.

Strength

The strength of all neurologically intact muscles is imperative, particularly for the functionally active patient with tetraplegia. The shoulder girdle and the arms will become the weight-bearing structure for transfers and the ambulatory limb when propelling the wheelchair. The neck and shoulder girdle muscles will be important for postural control. Mr SP's functional achievements are performed with comparatively few muscles in the upper limbs and with little intact sensation. Therefore he requires knowledge of movement and a heightened spatial awareness to enable him to utilize the biomechanical principles that will facilitate isolated movements and complete functional tasks.

Some specific skills that are central to the rehabilitation of the patient with a complete C6 have been described in detail by Bergström and Rose (1992 **C**). Strengthening exercises can and should be undertaken in a variety of ways. Initially this is done manually to help stabilize paralysed joints and to achieve the end range of movement. Mechanical weight-training systems in conjunction with splinting or strapping will later allow the patient to increase the time spent on strengthening exercises. It will also give him the opportunity to assess how he can continue this with minimal assistance in the future.

For the stability of the joints and for long-term care, primarily of the shoulder girdle, it is important to remember antagonist muscles. Daily life functions will be carried out using the same muscles as in pushing the chair and transferring, and little effort is spent by the antagonists. Degenerative musculoskeletal problems of the shoulder are a common long-term problem in the ageing person with SCI and are particularly devastating as the independence will be severely curtailed.

Function

The morphology of the patient will affect his biomechanics. This is particularly apparent in the C6 tetraplegic patient (Bergström et al., 1985 **B**). For example males, compared with females, usually have better physical build with which to lift, roll and transfer their body as they have broader shoulders and narrower hips. Mr SP is of medium height and slim; he is also young and fit. In these circumstances the aim would be to achieve optimal function for his neurological level, for example independent level transfer, dressing and most tabletop activities.

Wheelchair skills are introduced immediately and will successively increase the independence and safety as he learns to push and manoeuvre the chair in different directions, put the brakes on and off and take the footplates off and sides out in preparation for transfers. As he gets stronger and fitter he will be challenged to push the wheelchair outdoors and over longer distances and different surfaces and to negotiate slopes and kerbs. For someone of Mr SP's level this would be greatly facilitated by a lightweight, high-performance wheelchair.

Pressure relief will initially be done by tilting the chair back or by leaning sideways or forward with the help of another person. Later this will be done unaided when he can lean and regain the starting position himself. These weight-relieving positions have to be maintained for 1–2 minutes to allow the skin to reoxygenate (Bromley and Rose, 1998 **C**).

Transfers will be started with maximal assistance where Mr SP initially will help by propping himself up on the arms. This will teach him in what position the arms have to be. It will increase his sense of security and confidence and prepare him for when other people have to be involved in helping with transfers. The ability of other people such as family and friends to help with the transfers will hasten and increase the opportunities to leave the hospital for social outings, which in itself is an important part of the rehabilitation. Mr SP will gradually learn to do more of the transfer independently and with fewer aids such as sliding board, sliding sheet and lifting belt. Eventually it will be expected for someone of Mr SP's level to use a sliding board only for split-level transfers and car transfers. In conjunction with the car transfer he will learn to put the chair into and take it out of the car if he has a lightweight wheelchair. He will also learn to do the transfers in many different settings and in as many different ways as possible to become truly independent.

If there are aspects of some skills that Mr SP needs assistance with he should practise to instruct the helping person in how to help him. He will then be confident in relying on friends, for example when going out. With the tenodesis grip Mr SP will learn to do many tabletop activities. With the aid of simple straps and splints to hold a toothbrush, cutlery and a pen he will regain independence in most activities of daily living.

Driving a car is an important aid to independence, particularly where communal transport is inaccessible from a wheelchair. At Mr SP's level of injury it is possible to drive an automatic car that is fitted with hand controls. It is prudent to choose the car carefully to make sure that both transfer into the car and getting the chair in are possible. The choice will be different for each person depending on their size and mobility in conjunction with the chair.

Standing is beneficial for several physiological reasons in the spinal cord injured person. Regular standing will prevent contractures of hip and knee flexors, the Achilles tendon, and to some extent the abdominal muscles. It is an easy and economical way to ensure stretching of these structures. Weight bearing, particularly through extended hips, has a dampening effect on increased tone in some patients and it may substitute the need for anti-spasm drugs. For standing to influence the degree of disuse osteoporosis, it has to be undertaken within the first few months of injury, during which time most of the demineralization takes place. In the spinal cord injured it has not proved to be fully reversible. Standing is done using a simple standing frame if the patient is able to do most of the lifting. Electric standing frames, tilt tables and 'stand up' chairs are possibilities for patients unable to assist in this way.

Successful rehabilitation is undertaken by a team for whom the patient is the key person. The programme is devised by the goal-planning team to ensure a synchronized approach by all members and that all aspects are addressed (Kennedy and Hamilton, 1999 **A**). It will help to divide the process up into manageable short-term goals without losing sight of the long-term goals. A teaching programme including all aspects of living with SCI is a vital part of empowering the patient with both skills and knowledge. It will enable him to meet new situations and solve problems. Most people with SCI are young at the time of injury and their lifestyle may change and develop in ways not foreseen at the time of initial rehabilitation. It is therefore important to equip Mr SP further than for today's needs but also be able to offer further short spells of rehabilitation when the need arises.

References

Ashworth B (1969) Preliminary trial of carisoprodol in multiple sclerosis. Practitioner 192: 540–2.

Bergström EMK, Frankel HL, Galer IAR, Haycock EL, Jones PRM, Rose LS (1985) Physical ability in relation to anthropometric measurements in persons with complete spinal cord lesion below the sixth cervical segment. International Rehabilitation Medicine 7: 51–5.

Bergström EMK, Rose LS (1992) Physical rehabilitation: principles and outcome. In Vinken PJ, Bruyn GW, Klawans HL (Eds), Frankel HL (Co-ed) Spinal Cord Trauma, Handbook of Clinical Neurology 17(61). Amsterdam: Elsevier, pp 457–78.

Bodley R, Jamous A, Short D (1993) Ultrasound in the early diagnosis of heterotopic ossification in patients with spinal injuries. Paraplegia 31: 500–6.

Bromley I (1998a) Patient centred practice. In Bromley I (Ed) Tetraplegia and Paraplegia: A Guide for Physiotherapists, 5th edn. Edinburgh: Churchill Livingstone, pp 17–21.

Bromley I (1998b) The acute lesion. In Bromley I (Ed) Tetraplegia and Paraplegia: A Guide for Physiotherapists, 5th edn. Edinburgh: Churchill Livingstone, pp 23–9.

Bromley I, Brownlee S, Rose L (1998) Respiratory therapy. In Bromley I (Ed) Tetraplegia and Paraplegia: A Guide for Physiotherapists, 5th edn. Edinburgh: Churchill Livingstone, pp 31–42.

Bromley I, Rose L (1998) Pressure – effects and prevention. In Bromley I (Ed) Tetraplegia and Paraplegia: A Guide for Physiotherapists, 5th edn. Edinburgh: Churchill Livingstone, pp 43–55.

Edwards S (1998) The incomplete spinal lesion. In Bromley I (Ed) Tetraplegia and Paraplegia: A Guide for Physiotherapists, 5th edn. Edinburgh: Churchill Livingstone, pp 167–96.

Frankel HL, Hancock DO, Hyslop G, Melzak J, Michaelis LS, Ungar GH, Vernon JDS, Walsh JJ (1969) The value of postural reduction in the initial management of closed injuries of the spine with paraplegia and tetraplegia. Paraplegia 7: 179–92.

Goldman JM, Rose LS, Williams SJ, Silver JR, Dension DM (1986) The effect of abdominal binders on breathing in tetraplegic patients. Thorax 41(12): 940–5.

Hammel KW (1995) Spinal Cord Injury Rehabilitation. London: Chapman & Hall.

Jackson SE (1983) IPPB. In Downie PA (Ed) Cash's Textbook of Chest, Heart and Vascular Disorders for Physiotherapists, 3rd edn. London: Faber & Faber.

Kennedy P, Hamilton LR (1999) The needs assessment checklist: a clinical approach to measuring outcome. Spinal Cord 37: 136–9.

Maynard FM Jr, Bracken MB, Creasy G, Ditunno JF Jr, Donovan WH, Ducker TB, Gaber SL, Marino RJ, Stover SL, Tator CH, Waters RL, Willberger JE, Young W (1997) International standards booklet for neurological and functional classification of spinal cord injury. Spinal Cord 32: pp 70–80.

Moberg E (1978) The Upper Extremity in Tetraplegia: A New Approach to Surgical Rehabilitation. Stuttgart, Germany: Thieme.

Incomplete spinal cord injury C7

Case Report – Mr PL

Background

Mr PL was 25 years old and lived with a friend in a basement flat in London. He is engaged to be married and was two months into an MSc course in nutrition at the time of the accident. He was an international rower, and in the previous year was in the Olympic team, was very healthy and led a very active and sporty life. He dived into shallow water from a diving platform and hit the bottom of the pool. He was dragged out by his friends and transferred to a local hospital and the following day transferred to a spinal unit.

Diagnosis

C6–7 spinal fracture resulting in an incomplete C7 Frankel grade B spinal cord injury.

Management

On admission skull traction applied which remained *in situ* for 10 weeks. Patient nursed on Egerton turning tilting bed for 12 weeks.

On Examination

Day 1:

- No respiratory problems: VC: 28L.
- Decreased ability to cough. Paradoxical breathing.
- Spinal shock. No motor power below the lesion, no reflex below the lesion, decreased tone and sensation below the lesion.

- Range of motion: full range in all joints but tight tendo Achilles.
- Bladder and bowel: indwelling catheter, and manual evacuation.

Day 3:

- Spinal shock resolved. Increased tone below the lesion, scored 4 on the Ashworth tone scale with extensor spasticity.

Day 4:

- Recovery of muscle power starting from the left extensor hallux longus.
- Persistent spasticity in left leg leading to an inability to accept the base of support in supine position.
- Persistent tightness of Achilles tendons bilaterally: R < Å but full range achievable.
- Extended posture in bed leading to muscle imbalance between back extensors and abdominals, resulting in an anterior pelvic tilt.

Day 10:

- Muscle power in most muscles (grade 1–2–3 Oxford scale) except for dorsiflexors, evertors, and hip external rotators.
- Decreased tone due to specific positioning in bed, but tone increases if there are bladder or bowel problems.
- Tendency to lose range of motion specially into posterior tilt, also hip extension, internal rotation of the hip, dorsiflexion and eversion of the feet.
- Asymmetrical trunk convex to the right and extended thoracic spine. Use of back extensors to stabilize trunk when using upper and lower limbs.

Week 10:

- Traction has been removed, Mr PL wears a soft collar but is still nursed on a turning bed.

Muscle power: between 2 and 4 in all muscles, weaker muscles being abdominals, hip abductors, tibialis anterior and evertors.

Range of motion: right Achilles tendons decreased front arch of foot due to muscle imbalance between extensor longus and tibialis, anterior tight rotation and lateral tilt of pelvis.

Selective activity: tendency to move through triple flexion or triple extension when trying to get a selective movement in a lower leg, poor proximal stability.

Sensation and proprioception: impaired pin prick, light touch and proprioception but improves regularly.

Week 12

On normal bed, can get up and sit in manual wheelchair.

- Incomplete spinal cord injury.
- Decreased range of motion due to 12 weeks' bed rest.
- Decreased side flexion and rotation of head.
- Increased cervical lordosis leading to protracted head.
- Poor selective activity and stability around trunk compensated by locking upper limb along trunk to maintain posture against gravity.
- Poor balance reactions.
- Decreased muscle length and soft tissue changes in back extensors, hip flexors, hamstrings and Achilles tendons.
- Increased tone with effort.
- Minimal assistance in all transfers and in lying to sitting to standing and vice versa with increased tone and effort.
- Bladder and bowel: normal recovery.

Discharged Home (5 $\frac{1}{2}$ months post-injury)

- Impaired balance reactions.
- Persistent tightness in tendo Achilles due to slight increased tone leading to:
  - decreased quality on heel off;
  - decreased quality on toes off with tendency of inversion;
  - poor quality on swing phase.

Able to:

- get from lying to sitting;
- get from sitting to stand;
- walk: 10 m walk 4.6 sec (compared with 100 sec 16 weeks post-injury);
- get up and down stairs, slopes and kerbs.

Unable to run, with poor balance on one-leg stance and on tiptoes.

Treatment and Management of a Patient with Incomplete Spinal Cord Injury C7

SUSAN EDWARDS

Background

The number of people with incomplete spinal cord lesions is increasing. In a recent study reporting changes over a 13-year period in America, of the total number of patients with spinal cord injury, the number of incomplete lesions increased from 43.6% to 51.4% (De Vivo et al., 1992 **A**). Data relating to spinal cord injuries are usually from specialist spinal units rather than the general literature. However, it is important to recognize that many patients with spinal cord damage are never admitted to a spinal injuries unit and therefore they are not included in these statistics. Incomplete spinal cord lesions are said to account for 1.2% of all neurology outpatient consultations (Stevenson et al., 1996 **A**).

From a therapy perspective, the treatment of patients with incomplete lesions differs significantly from that of a patient with a complete lesion. Stevenson et al. (1996 **A**) suggest that patients with incomplete spinal cord lesions, particularly those caused by slowly evolving pathologies, may be best managed in a neurological rehabilitation unit where therapists are used to managing more diverse types of disability. This is as opposed to patients being managed in a spinal injuries unit, where therapists develop expertise in the management of the complete lesions but may not have experience with the more varied clinical pictures found within the field of general neurology. However, while this may be valid with regard to physiotherapy and occupational therapy, the problems relating to disruption of bladder and bowel function invariably require the specific expertise of spinal injury units. These issues highlight the need for greater liaison and transference of skills between therapists and other staff working in spinal injury and neurological rehabilitation units (Edwards, 1998 **C**).

Patients with incomplete spinal cord injuries demonstrate many diverse disabilities, depending on the level and extent of the lesion. Normal movement may be the idealistic goal of rehabilitation, but all too often this is not achievable for patients with extensive neurological damage. Compensatory strategies may be necessary for patients to realize their functional potential. Indeed, it has been suggested that 'changed motor patterns should be considered not pathological but rather adaptive to a primary disorder and may even be viewed as optimal for a given state of the system of movement production' (Latash and Anson, 1996 **C**, p. 55).

General Principles

These may be broadly divided into those relating to the early and later stages of management.

Early Management

- To ensure adequate ventilation and prevent respiratory complications.
- To maintain proximal range of movement within the limits imposed by the rigid immobilization of skull traction. The patient cannot use gross body movements such as rolling from side to side or moving from lying to sitting. The Egerton bed on which this patient is nursed turns the patient *en bloc* to ensure stability at the fracture site.
- To maintain range of movement within the limbs.
- To assess and monitor recovery of function through objective measurement.

Later Stage Management

- To ensure the optimal functional outcome on the basis of a damaged central nervous system. At six months post-injury, when Mr PL is discharged from hospital, he still has a residual disability and must be able to function effectively within the confines of his disability.
- To teach appropriate compensatory strategies to maximize function.
- To monitor and review exercise programmes undertaken by the patient to ensure that these continue to meet his needs.
- To monitor and review appliances or equipment issued to the patient such as wheelchair and splints.
- To select appropriate measures to evaluate outcome.

Treatment

This case report describes specific changes in Mr PL's condition during hospitalization. His impairment was that of an incomplete spinal cord injury at the level of C7. I propose to take each aspect of the developing disabilities and handicaps and suggest interventions that may prove of benefit in optimizing the functional outcome.

Measurement

Given the diversity of symptoms arising from an incomplete spinal cord injury, it is essential to monitor recovery of function throughout all stages of rehabilitation.

The Oxford scale (Wade, 1992) is frequently used, as in this case, to determine muscle power, although its suitability to measure strength when there is increased tone is sometimes questioned by clinicians (*Synapse*, 1998 **C**). I find this a useful tool to monitor recovering muscle activity not least because it demands that the therapist assess a wide selection of individual muscles affected by the level of lesion and early flickers of movement may be identified only with this specific analysis.

More functional scores such as the Functional Independence Measure (Dodds et al., 1993) and the Barthel index (Shah and Cooper, 1993) may be used to assess outcome once the patient is able to participate in an active rehabilitation programme.

Management while in Bed

Positioning

The position of the patient in bed was limited by the application of skull traction, which remained *in situ* for 10 weeks, and by the fact that Mr PL was nursed on an Egerton electrical turning tilting bed. Alignment of the head on trunk was of paramount importance to prevent any movement at the fracture site and subsequent further neurological deficit.

The Egerton bed enables greater ease of nursing care in that the patient lies constantly on his back with pressure being redistributed by turning the individual segments of the bed into a modified side-lying position at the touch of a button. Positioning fully in side lying is usually carried out only once a day for the purpose of washing the posterior aspect of the body and for bowel management.

By the third day it was reported that the spinal shock had resolved and that there was increased tone below the level of the lesion, grade 4 on the Ashworth scale, with extensor spasticity. Clinical opinion is that supine lying exacerbates extensor tone (Bobath, 1990 **C**; Davies, 1994 **C**; Edwards, 1996 **C**) and yet, where immobilization of the spinal column is of primary import-ance, there is little choice but to nurse the patient in the manner described above.

Positioning with the legs in abduction and lateral rotation, often referred to as the frog position, has been advocated (Edwards, 1998 **C**) but this position is often difficult to maintain in the presence of extensor spasticity. The intermittent use of a T-roll, as described by Pope (1992 **C**) and Edwards (1996 **C**), for example, putting it in place and removing it at each four-hourly turn, may prove of benefit at this stage of the patient's management. This roll (see Figure 1) provides greater support and control to maintain the legs in flexion and abduction. However, it is important to alternate between hip flexion and hip extension as contractures of the hip flexor muscles have been reported to be a common complication following upper motor neurone lesions (Yarkony and Sahgal, 1987 **A**).

Positioning the patient lying provides no stimulus to the development of proximal muscle activity as the body is constantly supported and does not have to cope with the effects of gravity. The poor proximal stability described by week 10 post-injury is indicative of this lack of stimulation. In animal studies it has been shown that the maintenance of slow-twitch muscle fibres is dependent upon mechanical stretch and their use in a supportive capacity (Goldspink et al., 1992 **B**; Vrbova et al., 1995 **B**; Pette and Staron, 1997 **B**). Clearly proximal activity against gravity cannot be carried out until the patient is able to mobilize out of bed, and resisted exercises of the limbs, which may produce overflow into the trunk, are not indicated given the danger of movement at the cervical spine.

The T-roll is used specifically to improve pelvic and hip alignment and to modify the extensor tone in the legs. Other adaptations such as the use of

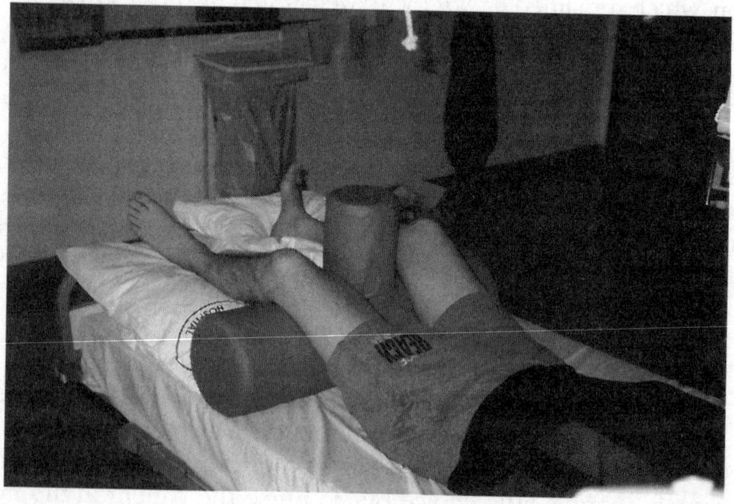

Figure 1: The T-roll.

additional pillows or wedges may be considered to influence the poor proximal activity and the resultant muscle imbalance. However, such intervention is inevitably restricted by the potential instability of the cervical spine.

Movement

The assessment on the first day reports that the patient was in spinal shock with no motor power below the level of the lesion. In the absence of activity, passive movements are indicated to preserve range of movement of all muscles and joints affected by the lesion (Bromley, 1998 **C**). These movements must be carried out with care and sensitivity. Mr PL, who is classified as being a Frankel grade B lesion, also grade B on the ASIA (American Spinal Injury Association) scale, has decreased sensation, possibly pain and lacks the motor ability to restrict any excessive force. The identification of 'decreased sensation below the lesion' implies that there was some sparing, an early indication that this is an incomplete lesion. It has been suggested that by facilitating appropriate patterns of activity, this will assist in establishing functional connections between regenerating supraspinal axons and spinal neurones (Muir and Steeves, 1997 **C**).

'Passive' movements should always be carried out with oral instruction to the patient and encouragement for him to participate in the movement. Reports of the benefits of mental imagery provide evidence that motor learning can be enhanced with visualization and participation in the desired movement sequence (Gandevia and Rothwell, 1987 **A**; Jeannerod and Decety, 1995 **A**; Lee and van Donkelaar, 1995 **A**).

These movements should not be limited to the limbs, in that proximal tone and stiffness may severely compromise function when the patient is able to mobilize. Rotational movements of the pelvis against the upper body, stabilized by an assistant at the shoulder girdles to prevent neck movement, will go some way to modifying the almost inevitable muscle imbalance that occurs with the restrictive features of the Egerton bed.

Splinting

In spite of the lack of motor power and decreased tone, the Achilles tendons were reported to be 'tight' even on the first day, this tightness persisting up to the time of his discharge from hospital. This early tightness is indicative of the contribution of the mechanical properties of muscle.

Mr PL was an international rower. Rowing is an activity that requires sustained powerful effort, and endurance exercise training has been shown to produce adaptations of fast to slow fibre types (Pette and Staron, 1997 **B**).

The plantar flexion force as the oarsman makes his stroke may well have led to this change in the posterior crural muscle group with a resultant predominance of slow oxidative fibres. These slow-twitch fibres have more collagen and are therefore less compliant than muscles with more predominant fast-twitch fibres (Goldspink and Williams, 1990 **B**; Given et al., 1995 **B**).

Immobilization leads to muscle atrophy. This has been shown to be greater in slow oxidative fibres than in the fast-twitch fibres in patients following stroke or spinal cord injury (Given et al., 1995 **B**; Vrbova et al., 1995 **B**; Gordon and Mao, 1994 **B**) and shortening of muscle fibre length is accelerated when the muscle is immobilized in a shortened position (Herbert, 1988 **A**).

The use of casting to maintain range of movement in patients with neurological dysfunction has been advocated by many authors (Conine et al., 1990 **A**; Davies, 1994 **C**; Edwards and Charlton, 1996 **C**). Clinical guidelines for the use of splinting in adults with neurological disability have been produced by the Association of Chartered Physiotherapists Interested in Neurology (ACPIN) (1998 **C**) where an extensive literature search carried out at that time revealed only four papers with scientific data to support the use of casting in the management of these patients (Imle et al., 1986 **A**; Sullivan et al., 1988 **A**; Conine et al., 1990 **A**; Moseley, 1993 **A**).

Whilst it is indisputable that splinting will cause immobilization, for this is its purpose, it would appear logical to provide the optimal, if not perfect, intervention by maintaining joint position and muscle length within a functional range. Tardieu et al. (1988 **A**) demonstrated that the short soleus muscle in children with cerebral palsy required six hours of stretch to maintain range of movement.

I consider that splinting as a prophylactic measure, to maintain the range of movement at the ankle joint, is an essential adjunct to this patient's physiotherapy management. I would apply bilateral, removable below-knee casts (see Figure 2) as soon as was practicable and certainly within the first 48 hours of his admission to hospital.

The case report identifies increasing difficulty in controlling spasticity and maintaining range of movement during the early weeks of this patient's management while he was nursed in bed. Muscle imbalance between the back extensors and abdominal muscles was reported to be in evidence as early as the fourth day and it was also at this time that recovery of motor power was noted.

The treatment interventions described should address these problems but it must be recognized that it is impossible to replicate the full gamut of normal movement where there is a combination of impaired tone and marked muscle weakness leading to muscle imbalance, and where

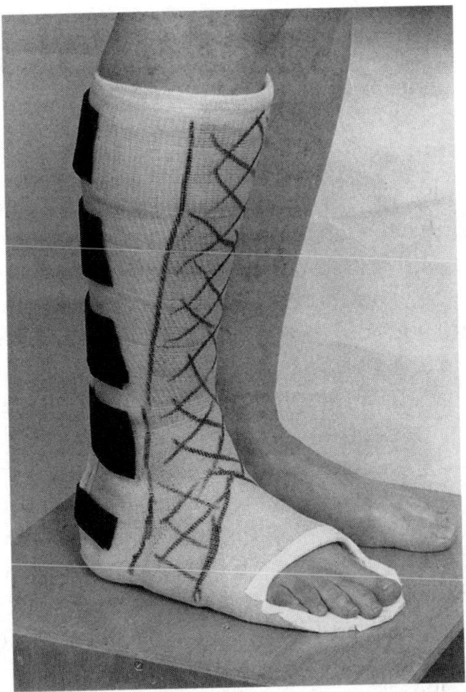

Figure 2: Removable below knee cast.

treatment of these impairments is compromised by the need to maintain alignment of the spinal column at all costs.

Management Following Stabilization of Spinal Fracture

Positioning and Bed Mobility

Alternate positioning once the cervical spine is stable should be encouraged, to produce greater flexibility within the trunk and pelvis in particular. Sequences of movement such as supine lying to side or prone lying, and lying to sitting and vice versa should be commenced ensuring rotation of segments as opposed to movement *en bloc*. These activities would also serve to increase strength and control of the abdominal muscles, which are identified as being weak at week 10.

It is inevitable that there will be stiffness of the cervical spine as a result of the fracture and the imposed immobility in the management of this fracture. The lack of movement will cause some restriction to gross body movement such as rolling, as rotation of the head is a primary feature of this movement sequence. Mr PL should be encouraged not only to practise the gross activities of rolling to either side, turning into prone and sitting up from lying, but also to work specifically to increase the available range of movement at the cervical spine.

Wheelchair Provision

The patient was transferred on to a normal bed after 12 weeks and allowed to get up and sit in a wheelchair. The type of wheelchair is not described, but ideally this should have been a lightweight model enabling greater freedom of movement and thereby independence. Suitable adaptations to provide appropriate support to accommodate for his poor activity and for stability within the trunk should have been incorporated into the chair.

The means by which Mr PL propels the chair would be determined by the level of impairment and the extent of recovery. Throughout the case report, no mention is made of his hand function and yet if a complete C7 injury, this would be severely affected. On the basis of the information provided relating to Mr LP's level of disability, I am assuming that his hands were unaffected. On this basis, I would endeavour to position him in his wheelchair in such a way as to allow him to use his legs for self-propulsion.

There is concern that self-propulsion of wheelchairs for patients following stroke may lead to the establishment of abnormal patterns of movement or 'associated reactions' (Cornall, 1991 **C**). As Mr PL has poor proximal trunk control and increased tone, some may argue that he too may be at risk of developing compensatory strategies, which may ultimately prevent him attaining his optimal level of function. However, in this case, as with many people with incomplete spinal cord injury, several factors contribute to his movement disorder:

- Weakness, which may be a negative feature of the upper motor neurone syndrome or the result of lower motor neurone damage or more probably a combination of the two.
- Increased tone, which may be due to spasticity/hyperreflexia, spastic dystonia (Sheean, 1998 **C**) or mechanical changes in the affected muscles. Again all three are likely to contribute.
- Muscle imbalance, whereby co-ordinated activity between agonists and antagonists is impaired.

Following a thorough assessment and in consultation with Mr PL, appropriate strategies should be determined to allow him to self-propel without causing adverse effects. Certainly during the early stages of his rehabilitation, he is spending a great deal of time in his wheelchair. The idea that he should not use this time in his chair to improve his strength and movement control, because of an ill-defined risk that this may lead to compensatory strategies which may impair later function, I find quite incomprehensible.

Mr PL is a well-motivated sportsman used to the discipline of training up to international level. He is best placed to monitor the effects of activity such as propelling his wheelchair providing the physiotherapist indicates potential problems and is prepared to hand over this responsibility.

Transfers

Transfers to and from his wheelchair become an essential part of Mr PL's rehabilitation programme once he is allowed out of bed. It is reported that by week 12 he required minimal assistance with all transfers but that he had 'increased tone with effort'. I presume that he was able to transfer through standing at this time and that the increased tone with effort was probably the result of his weakness and poor balance reactions.

I would work specifically to improve his control and thereby his confidence when transferring in varied situations – transfers from different heights and to and from different surfaces, for example, toilet transfers, car transfers and on to and off the floor. I would encourage him to use his arms to provide greater security, which would subsequently reduce the amount of effort required.

The shortening of Mr PL's Achilles tendons and increased tone will contribute to his sense of insecurity as it will be difficult for him to place his feet appropriately for effective weight bearing as he stands. The splints that I advocated at the start of his management may be of value in controlling the foot position and providing a more stable base of support. However, I would use these intermittently as he must also learn to accommodate to the supporting surface without the support of the splints.

Any necessary function should be utilized to improve muscle strength, range of movement and general fitness. Transfers should be seen in this light. He has to carry these out on a regular basis and the manner in which he does so can greatly enhance his performance.

Movement

Mr PL is described as having generally decreased range of motion as a result of 12 weeks of bed rest. In addition, specific loss of range of movement and soft tissue changes are reported in the back extensors, the hip flexors, hamstrings and in the Achilles tendons. His tone was said to increase with effort but information regarding the severity of tone as measured on the Ashworth scale is not provided. The extent to which spasticity contributes to the movement disorder continues to evoke great debate and controversy (Brown, 1994 **C**; Rothwell, 1994 **C**).

The increased mechanical resistance to movement is the result of the combined contributions of passive tissues and active contractile properties of the muscle–tendon complex, and physiological and histochemical changes in muscle fibres. The presence of increased stiffness cannot automatically be attributed to an enhanced stretch reflex (Given et al., 1995 **A**; Dietz, 1992 **A**). O'Dwyer et al. (1996 **A**) reported that the major functional deficits following stroke were largely the result of weakness and loss of dexterity as opposed to spasticity. In this case of incomplete spinal cord injury weakness, changes in the mechanical properties of muscle and increased tone are factors that impact on the patient's functional ability.

The changes in the mechanical properties of muscle are a major determinant of outcome. The maintenance of mobility and alignment of the muscle tendon complex is vitally important to maximize the residual muscle activity influenced by increased tone from the upper motor neurone (UMN) lesion and weakness due to both the UMN lesion and damage to the grey matter of the cord (Gordon and Mao, 1994 **A**).

Changes in the mechanical properties of muscle need to be addressed but it is essential that changes in muscle length, which may result from specific mobilizations, be incorporated into functional tasks. For example, the decreased muscle length and soft-tissue changes in his back extensors may well respond to specific mobilization but the patient must then be encouraged to use this gain by reaching down in his wheelchair to adjust his footplates or by putting on his shoes and socks from a seated position.

I consider that an effective stretching programme to target the shortened muscles is essential to obtain any lasting change in muscle length. People with spinal cord damage have no cognitive or perceptual problems and are invariably only too keen to participate actively in their therapy management. Therapy sessions are of limited duration and it is imperative that gains made during a therapy session are supplemented with practice on the part of the patient to enable effective learning and carry-over into everyday function.

Gait Re-education

The residual disabilities and handicaps reported on discharge indicate that this young man has persistent difficulties with walking. No detail is provided as to specific treatment strategies carried out to improve his gait pattern but he clearly made significant gains as illustrated by his improved timed 10-metre walk.

Mr PL's residual problems, as documented $5\frac{1}{2}$ months post-injury, included impaired balance reactions, persistent tightness in both Achilles tendons, poor balance standing on one leg and on tiptoes and an inability to run. On a positive note, he was able to get up and down stairs and manage slopes and kerbs.

Treadmill Training

The use of a treadmill with the body weight supported in a harness in the rehabilitation of the spinal cord injured patient is well documented and has shown promising results (Fung et al., 1990 **A**; Dobkin, 1994 **A**; Dietz et al., 1995 **A**; Muir and Steeves, 1997 **A**). The spinal cord has the capacity not only to generate a locomotor pattern but also to 'learn' (Dietz et al., 1995 **A**) and it is suggested that spasticity and some of the functional consequences of disordered motor control may be reduced by this intervention (Dobkin, 1994 **A**). However, in spite of the scientific evidence to support this treatment and its use in many countries, to my knowledge there are no spinal cord injury units in the United Kingdom to date that have a treadmill.

The central networks generating rhythmic behaviours such as locomotion do not exist in a vacuum but are subject to continual sensory input from proprioceptors monitoring muscle stretch and joint position (Harris-Warwick and Sparks, 1995 **C**). If the rhythmical action of walking can be facilitated by means of a treadmill then it would appear to be eminently sensible to use this treatment strategy.

I have not yet had the opportunity at first hand to evaluate the effectiveness of this intervention for this client group but on the basis of the evidence I would certainly wish to use this treatment modality with Mr PL.

The Use of Botulinum Toxin

Botulinum neurotoxin A (BoNT/A) is a potent neurotoxin which produces temporary weakness in skeletal muscle by presynaptic inhibition of acetylcholine release at the neuromuscular junction (Anderson et al., 1992 **A**). The purpose of intervention with BoNT/A is to weaken the dominant spastic muscle or muscles to enable clearly identified treatment goals to be accomplished. In this case botulinum toxin may prove effective in weakening the calf muscles, enabling an improved gait pattern for the duration of the toxin's effect as reported by Scrutton et al. (1996 **A**) in a single case study.

The persistent tightness of the Achilles tendons is reported to be 'due to slight increased tone'. It would be important to determine the contribution of heightened, excessive activity in the posterior crural muscle group as opposed to changes that may be attributed to altered mechanical properties of muscle to this increased tone.

EMG should be used to distinguish between these two factors (Sheean, 1998 **C**). It is possible to identify the more superficial muscles with surface

EMG electrodes, but the more deeply sited muscles require needle EMG to ensure accurate administration of the toxin. If increased muscle activity of the calf muscles is contributing to the movement disorder, administration of BoNT/A may be indicated. However, if there is no excessive activity, the increased tone in this muscle group can be almost wholly attributed to altered mechanical properties of muscle. In this case, BoNT/A is not indicated.

Splinting is often of value to supplement the effects of the toxin. If this is the case, application of the splint should be delayed until the effects of the toxin are apparent, approximately 10 days after injection.

In this case, the tightness of Mr PL's Achilles tendons was reported on the first day post-injury and therefore he would almost certainly benefit from a splint. This splint may be used throughout the day in an attempt to maintain some dorsiflexion at the ankle and to enhance a more fluent gait pattern. Alternatively, he could use the splint at certain times of the day. The duration of wear would be determined primarily by when the toxin was administered. If he was still an in-patient in hospital, continuing with his rehabilitation, he might well use the splint for longer periods. However, if the toxin were administered once he was at home and back at work, continuous use might be more problematic.

Implications

Different therapy approaches are advocated in the treatment of patients with neurological disability but as yet there is little scientific evidence to support the benefits of the proposed interventions. Even where evidence exists in the literature this may not be readily accepted by clinicians, some of whom consider that tried and tested methods that have served the therapist well for many years require no revision. In some instances, not only is there no clear evidence as to the effects of a particular neurological physiotherapy treatment approach, but the concepts are ill defined and do not appear to take into account the more elaborate concepts of modern motor neurophysiology.

A source of frustration for those describing current clinical management of neurological patients is the paucity of literature to support some of the clinical treatment concepts. For example, although the Bobath concept appears to be the most widely used treatment approach in Europe, there is little evidence to justify its prominence. Changes in emphasis, such as the use of specific inhibitory mobilization of muscle as opposed to 'inhibition' of pathological movement patterns, have not been documented and information as to the development of this concept within the field of adult neurology continues to be passed on by word of mouth.

It is essential that physiotherapy management of patients with neurological disability, such as that which may arise from spinal cord injury, is based on sound scientific evidence. A number of studies evaluating the efficacy of neurological therapeutic approaches have been published and reviewers have concluded that 'it does not matter which approach is chosen, any of the available therapeutic approaches will improve the patients' functional status' (Ernst, 1990 **R**; Kwakkel et al., 1999 **R**).

Clearly, further research is necessary to determine the most effective treatment intervention to ensure that patients with incomplete spinal cord injury are properly managed. The points raised by this case study that warrant further evaluation include:

- the need for greater liaison between spinal injury and neurological rehabilitation units;
- the involvement of the patient in the decision-making process;
- practice of recommended tasks to enable carry-over into everyday life;
- activity should not be discouraged on the assumption that this may produce harmful compensatory strategies.

References

Anderson TJ, Rivest J, Stell R, Steiger MJ, Cohen H, Thompson PD, Marsden CD (1992) Botulinum toxin treatment of spasmodic torticollis. Journal of the Royal Society of Medicine 85: 524–9.

Association of Chartered Physiotherapists Interested in Neurology (1998) Clinical Practice Guidelines on Splinting Adults with Neurological Dysfunction. London: Chartered Society of Physiotherapy.

Bobath B (1990) Adult Hemiplegia: Evaluation and Treatment, 3rd edn. London: Heinemann Medical Books.

Boorman GI, Lee RG, Becker WJ, Windhorst UR (1996) Impaired 'natural reciprocal inhibition' in patients with spasticity due to incomplete spinal cord injury. Electroencephalography and Clinical Neurophysiology 101: 84–92.

Bromley I (1998) The acute lesion. In Bromley I (Ed) Tetraplegia and Paraplegia: A Guide for Physiotherapists. Edinburgh: Churchill Livingstone.

Brown P (1994) Pathophysiology of spasticity. Journal of Neurology, Neurosurgery and Psychiatry 57: 773–7.

Conine T, Sullivan T, Mackie T, Goodman M (1990) Effect of serial casting for the prevention of equinus in patients with acute head injury. Archives of Physical Medicine and Rehabilitation 71: 310–12.

Cornall C (1991) Self-propelling wheelchairs: the effect on spasticity in hemiplegic patients. Physiotherapy Theory and Practice 7: 13–21.

Davies PM (1994) Starting Again: Early Rehabilitation after Traumatic Brain Injury or Other Severe Brain Lesions. London: Springer Verlag.

DeVivo MJ, Rutt RD, Black KJ, Go BK, Stover SL (1992) Trends in spinal cord injury demographics and treatment outcomes between 1973 and 1986. Archives of Physical Medicine Rehabilitation 73: 424–30.

Dietz V, Colombo G, Jensen L, Baumgartner L (1995) Locomotor capacity of spinal cord in paraplegic patients. Annals of Neurology 37: 574–82.

Dietz V (1992) Human neuronal control of automatic functional movements: interaction between central programs and afferent input. Physiological Reviews 72: 33–69.

Dobkin BH (1994) New frontiers in SCI rehabilitation. Journal of Neurological Rehabilitation. 8: 33–9.

Dodds TA, Martin DP, Stolov WC, Deyo RA (1993) A validation of the Functional Independence Measure and its performance among rehabilitation inpatients. Archives of Physical Medicine and Rehabilitation 74: 531–6.

Edwards S (1996) General principles of treatment. In Edwards S (Ed) Neurological Physiotherapy: A Problem-solving Approach. Edinburgh: Churchill Livingstone.

Edwards S (1998) The incomplete spinal lesion. In Bromley I (Ed) Tetraplegia and Paraplegia: A Guide for Physiotherapists. Edinburgh: Churchill Livingstone.

Edwards S, Charlton P (1996) Splinting and the use of orthoses in the management of patients with neurological disorders. In Edwards S (ed) Neurological Physiotherapy: A Problem-solving Approach. Edinburgh: Churchill Livingstone.

Ernst E (1990) A review of stroke rehabilitation and physiotherapy. Stroke 21: 1081–5.

Fung J, Stewart JE, Barbeau H (1990) The combined effects of clonidine and cyproheptadine with interactive training on the modulation of locomotion in spinal cord injured subjects. Journal of Neurological Sciences 100: 85–93.

Gandevia SC, Rothwell J (1987) Knowledge of motor commands and the recruitment of human motoneurones. Brain 110: 1117–30.

Given JD, Dewald JPA, Rymer WZ (1995) Joint dependent passive stiffness in paretic and contralateral limbs of spastic patients with hemiparetic stroke. Journal of Neurology, Neurosurgery and Psychiatry 59: 271–9.

Goldspink G, Scutt A, Loughna PT, Wells DJ, Jaenicke T, Gerlach GF (1992) Gene expression in skeletal muscle in response to stretch and force generation. American Journal of Physiology 262: R356–63.

Goldspink G, Williams P (1990) Muscle fibre and connective tissue changes associated with use and disuse. In Ada L, Canning C (Eds) Key Issues in Neurological Physiotherapy: Physiotherapy Foundations for Practice. Oxford: Butterworth Heinemann.

Gordon T, Mao J (1994) Muscle atrophy and procedures for training after spinal cord injury. Physical Therapy 74: 50–60.

Harris-Warwick RM, Sparks DL (1995) Neural control: editorial overview. Current Opinion in Neurobiology 5: 721–6.

Herbert R (1988) The passive mechanical properties of muscle and their adaptations to altered patterns of use. Australian Journal of Physiotherapy 34: 141–9.

Imle PC, Eppinghaus CE, Roughton AC (1986) Efficacy of non-bivalved and bivalved serial casting in head injured patients in intensive care. Physical Therapy 66: 738 (abstract).

Jeannerod M, Decety J (1995) Mental motor imagery: a window into the representational stages of action. Current Opinion in Neurobiology 5: 727–32.

Kwakkel G, Kollen JB, Wagennaar RC (1999) Therapy impact on functional recovery in stroke rehabilitation. Physiotherapy 85: 377–91.

Latash ML, Anson JG (1996) What are 'normal movements' in atypical populations? Behavioral and Brain Sciences 19: 55–106.

Lee RG, van Donkelaar P (1995) Mechanisms underlying functional recovery following stroke. Canadian Journal of Neurological Science 22: 257–63.

Moseley AM (1993) The effect of a regimen of casting and prolonged stretching on passive ankle dorsiflexion in traumatic head-injured adults. Physiotherapy Theory and Practice 9: 215– 21.

Muir GD, Steeves JD (1997) Sensorimotor stimulation to improve locomotor recovery after spinal cord injury. TINS 20: 72–7.

O'Dwyer NJ, Ada L, Neilson PD (1996) Spasticity and muscle contracture following stroke. Brain 19: 1737–49.

Pette D, Staron RS (1997) Mammalian skeletal muscle fibre type transitions. International Review of Cytology 170: 143–223.

Pope PM (1992) Management of the physical condition in patients with chronic and severe neurological pathologies. Physiotherapy 78: 896–903.

Rothwell J (1994) Control of Human Voluntary Movement, 2nd edn. London: Chapman & Hall.

Scrutton J, Edwards S, Sheean G, Thompson A (1996) A little bit of toxin does you good? Physiotherapy Research International 3: 141–7.

Shah S, Cooper B (1993) Commentary on 'A Critical Appraisal of the Barthel Index'. British Journal of Occupational Therapy 56: 70–2.

Sheean G (1998) Pathophysiology of spasticity. In Sheean G (Ed) Spasticity Rehabilitation. Europe: Churchill Communications (available from Ipsen).

Stevenson VL, Playford ED, Langdon DW, Thompson AJ (1996) Rehabilitation of incomplete spinal cord pathology: factors affecting prognosis and outcome. Journal of Neurology 243: 644–7.

Sullivan T, Conine T, Goodman M, Mackie T (1988) Serial casting to prevent equinus in acute traumatic head injury. Physiotherapy Canada 40: 346–50.

Synapse (1998) To Oxford or not! Synapse, Journal and Newsletter of the Association of Chartered Physiotherapists Interested in Neurology (ACPIN).

Tardieu C, Lespargot A, Tabary C, Bret MD (1998) For how long must the soleus muscle be stretched each day to prevent contracture? Developmental Medicine and Child Neurology 30: 3–10.

Vrbova G, Gordon T, Jones R (1995) Nerve–Muscle Interaction. London: Chapman & Hall.

Wade D (1992) Measurement in Neurological Rehabilitation. Oxford: Oxford University Press.

Yarkony G, Sahgal V (1987) Contractures: a major complication of craniocerebral trauma. Clinical Orthopaedics and Related Research 219: 93–6.

Section 2
Progressive Disorders

Parkinson's Disease

Case report – Mr LH

Background

Mr LH is a 71-year-old man who lives with his wife in a semi-detached house. They have two children who live locally and visit regularly. Mr LH was a coach driver for 20 years but retired six years ago. He used to enjoy driving but now takes the car out only occasionally; his wife does not drive. He used to be a keen gardener but has recently lost interest; however, he does walk to the local shops. His wife is very anxious about him and constantly thinks he will fall. Mr LH does not smoke and rarely drinks alcohol. He attends an outpatient clinic every six months.

Main Diagnosis

Parkinson's disease diagnosis made in 1993.

Impairments

- Currently Hoehn and Yahr grade III.
- Mild bradykinesia and mild rigidity.
- Mild resting tremor in both hands (worse in right); described as constant.

Activity Restriction and Participation

- Unsteady, has fallen twice in the previous nine months, but without sustaining an injury.
- Wife reluctant to leave him at home alone.
- Finds stairs difficult.
- Dressing and getting in and out of bath becoming difficult.
- Turning over in bed and getting in and out of bed increasingly difficult, has fallen out of bed a number of times.
- Complains of feeling dizzy and very tired.

- Some problems in rising from a chair.
- His dominant right hand is the side worse affected.

Other Conditions

- Prostate operation last year (TURP).
- Low back pain for many years.
- Blood pressure monitored six monthly (by GP).
- Fully oriented but gets depressed at times and complains of fatigue.

Medication

Anti-PD medication is Sinemet Plus four times daily.
Also taking Co-proxamol, Adalat and Temazepam.

Physical Examination

- Decreased arm-swing and heel strike bilaterally.
- Hesitation at doorways and when turning.
- Decreased cervical spine rotation bilaterally (pain free).
- Speech is quiet but clear.
- Facial expression is slightly decreased.
- Moderate difficulty in performing repeated movements (finger-tap, fist open/close, pro-/supination).
- Posture erect, but tends to lean forward when tired.
- Full range of movement at ankles, knees and hips.
- Needs repeated attempts to stand up without using arms.

Treatment and Management of a Patient with Parkinson's Disease (1)

MARGARET SCHENKMAN

General Principles

Intervention for this patient with Parkinson's disease (PD) is designed to improve his function, improve his safety, and delay loss of independence. The intervention begins with an assessment of his functional limitations and his goals for treatment. Next analysed are underlying impairments and their relationship to his functional limitations. Intervention strategies are chosen based on an assessment of those impairments and functional limitations that are likely to improve with therapy, those that will require compensatory strategies, and those for which preventive intervention is indicated (Schenkman, 2000 **C**). This analysis is based on a detailed examination with a careful interpretation of findings. The intervention then follows logically from the interpretation of examination findings.

Examination

In addition to the examination findings provided at the beginning of this section of the text, additional important information should be obtained regarding the patient's musculoskeletal, cardiopulmonary and neurological systems. Loss of musculoskeletal flexibility (of both the extremities and axial structures), pain and cardiovascular deconditioning often occur as sequelae and can be considered *indirect effects* of the disease or secondary impairments (Schenkman, 1992 **B**, 1999; Schenkman and Butler, 1989 **B**).

Tests and Measures

Because PD is a chronic progressive disorder, it is important to establish a quantitative baseline to monitor the course of the disease and its functional consequences. These objective measures of function and impairments can be critical in assessing this patient's changes over time. I made assumptions, summarized in Table 1 and described below, regarding objective findings. These assumptions are based on data available in the literature (Schenkman, Clark et al., 2001 **B**).

Musculoskeletal

Clinical experience as well as scientific evidence suggests that, even early in PD, patients may have significant limitations in both spinal and extremity flexibility (Schenkman, Cutson et al., 1996 **B**). Furthermore, loss of flexibility is associated with functional limitations in community dwelling adults both with and without PD (Schenkman, Shipp et al., 1996 **A**; Schenkman et al., 1999 **A**). Mr LH is therefore assumed to have decreased rotation throughout the spine, which is evident when he twists to look toward the right or left. Loss of flexibility is presumed to contribute to his functional limitations.

Impairments of force production have been identified with PD (Berardelli et al., 1986 **A**; Koller and Kase, 1986 **A**; Corcos et al., 1996 **A**; Teasdale et al., 1990 **A**). A brief examination suggests that Mr LH's lower extremity strength is within normal limits. At some future time it may be important to establish a baseline for lower extremity strength. On the other hand, Mr LH 'bends forward' when he is tired, suggesting that extensor strength of the back might be impaired, as has been described by Bridgewater and Sharpe (1998 **A**).

Pain

A growing body of evidence suggests that people with PD frequently have pain of either extremities or back and sometimes both (Koller, 1984 **A**; Goetz et al., 1986 **A**; Snider, 1992 **A**; Stein and Read, 1997 **A**; Schenkman, Zhu et al., 2001 **A**). Pain can be exhausting and functionally limiting, even for people without PD (Gold, 1994 **A**). Given Mr LH's 15-year history of back pain, I probe regarding pain. I make the assumption that back pain is not a significant factor at this time.

Cardiopulmonary

There is growing evidence that patients in early to middle stages of PD may experience cardiovascular deconditioning and that these patients can tolerate cardiovascular exercise without interfering with dopamine absorption (Carter et al., 1992 **A**; Goetz et al., 1993 **A**; Protas et al., 1996 **A**; Canning et al., 1997 **A**). Furthermore, cardiovascular function is related to functional ability even in the absence of PD (Morey et al., 1998 **A**). This patient indicated that walking to the store, a mile away, is an effort. A baseline value for endurance is indicated. The six-minute walk distance (Guyatt et al., 1985 **A**) is used.

Table 1: Impairments, functional limitations, and quality of life

Measures	Session	1	2	3	4	5	6	7	8	9	Community adults ages 65–74 without PD
Date		**Initial evaluation**									
Impairments											
Spinal flexibility											
(Functional axial rotation)											
FAR-p, right (degrees)		95									125[1]
FAR-p, left (degrees)		100									
Extremity flexibility[2]											
Hamstring length (degrees)											
right		39									
left		43									
Ankle dorsiflexion (degrees)											
right		5									
left		5									
Spinal endurance											
timed loaded standing (sec)											
Cardiovascular											
Six-minute walk (feet)		1050									
Functional limitations											
Balance control											
Functional reach (inches)		10									13.8[1]
Berg balance (56 total)		42									(56)
Get up and go (sec)		14.8									<10[3]
360° turn (steps)											
steps to right		9									6.3[1]
steps to left		10									
UPDRS sub-scores (124 possible)											
Activities of daily living (13–52)		16									
Motor examination (14–56)		20									
PDQ39 score (156 possible)		75									
Modified Schwab & England		80%									

Notes: 1. Schenkman, Shipp et al. (1996). 2. No data specific to people ages 60–70 were available. Data for healthy adults generally are available (See Norkin CC, White DJ [1985] Measurement of Joint Motion: A Guide to Goniometry. Philadelphia, PA: FA Davis, pp 138–40). 3. Shumway-Cook and Woollacott (1995).

Neurological

Impaired motor planning also typically occurs with PD and is manifested as difficulty in performing simultaneous and sequential motor tasks. Mr LH exhibits early signs of impaired motor planning as evidenced by trouble carrying out two activities simultaneously such as opening a door and proceeding through in one smooth movement.

Overall symptoms and stage of disease

The Unified Parkinson's Disease Rating Scale (UPDRS) (Box 1, Table 1) (Fahn et al., 1987 **A**) is used to quantify overall symptoms (including neurological impairments) and functional limitations. This standardized examination has six subcategories, including motor signs and activities of daily living, which are particularly relevant to the physiotherapist. In terms of 'motor signs', Mr LH has mild right-sided rigidity and moderate right upper extremity tremor (Table 1). His movements are slow with a deliberate quality, which is evidence of bradykinesia. This problem is particularly apparent when he performs repeated movements such as finger-taps and hand opening and closing. His overall score on the UPDRS motor and activities of daily living subscales are 16 and 20 respectively, consistent with his substantial problems in these areas. The modified Hoehn and Yahr (H & Y) scale is used to identify general stage of disease (Hoehn and Yahr, 1967). His score of 3 is based on a combination of cardinal signs and physical disability (Box 2).

Mr LH has significant postural instability. When pulled posteriorly from his pelvis or shoulders, he would fall over if not caught by the examiner. His balance control can be further quantified. His score of 46 on the Berg Balance test (Berg et al., 1995), a hierarchically organized series of functionally relevant tasks, indicates that he is on the borderline for requiring an assistive device for safety (Shumway-Cook and Woollacott, 1995 **A**). His Functional Reach score (Duncan et al., 1990 **A**) of 10 inches indicates that he is at some risk for falls. (Those with a reach of six to 10 inches are twice as likely to fall as those with a reach distance of greater than 12 inches (Duncan et al., 1992 **A**).) Quantitative measures can be used to track improvement with intervention and decline as the disease progresses. Qualitative information also is important in deciding the circumstances under which Mr LH tends to lose his balance. He indicates difficulty getting out of bed at night to go to the bathroom, turning quickly toward the right, and when stepping over a low curb.

Measures are chosen to quantify spinal flexibility, trunk extensor strength and endurance. Functional axial rotation (FAR) (Schenkman et

Box 1: Unified Parkinson's Disease Rating Scale*

I. Mentation, Behaviour and Mood (4 items)
Intellectual impairment, thought disorder, depression, and motivation

II. Activities of Daily Living (13 items)
Speech, salivation, swallowing, handwriting, cutting food, dressing, hygiene, turning in bed, falling (unrelated to freezing), freezing, walking, tremor, sensory complaints

III. Motor Exam (14 items)
Speech, facial expression, tremor at rest, action or postural tremor of hands, rigidity, finger taps, rapid alternating movements of hands, leg ability, arising from the chair, posture, gait, postural stability, body bradykinesia and hypokinesia

IV. Complications of Therapy (in the past week) (10 items)
Dyskinesias (4 items)
Clinical fluctuations (4 items)
Other (2 items)

V. Modified Hoehn and Yahr Stage

VI. Modified Schwab and England Activities of Daily Living

Notes: * Items of the UPDRS are outlined. Each item in subcategory I – IV has five choices, scored from 0 (no symptoms) to 4 (most severe symptoms). The possible responses are provided for each item, based on the expected symptoms. The Modified Hoehn and Yahr scale is scored as illustrated in Box 2. The Schwab and England ADL Scale gives a single score identifying level of dependence. (See Fahn S, Elton RL, and Members of The UPDRS Development Committee [1987] Unified Parkinson's disease rating scale. In Fahn S, Marsden CD, Calne D, Goldstein M, eds. Recent Developments in Parkinson's Disease, vol. 2. Florham Park, NJ: Macmillan Healthcare Information, pp 153–63.) (Reprinted from Schenkman M [1998] Seleginline and PT intervention in early Parkinson's disease. *PT Magazine* 6: 50–60.)

al., 1995) is used to quantify his ability to twist and visualize objects posterior to him while sitting. The six-minute walk test is used to quantify endurance (Guyatt et al., 1985) (Table 1). Reliability of these measures, for a sample of patients with PD, has been established (Schenkman et al., 1997 **A**). Timed loaded standing, a measure of ability to hold objects in the outstretched arms, is used to quantify back strength. Although this measure has not been applied to people with PD, it has been shown to be a reliable and valid measure for use with osteoporotic women (Shipp et al., 1998 **A**).

Box 2: Modified Hoehn and Yahr Scale

Stage 0:	No signs of disease
Stage 1:	Unilateral disease
Stage 1.5:	Unilateral plus axial involvement
Stage 2:	Bilateral disease, without impairment of balance
Stage 2.5:	Mild bilateral disease; recovery on pull test
Stage 3:	Mild to moderate bilateral disease; some postural instability; capacity for living independent lives
Stage 4:	Severe disability; still able to walk or stand unassisted
Stage 5:	Wheelchair bound or bedridden unless aided

Notes: Signs of disease include rigidity, tremor and bradykinesia. Postural instability is determined by pulling the patient backwards suddenly from the shoulders. Patients with normal responses recover balance with ≤ 3 steps. Recovery on pull test indicates that the patient can recover balance, but requires > 3 steps. Patients with instability would fall if not caught. See Fahn S, Elton RL, and Members of The UPDRS Development Committee [1987] Unified Parkinson's disease rating scale. In Fahn S, Marsden CD, Calne D, Goldstein M, eds. Recent Developments in Parkinson's Disease, vol. 2. Florham Park, NJ, Macmillan Healthcare Information, pp 153–63. (Reprinted from Schenkman M [1998] Seleginline and PT intervention in early Parkinson's disease. *PT Magazine* 6: 50–60.)

Physical Performance

Measures of physical performance include both time to complete activities and a description of the movement strategies used. The 'Timed Get Up and Go' (Podsiadlo and Richardson, 1991) quantifies Mr LH's ability to stand up from a chair, walk 10 metres, turn, return to the chair, and sit back down. This functionally relevant measure incorporates balance control and the ability to transition between two separate activities (standing from a seated position and walking). Its utility for those with PD has been described (Thompson and Medley, 1998). Community-dwelling adults without specific disorders should be able to accomplish the task in under 10 seconds (Shumway-Cook and Woollacott, 1995 **A**). This patient's score of 14.8 seconds indicates that he is beginning to have problems with this essential functional activity.

The number of steps and time to complete a 360° turn in standing also is measured. This test is quick and easy to administer, and appears to be sensitive to change in those with PD (Schenkman, Cutson et al., 1998 **A**). The six-minute walk test (Guyatt et al., 1985) was applied as a measure of endurance but also provides information regarding the patient's functional status.

Descriptions are used for functional movements including transitional movements (turning over in bed, rising from supine to sitting, sitting to standing, getting up from the floor), gait, reaching activities (a glass from the cupboard), and carrying activities (a glass of water and a book). With regard to transitional movements, Mr LH typically omits the postural adjustments that should accompany the movements (such as repositioning feet and pelvis before coming from sitting to standing); he has little rotation of the thorax relative to the pelvis. When reaching for objects he often neglects to move close enough to the object, straining to position his arm far enough forward. He exhibits difficulty when carrying objects while trying to perform a second activity. For example, he may have to put down an object that he holds in one hand before using the other hand to open a door.

During gait, Mr LH tends to stay forward, never achieving full hip extension; there is no heel-strike, and he is inherently unstable. He has little arm-swing and almost no rotation of the thorax with respect to pelvis. His step length is small, his base of support narrow. When asked to stop suddenly, Mr LH tends to take a few extra steps and appears unsteady. He has more difficulty with turns to the right than left, with a tendency for his right foot to 'stick' to the floor. He is able to negotiate stairs safely if he uses the handrail. Performance on stairs will be monitored to assure continued safety as his bedroom is on the second floor.

Overall Quality of Life

Mr LH will complete a PD-specific quality of life questionnaire, the PDQ39 (Jenkinson et al., 1995; Peto et al., 1995; Fitzpatrick et al., 1997) which he will bring on his next visit. The PDQ39 has eight subscales including both physical and psychosocial domains (Box 3). This questionnaire provides additional important information regarding how Mr LH views his situation.

Evaluation

Evaluation refers to interpretation of examination findings and determination of priorities. Priorities include patient safety, optimizing function, and – to the extent possible – preventing further functional or physiological decline. This analysis is used to set goals and determine the treatment strategy.

One of the top priorities at this time is to improve Mr LH's stability and general safety as he has already experienced several recent falls. Although Mr LH himself does not seem particularly worried, his wife is especially concerned about his falls from bed. Furthermore, postural instability and falls are likely to increase as the disease progresses.

Box 3: Parkinson's Disease Quality of Life (PDQ 39)

I. Mobility (10 items)
Leisure activities, care for home, carrying shopping bags, walking 1/2 mile, walking 100 yards, getting around the house, getting around public places, need someone to accompany when out, confined to house, worried about falling

II. Activities of Daily Life (6 items)
Washing, dressing, buttoning, writing, cutting food, holding a drink

III. Emotional Well-being (6 items)
Depressed, isolated and lonely, tearful, angry or bitter, anxious, worried about the future

IV. Stigma (4 items)
Conceal PD, avoid eating/drinking in public, embarrassed by PD, worried about others' reactions

V. Social Support (3 items)
Close relationships, support from spouse/partner, support from friends/family

VI. Cognition (4 items)
Unexpectedly falls asleep during day, concentration, memory, hallucinations

VII. Communication (3 items)
Speech, communication, ignored by people

VIII. Bodily Discomfort (3 items)
Painful cramps/spasms, aches or pains, hot/cold

Notes: The categories and items of the PDQ39 are summarized. Each item is scored from 1 (never) to 4 (always).
(For the full test, see Peto et al. [1995].)

It also is critically important to assist Mr LH to improve performance and efficiency of basic activities of daily living so that he does not also lose his independence. Even the simplest activities, such as turning over in bed, are increasingly burdensome for Mr LH. He exhibits an *en bloc* pattern of movement (that is, he tends to move as if his torso is a solid block, with only limited rotation and lateral flexion). Mr LH has already stopped participating in leisure activities, such as gardening, that he previously enjoyed.

The third area of concern is Mr LH's endurance. Endurance could be limited by the effort expended to complete functional activities, by cardiovascular deconditioning, or possibly by underlying depression. Depending on his response to treatment, endurance training and discussion with other professionals may be indicated.

Finally, Mr LH is in the mid-stage of PD; at this time it is important to include critical preventive strategies related to respiratory status, falls and further musculoskeletal impairments (Cutson et al., 1995 **C**).

Interrelationships

To meet the above priorities efficiently, it is necessary to understand interrelationships between functional limitations and underlying impairments and among the different underlying impairments. Specifically, contributions that are *direct effects* of PD (primary impairments) are differentiated from *indirect effects* (sequelae, secondary impairments) of the musculoskeletal or cardiovascular systems. *Co-morbid conditions* are identified which might contribute to the patient's functional limitations and disability. The influence of other factors is interpreted (such as the impact of his wife's responses to his disease) on both impairments and functional limitations (Verbrugge and Jette, 1994 **B**). Based on this analysis, an overall diagnosis is determined for the patient and his probable response is predicted with respect to the physical intervention. A general approach to intervention is then determined, including expected frequency of treatment and predicted outcomes. These interrelationships are analysed.

Rigidity, Loss of Flexibility, and En Bloc Movements

Loss of flexibility, resulting in *en bloc* patterns of movement is limiting almost all of Mr LH's functional activities. This loss is interpreted to occur from a combination of rigidity, bradykinesia and loss of automaticity of movement (Schenkman and Butler, 1989 **C**; Schenkman, 1992 **C**). Over time, contractures result so that available range of motion and muscle flexibility is limited. Loss of flexibility and limitations in range of motion must be addressed in treatment. His functional ability and efficiency should improve as his flexibility increases.

Postural Instability

When Mr LH is displaced he attempts to regain postural control. However, his responses are delayed and ineffective, suggesting that the postural response mechanism is impaired. Limited spinal flexibility further exacerbates his difficulty in generating appropriate responses. These problems are compounded by his tendency to stand with hips flexed, thus positioning his centre of mass excessively forward. Postural malalignment and limited spinal flexibility should respond to physical intervention. In contrast, the primary contributions to postural instability are likely to be resistant to correction and may worsen over time. Therefore, an intervention strategy should include corrective techniques to improve overall flexibility and to enhance postural responses under a variety of conditions. Compensatory strategies are also needed so that Mr LH avoids situations that are likely to result in falls.

Slow and Awkward Functional Movements

Bradykinesia, loss of velocity and inefficient movement strategies can contribute to slowness of functional movements. Mr LH exhibits bradykinesia. He often uses inefficient movement strategies (for example, he often sits straight up from supine, expending a great deal of energy). Sometimes he also has akinetic blocks, as evidenced by episodes of arrested movement or 'freezing'. For example, to turn from supine to side lying he sometimes begins to bend his knees, but freezes with his hips flexed so that his legs are in the air. He will require compensatory strategies for these primary impairments of bradykinesia sequencing.

Restricted spinal rotation and lateral flexion further contribute to overall slowness of movement. Clinical experience suggests that Mr LH's loss of flexibility during function relates in part to overactive muscles. As he improves his ability to relax overactive muscles, move in a more relaxed state and incorporate this relaxed movement into functional activities, he should improve flexibility and co-ordinated movement. Relaxation of overactive muscle groups also should lead to improved flexibility and muscle extensibility.

Finally, difficulty with balance control can contribute to slow and awkward movements. For example, Mr LH takes almost 10 steps to turn while standing. The use of many steps could result from bradykinesia and motor planning problems but also probably results from inadequate balance control and loss of spinal flexibility.

Endurance

As noted, several factors may contribute to Mr LH's low endurance. His endurance may improve as his ability to perform tasks improves. If endurance does not improve, it may be necessary to initiate a cardiovascular conditioning programme; it also may be important to consult with other professionals regarding possible underlying depression.

Tremor

Tremor is a direct effect of PD and is unlikely to respond to physical intervention. Compensatory strategies for tremor will be necessary should it continue to worsen. These strategies will be designed to assist Mr LH to continue to carry out daily functional activities despite the tremor.

Diagnosis and Prognosis

Mr LH has been diagnosed with PD for over four years. According to his history, he had significant problems with rigidity and bradykinesia from the beginning. This pattern of development of PD symptoms is associated with faster progression of symptoms and worse prognosis than is the case when tremor is the initial presenting symptom (Zetusky et al., 1985 **A**; Gerstenbrand and Poewe, 1990 **A**; Roos et al., 1996 **A**). Indeed, Mr LH's disease seems to be progressing relatively quickly. On the positive side, his functional limitations appear to result in part from impairments of spinal flexibility and strength, both of which should respond to physical intervention. Furthermore, with movement re-education he should be able to compensate for some of the impairments of neurological processing that interfere with his function.

Several factors suggest that Mr LH will respond well to physical intervention. He appears to be motivated. Within the first session improvements were apparent in flexibility and he was able to use more appropriate movement strategies with cues, both of which contribute to a favourable prognosis. Based on previous clinical experience with patients at a similar stage of PD, these observations indicate probable improvements of balance control and functional ability.

Another important factor is the role of Mr LH's wife. She appears supportive, although impatient, perhaps because of a limited understanding of the impact of his disease. It will be important for Mrs LH to better understand PD so that she, in turn, can assist her husband. Thus family education will be critical.

Plan of Care

The intervention will include exercises to improve spinal and extremity flexibility (Schenkman et al., 1994 **B**; Laub and Schenkman, 1995 **B**) and movement re-education to improve organization of functional movements and balance control activities (Whipple, 1998 **A**). An aerobic exercise programme (walking and cycling) may be added later, depending on how endurance improves with the initial programme. Education also is critical so that Mr LH will understand the reasons for the exercises, their correct performance, and guidelines for monitoring his performance. For lasting benefit, Mr LH must assume responsibility for his programme and must become independent and regular in performing the exercises. Family education is also important so that Mrs LH will be better able to understand her husband's limitations.

Expected Frequency of Visits

Mr LH will be seen for 45 minutes three times per week for two weeks to establish the exercise programme. Assuming he responds well to the exercises and learns to monitor his movement strategies, he will be seen twice weekly thereafter for an additional four weeks, then weekly and finally monthly. The frequency is estimated from prior clinical experience. The exact frequency will depend on how quickly Mr LH learns the initial exercises and becomes proficient at correcting his movement strategies. After discharge, Mr LH will be encouraged to seek follow-up visits at regular intervals for monitoring of his exercise programme and for modifications as his condition changes.

Intervention

Several authors have offered conceptual suggestions for treatment of people in early and mid-stages of PD based on both empirical evidence and expert opinion (Dibble and Nicholson, 1997; Glendinning, 1997; Morris and Iansak, 2000; Schenkman, 1998, 1999). Clinical investigations demonstrate that impairments and physical performance may improve when people in early and mid-stages of PD participate in exercise programmes (Szeleky et al., 1983 **A**; Palmer et al., 1986 **A**; Comella et al., 1994 **A**; Dam et al., 1996 **A**; Mohr et al., 1996 **A**; Schenkman, Cutson, et al., 1998 **A**; Thaut et al., 1996 **A**; MacIntosh et al., 1997 **A**; Müller et al., 1997 **A**). Most of these studies either have focused on correction of a specific underlying impairment (Schenkman, Cutson et al., 1998 **A**), or have tested whether a specific type of feedback is effective (Dam et al., 1996 **A**; Thaut et al., 1996 **A**). A few studies have tested more global exercise programmes (Szeleky et al., 1983 **A**; Palmer et al., 1986 **A**; Comella et al., 1994 **A**). Taken together, these investigations provide insight into strategies and techniques that might be useful for Mr LH. Coupled with clinical experience, they provide guidance in developing his exercise programme. Conceptual issues are reviewed first, including an analysis of the particular sequence of exercises chosen and decisions regarding use of feedback. Strategies are then described in detail for selected functional activities.

Conceptual Considerations

Impairments vs. Function

An important decision is the extent to which treatment goals can be accomplished by addressing function and ability directly, and the extent to which underlying impairments should be treated first. Specific underlying impairments should be treated if they interfere with physical performance or if they are likely to lead to injury or functional loss at a later time (Schenkman and Riegger-Krugh, 1997 **C**). Furthermore, by increasing physiological reserves in other systems, such as the cardiovascular system, it may be possible to improve function even when there are no specific impairments (Schenkman, 2001 **C**). The approach to Mr LH's treatment reflects a synthesis of these concepts.

Mr LH's programme begins with flexibility training. Because his flexibility is quite limited, it is not sensible to begin with movement strategies. For example, it might be tempting to teach Mr LH to swing his arms while walking. Although arm-swing is appropriate during gait when the torso rotates relative to the pelvis, it is artificial, probably energy consuming, and frustrating to the patient if there is inadequate flexibility for the thorax to rotate relative to the pelvis. In fact, clinical experience shows that arm-swing often improves spontaneously when thoracolumbar flexibility and relaxed mobility improve.

Conversely, it will do Mr LH little good to gain flexibility unless exercises are included that incorporate improved flexibility into function. Sit-to-stand illustrates this issue. Mr LH usually attempts to stand from excessive posterior pelvic tilt. As his thoracolumbar extension improves, he should be taught to position himself in neutral or slight anterior pelvic tilt before beginning to stand. Further, he should retain neutral pelvic alignment, with his centre of mass close to his base of support, throughout the activity. Therefore, movement re-education will be incorporated as flexibility improves to meet Mr LH's functional needs.

As function, balance control and movement strategies improve it is necessary to challenge Mr LH's balance control and gait using higher-level postural control exercises. As with sit-to-stand, these exercises are likely to be most effective *after* Mr LH has developed the necessary physiological capabilities. For example, flexibility of hip musculature is needed first so that he can stand with his hips in neutral alignment or in slight extension. Exercises are then introduced to help him to re-learn movement strategies that allow him to move his centre of mass around his base of support while retaining an erect posture. As these abilities improve, more aggressive balance control activities can be introduced when standing. Note that balance activities can also be used to facilitate hip muscle flexibility; sit-to-stand activities might be used to improve lumbar flexibility. When balance activities are used for this purpose, careful attention must be directed to Mr LH's performance to assure that he achieves the desired kinematic response and not just the desired functional response.

In summary, based on the above analysis, Mr LH's treatment will begin with flexibility and trunk strength training. Movement re-education, functional training and balance activities will be included as flexibility increases. More aggressive gait and balance-control activities will be introduced once flexibility and strength have improved sufficiently. Cardiovascular conditioning, while important, will be delayed so that Mr LH is not burdened with too much exercise too fast.

Feedback

Another conceptual issue to consider is the use of feedback. The literature indicates that external sensory cueing can enhance movement performance of people who have PD (Dam et al., 1996 **A**; Thaut et al., 1996 **A**; Dibble and Nicholson, 1997 **A**). Studies, carried out under controlled laboratory conditions, demonstrate improvements in gait at the time that the study is completed. From these studies, one *cannot* infer that the use of auditory or visual cues as a form of therapy will lead to improved motor output if those sensory stimuli are removed (Schenkman, 2001 **C**). To determine the long-term impact of sensory cueing on functional performance, experimental studies are needed.

Patients are unlikely to use external cues if those cues interfere with their ability to carry out daily functional activities. For example, while music can improve gait velocity, it may be unrealistic to ask Mr LH to attend to the beat of music as a corrective strategy while simultaneously trying to negotiate obstacles in a supermarket, interact with family members, or prepare a meal. On the other hand, Mr LH might be able to utilize music when walking for aerobic conditioning or to specific destinations.

From clinical experience, it appears that verbal input can assist patients to *re-learn* more efficient movement strategies for tasks such as turning in bed and getting up from the seated position. Cues (either said out loud or silently) can be used as a daily routine to assist patients during selected tasks that do not require divided attention. Specific examples are provided below. Because patients may require ongoing use of these compensatory strategies, it is important to restrict use to the most critical aspects of function in order to enhance function while limiting the burden on the patient.

As the disease progresses, symptoms may wax and wane depending on when medications are taken. If Mr LH experiences these fluctuations in symptoms, it will be important to time treatment sessions to those periods of the day when he is at his 'best' ability to perform. Unfortunately this also may be the time when he is most able to accomplish necessary daily tasks or to enjoy leisure activities. Mr LH and his wife will need to work with me to determine a schedule of treatment that best meets all of his needs.

Specific Treatment Strategies for Underlying Impairments

Flexibility and Relaxation

Based on proposed interrelationships of rigidity and loss of flexibility, we had previously hypothesized that improvements in flexibility might best be achieved through relaxed movement as opposed to forceful stretching (Schenkman and Butler, 1989 **C**; Schenkman et al., 1989 **C**; Schenkman, 1992 **C**). Furthermore, anecdotal reports from clinicians and their physicians, as well as my own observations, suggest that an emphasis on relaxed movement may result in an overall reduction of rigidity when the patient uses this approach on a regular, long-term basis. Therefore, the treatment strategy used with Mr LH will be based on relaxed, rhythmical motion using kinesiologically defined movements.

My colleagues and I developed an exercise programme based on these concepts and designed to improve spinal and extremity flexibility as well as functional movement strategies of people with PD (Schenkman et al., 1994; Laub and Schenkman, 1995 **C**). The exercises are based on a kinesiological analysis of movements during functional activities with emphasis of participation of the axial structures. They are designed to enhance participation of appropriate synergistic muscles and use relaxed movement, as opposed to forceful stretching, to increase range of motion. Functional training is incorporated so that the participant learns to incorporate movement into related daily activities.

Using a randomized controlled intervention study, we compared the flexibility programme with 'usual care' (no specific exercise) (Schenkman, Cutson et al., 1998 **A**). Those who received the intervention had significantly better spinal flexibility and balance control compared with those in the 'usual care' group. I have used the general approach to exercise with close to 100 patients who have PD of various stages. I find the approach successful when I tailor the programme to the patient's exact needs and incorporate other aspects of treatment as appropriate to the specific patient.

Trunk Strength

Trunk strength exercises will be used, including sitting extension activities with a Theraband™ or holding weights in the hands while extending the thoracic spine. For some patients, prone extension exercises might also be incorporated, beginning with arms at the side and progressing to shoulder abduction with elbow flexion. Because Mr LH already has substantial limitations in flexibility, this activity may be contraindicated.

Functional Training

No studies report specifically on functional training for people with PD. To determine the optimum movement strategy for Mr LH, it is important first to observe how he carries out each task and determine whether musculoskeletal limitations preclude a more appropriate strategy. If so, flexibility and strengthening exercises will be introduced to provide the necessary prerequisites for the movement. Specific movement strategies will then be identified that are most efficient for Mr LH. During treatment, decisions will be made regarding whether and how to incorporate oral or visual cues. In my experience treating patients with motor planning impairments, such as those exhibited by Mr LH, it may be necessary to teach a single strategy, with frequent repetition and *without* attempts at generalization. Some examples are given below based on my experience with patients similar to Mr LH. These suggestions are guided by a kinesiological analysis of different functional tasks combined with clinical experience.

Bed Mobility

Mr LH uses an *en bloc* strategy to turn over in bed, shift position, and get in and out of bed. These activities will be easier if he incorporates spinal movements that typically accompany this task. Although there is no single 'correct way' to perform this task (van Sant and Newton, 1989 **A**), clearly some spinal motion will facilitate Mr LH's ability to do so easily and efficiently. Therefore, the programme begins with spinal and extremity flexibility exercises when both supine and side lying. As Mr LH becomes proficient in these exercises, functional training is incorporated. Oral cues are used such as the following: 'Bend your hips and knees (to hook lying), now drop your knees to the side, reach across your body with your arm and roll on to your side.' Once Mr LH learns the general strategy, the cues are simplified ('Bend your legs, drop your knees, reach, now roll'). Mr LH is encouraged to practise this activity saying the cues himself, either out loud or silently, whichever is more effective. With time he may no longer need the cues. Many patients report that they can move in bed more easily if they use satin sheets. This suggestion may be helpful to Mr LH, either now or in the future.

A similar strategy is used for reaching for a bedside lamp and adjusting the bed sheets. For each activity, we identify an efficient strategy, then break the task into a few manageable components and use simple but descriptive verbal cues.

Transfers to and from Bed

Getting out of bed is particularly problematic for Mr LH. He needs adequate spinal flexibility, including lateral flexion in addition to rotation. Even with adequate spinal flexibility, he may still attempt to sit up over the edge of the bed while the body's centre of mass is too far posterior. Alternatively, he may attempt to sit up without lateral flexion. Both these problems make this task more difficult than necessary. I shall teach Mr LH how to control his centre of mass in order to minimize the moment arm of his torso. I shall provide gentle guidance from the occiput until he is comfortable keeping his torso forward. I also remind him to let his legs slide off of the bed *in co-ordination with* bringing his thorax forward. When these two activities are smoothly co-ordinated, an efficient trajectory of movement develops, facilitating Mr LH's ability to come to sitting from lying down. Because Mr LH has had several falls while getting out of bed at night, I shall identify verbal cues that he can use to remind himself of a safe strategy. Clinical experience with patients who have a similar problem suggests that he will stop falling out of bed as his flexibility and movement strategies improve.

Sitting to Standing

In coming from sitting to standing, Mr LH, like many patients with PD, keeps his weight too far posteriorly. He compounds the problem by failing to move his feet closer to his body and failing to bring his hips forward in the chair seat. As a result, his body weight pulls him back down into the chair. Adequate flexibility is required throughout the spine to bring the pelvis into more neutral alignment. Once this is achieved it should be an easy matter to teach Mr LH to organize the sitting-to-standing activity more appropriately. Appropriate and simple verbal cues can facilitate both learning and retaining the activity. For example, I might say 'Slide forward, lean forward, keep coming forward', while providing light tactile input at the occiput. Similarly, Mr LH learns to control his return from standing to sitting. Cues such as 'Pretend you are about to sit on a crate of eggs' can provide helpful reminders. Again, a light touch at the occiput may be helpful while he learns the strategy.

In cases where mobility is lacking and cannot be regained, it may be necessary to teach patients to generate momentum by rocking in order to stand up from seated positions. However, rocking motions can be destabilizing and may put the patient at risk for falls. Therefore, it is important for the clinician to use such compensatory strategies judiciously. As an alternative, the clinician might recommend a lift for the patient's most frequently used chair.

Getting on to and off the Floor and in and out of the Bath

All patients should be able to get down to and up from the floor, especially if falling has been a problem. Observational analysis of the task highlights the particular importance of lateral flexion of the spine, anterior and posterior motion of the pelvis, and adequate hip and ankle flexion. In addition, adequate quadriceps strength is required. Mr LH's history of back pain is also considered in devising an appropriate strategy. At the same time, I can problem solve with Mrs LH to identify the best strategy for getting in and out of the bathtub safely. He may require grab bars for safety. If a shower is available, he should be encouraged to take showers rather than baths.

Walking

Mr LH walks with forward flexion, limited heel-strike, small base of support, and short stride length, as is typical for many patients with PD (Turnbull, 1993 **C**). He needs adequate flexibility to accomplish the task from a more upright posture. Further, Mr H needs to relearn how to use that flexibility. The series of exercises in the Axial Mobility Exercise Program (Schenkman et al., 1994; Laub and Schenkman, 1995) is designed to provide Mr LH with adequate spinal and extremity flexibility for a more efficient and stable pattern of gait. The early stages provide prerequisite flexibility; the latter stages of the programme (Stages 6 and 7) provide movement re-education for components of the activity.

Learning to control the components of gait in and of themselves is not enough. To assure good functional gait, it will be necessary for Mr LH to practise walking efficiently under a variety of conditions. Therefore, once he is able to remain upright, take steps of appropriate length and transfer weight appropriately from side to side, he will need to practise walking under the many circumstances that he will face (for example, slowly, quickly, on busy streets, uneven surfaces, ice).

For Mr LH, safety is of paramount importance (Cutson et al., 1995 **C**), and some compensatory strategies also will be required. For example, Mr LH tends to 'freeze' when he turns in small spaces, but not when the turn takes place over a greater radius. His right foot tends to 'stick' to the floor and he is more likely to lose balance if he turns to the right rather than the left. I teach Mr LH to use larger turns to the *left*. I also teach him to break movement sequences down into components (Morris and Iansek, 1997 **C**) (such as stand up, walk forward a few steps, then turn) in order to make the transition from a seated position to walk out of the door located to the right of his chair. In addition, I assist him to modify his home environment. For example, I recommend that he reposition furniture to facilitate appropriate turning and sit-to-stand-to-walk strategies within his home. I also suggest that he remove excess clutter, which could trigger akinetic blocks, and loose carpets that could precipitate falls (Morris and Iansek, 1997 **C**).

Eventually Mr LH may require an assistive device while walking. At that time I shall play a crucial role in deciding when and which device to use. I shall help him weigh the pros and cons of using a cane. Although the cane may provide him with greater stability, holding the cane will interfere with his function to some extent. Furthermore, his difficulties with motor organization may make use of a cane problematic, in which case a walker may be preferable.

Balance Control

As flexibility and strength improve and Mr LH learns strategies for carrying out critical functional tasks, we begin to incorporate more aggressive balance retraining into his programme. We begin with activities that narrow his base of support, then proceed to walking while moving his head. We perform directed movements while standing on uneven surfaces or on support surfaces of different textures, and similarly challenging activities (Whipple, 1998 **C**). If available, I may choose to work with Mr LH in a pool, which can be used to increase balance control, as well as for cardiovascular conditioning (Schenkman and Riegger-Krugh, 1997 **C**).

The Home Programme

Exercise benefits depend upon continued participation long after formal training is completed. For this reason, intervention without patient follow-through may be of little long-term benefit. It is therefore imperative to work with Mr LH and family members to ensure that they understand the issues involved so they will be able to continue the programme independently after the formal treatment sessions are completed.

Discharge

Mr LH will be discharged from this episode of physiotherapy when he is able to perform his exercise programme independently and when his spinal flexibility, balance control and functional movements are improved sufficiently for him to function safely and independently. However, Mr LH should receive intermittent treatment throughout the course of the disease. Both Mr and Mrs LH will need to monitor his flexibility and physical performance. They should be able to identify changes in impairments or function that require further examination and treatment. When necessary, he should be seen by a physiotherapist again so that his programme can be modified to better meet his needs.

Implications

This case analysis demonstrates a strategy for making decisions regarding physical intervention for a patient with PD. This strategy can be applied to any patient with neurological dysfunction (Schenkman, Bliss, et al., 2000 **C**), and indeed could be applied to management of patients with non-neurological disorders as well. In using this strategy, the clinician determines cause and effect interrelationships among the patient's impairments and functional limitations. She determines which impairments must be changed in order to improve function, which should be changed to prevent future decline, and which impairments cannot be changed using physical intervention strategies. She also uses clinical judgement coupled with available literature to predict the changes in function that can be achieved and to estimate the time that will be required. The treatment plan then follows logically from the above analyses. Finally, clinical judgement that a patient is 'progressing' may or may not provide an accurate assessment of the changes that occur with treatment. Objective outcome measures can be critical in establishing the extent to which changes have occurred.

References

Berg K, Wood-Dauphinee S, Williams J (1995) The balance scale: reliability assessment with elderly residents and patients with an acute stroke. Scandinavian Journal Rehabilitation Medicine 27: 27.

Berardelli A, Dick JPR, Rothwell JC, Day ABL, Marsden CD (1986) Scaling of the size of the first agonist EMG burst during rapid wrist movements in patients with Parkinson's disease. Journal of Neurology, Neurosurgery and Psychiatry 49: 1273–9.

Bridgewater KJ, Sharpe MH (1998) Trunk muscle performance in early Parkinson's disease. Physical Therapy 78: 566–76.

Canning C, Alison JA, Allen NE, Goreller H (1997) Parkinson's disease: an investigation of exercise capacity, respiratory function, and gait. Archives of Physical Medicine Rehabilitation 78: 199–207.

Carter JH, Nutt JG, Woodward WR (1992) The effects of exercise on levodopa absorption. Neurology 42: 2042–5.

Comella CC, Stebbins GT, Brown-Toms J, Goetz CG (1994) Physical therapy and Parkinson's disease: a controlled clinical trial. Neurology 44: 376–8.

Corcos DM, Chen C-M, Quinn NP, McAuley J, Rothwell JC (1996) Strength in Parkinson's disease: relationship to rate of force generation and clinical status. Annals of Neurology 39: 79–88.

Cutson TM, Laub KC, Schenkman M (1998) Pharmacological and nonpharmacological interventions in the treatment of Parkinson's disease. Physical Therapy 75: 363–73.

Dam M, Tonin P, Casson S, Bracco F, Piron L, Pizzolato G, Battistin L (1996) Effects of conventional and sensory-enhanced physiotherapy on disability of Parkinson's disease patients. Advances in Neurology 69: 551–5.

Dibble LE, Nicholson DE (1997) Sensory cueing improves motor performance and rehabilitation in persons with Parkinson's disease. Neurology Report 21: 117–24.

Duncan PW, Weiner DK, Chandler J, Studenski SA (1990) Functional reach: a new clinical measure of balance. Journal of Gerontology 45: M192–7.

Duncan PW, Studenski SA, Chandler J, Prescott B (1992) Functional reach: predictive validity in a sample of elderly male veterans. Journal of Gerontology 47: M93–8.

Fahn S, Elton RL, and Members of the UPDRS Development Committee (1987) Unified Parkinson's disease rating scale. In Fahn S, Marsden CD, Calne D, Goldstein M (Eds) Recent Developments in Parkinson's Disease, vol. 2. Florham Park, NJ: Macmillan Healthcare Information, pp 153–63.

Fitzpatrick R, Peto V, Jenkinson C, Greenhall R, Hyman N (1997) Health-related quality of life in Parkinson's disease: a study of outpatient clinic attenders. Movement Disorders 12: 916–22.

Gerstenbrand F, Poewe WH (1990) The classification of Parkinson's disease. In Stern G (Ed) Parkinson's Disease. Baltimore: Johns Hopkins University Press, pp 315–32.

Glendenning D (1997) A rationale for strength training in patients with Parkinson's disease. Neurology Report 21: 132–5.

Goetz CG, Tanner CM, Levy M, Wilson R, Garron DC (1986) Pain in Parkinson's disease. Movement Disorders 1: 45–9.

Goetz CG, Thelen JA, MacLeod CM, Carvey PM, Bartley EA, Stebbins GR (1993) Blood levodopa levels and Unified Parkinson's Disease Rating Scale function: with and without exercise. Neurology 43: 1040–2.

Gold DT (1994) Chronic musculoskeletal pain: older women and their coping strategies. Journal of Women and Aging 6: 43–58.

Guyatt GH, Sullivan MJ, Thompson PJ (1985) The 6 minute walk: a new measure of exercise capacity in patients with chronic heart failure. Canadian Medical Association Journal 32: 919–23.

Hoehn MM, Yahr MD (1967) Parkinsonism: onset, progression, and mortality. Neurology 17: 427–42.

Jenkinson C, Peto V, Fitzpatrick R, Greenhall R, Human N (1995) Self-reported functioning and well-being in patients with Parkinson's disease: comparison of the Short-form Health Survey (SF-36) and the Parkinson's Disease Questionnaire (PDQ-39). Age and Aging 24: 505–9.

Koller WC (1984) Sensory symptoms in Parkinson's disease. Neurology 34: 957–9.

Koller WE, Hubble JP (1992) Classification of Parkinsonism. In Koller WC (Ed) Handbook of Parkinson's Disease, 2nd edn. New York: Marcel Dekker, pp 55–103.

Koller W, Kase S (1986) Muscle strength testing in Parkinson's disease. European Neurology 25: 130–3.

Laub KC, Schenkman M (1995) The Axial Mobility Exercise Program (Participant and Instructor's tapes). Videotapes, produced by Claiborne Clark; Duke University, Claude D. Pepper Older Americans Independence Center.

MacIntosh GC, Brown JH, Rice RR, Thaut MH (1997) Rhythmic auditory motor facilitation of gait patterns in patients with Parkinson's disease. Journal of Neurology, Neurosurgery and Psychiatry 62: 22–6.

Mohr B, Müller V, Mattes R, Rosin R, Federmann B, Strehl U, Pulvermüller F, Müller F, Lutzenberger W, Birbaumer N (1996) Behavioral treatment of Parkinson's disease leads to improvement of motor skills and to tremor reduction. Behavioural Therapy 27: 235–55.

Morey MC, Pieper CF, Cornoni-Huntley J (1998) Physical fitness and functional limitations in community-dwelling adults. Medicine and Science in Sports and Exercise 30: 715–23.

Morris ME, Iansek R (1997) Gait disorders in Parkinson's disease: a framework for physical therapy practice. Neurology Report 21: 125–31.

Müller V, Mohr B, Rosin R et al. (1997) Short-term effect of behavioral treatment on movement initiation and postural control in Parkinson's disease: a controlled clinical trial. Movement Disorders 12: 306–14.

Palmer SS, Mortimer JA, Webster DD, Bistevins F, Dickinson GL (1986) Exercise therapy for Parkinson's disease. Archives of Physical Medicine and Rehabilitation 67: 741–5.

Peto V, Jenkinson C, Fitzpatrick R, Greenhall R (1995) The development and validation of a short measure of functioning and well-being for individuals with Parkinson's disease. Quality of Life Research 4: 241–8.

Physical Therapy (1997) Guide to Physical Therapist Practice, Parts one and two. Physical Therapy 77.

Podsiadlo D, Richardson S (1991) The timed 'Up and Go': a test of basic functional mobility for frail elderly persons. Journal of the American Geriatric Society 39: 142–8.

Protas EJ, Stanley RK, Jankovic J, MacNeil B (1996) Cardiovascular and metabolic responses in upper- and lower-extremity exercise in men with idiopathic Parkinson's disease. Physical Therapy 76: 34–40.

Roos RAC, Jongen JCF, van der Velde EA (1996) Clinical course of patients with idiopathic Parkinson's disease. Movement Disorders 11: 236–42.

Schenkman M (1992) Treatment of the ambulatory patient. In Turnball GI (Ed) Physical Therapy in Management of Parkinson's Disease. New York: Churchill Livingstone, pp 137–92.

Schenkman M (1998) Selegiline and PT intevention in early Parkinson's disease. Physical Therapy 6: 50-60.

Schenkman M (1999) Parkinson's disease. Update on clinical features, physiology, and treatment. In Riolo L (Ed) In Touch Home Series. Alexandria, VA: American Physical Therapy Association.

Schenkman M, Bliss S, Day L, Susan Kemppainen S, Morse J, Pratt J (2000) Model for management of neurologically impaired patients. Update and case analysis. Neurology Report 1999. Journal of Gerontological Medical Science, July.

Schenkman M, Butler RB (1989) A model for the evaluation, interpretation, and treatment of individuals with Parkinson's disease. Physical Therapy 69: 932–43.

Schenkman M, Cutson TM, Morey M (1996) Axial mobility, axial configuration, and physical performance of community dwelling elders with and without Parkinson's disease. Physical Therapy 76: S71.

Schenkman M, Cutson TM, Chandler JC, Kuchibhatla M, Pieper C (1997) Reliability of impairment and physical performance measures for persons with Parkinson's disease. Physical Therapy 77: 19–27.

Schenkman M, Donovan J, Tsubota J, Kluss M, Stebbins P, Butler RB (1989) Management of individuals with Parkinson's disease - rationale and case studies. Physical Therapy 69: 944–55.

Schenkman M, Hughes MA, Bowden M, Studenski SA (1995) A new device for measuring functional axial rotation: technical report. Physical Therapy 75: 151–6.

Schenkman M, Keysor J, Chandler J, Laub KC, MacAller H (1994) Axial Mobility Exercise Program, An Exercise Program To Improve Functional Ability. Durham, NC: Center on Aging, Duke University Medical Center.

Schenkman M, Morey M, Kuchibhatla M (2001) Spinal flexibility and physical performance of community-dwelling adults with and without Parkinson's disease.

Schenkman M, Riegger-Krugh C (1997) Physical intervention for elderly patients with gait disorders. In Masdeu J, Sudarsky L, Wolfson L (Eds) Gait Disorders of Aging. Falls and Therapeutic Strategies. Philadelphia, PA: Lippincott-Raven, pp 327–53.

Schenkman M, Shipp KM, Chandler J, Studenski SA, Kuchibhatla S (1996) Relationships between mobility of axial structures and physical performance. Physical Therapy 76: 276–85.

Schenkman M, Clark K, Xic T, Kuchibhatla M, Shinbeig M, Roy L (2001) Spinal movement and performance of a standing reach task in patients with and without Parkinson's disease. Physical Therapy 81: 1400–11.

Sheridan MR, Flowers KA (1990) Movement variability and bradykinesia in Parkinson's disease. Brain 113: 1149–61.

Shipp K, Purser JL, Gold DT et al. (1998) The effect of an exercise intervention on timed loaded standing. Journal of Bone and Mineral Research 13(Suppl 5): S614.

Shumway-Cook A, Woollacott M (1995) Motor Control. Theory and Practical Applications. Baltimore, MD: Williams & Wilkins.

Snider SR (1992) Sensory dysfunction. In Koller WC (Ed) Handbook of Parkinson's Disease, 2nd edn. New York: Marcel Dekker, pp 217–26.

Stacy M, Jankovic J (1992) Differential diagnosis of Parkinson's disease and the parkinsonism plus syndrome. Neurologic Clinics 10: 341–59.

Stein WM, Read S (1997) Chronic pain in the setting of Parkinson's disease and depression. Journal of Pain and Symptom Management 14: 255–8.

Szekely BC, Kosanovich NN, Sheppard W (1983) Adjunctive treatment in Parkinson's disease: physical therapy and comprehensive group therapy. Rehabilitation Literature 43: 72–6.

Teasdale N, Phillips J, Stelmach GE (1990) Temporal movement control in patients with Parkinson's disease. Journal of Neurology, Neurosurgery and Psychiatry 53: 802–8.

Thaut MJ, McIntosh GC, Rice RR, Miller RA, Rathbun J, Brault JM (1996) Rhythmic auditory stimulation in gait training for Parkinson's disease patients. Movement Disorders 11: 193–200.

Thompson M, Medley A (1998) Performance of individuals with Parkinson's disease on the Timed Up and Go. Neurology Report 22: 16–21.

Turnbull GI (1993) The role of physical therapy intervention. In Turnbull GI (Ed) Physical Therapy Management of Parkinson's Disease. New York: Churchill Livingstone, pp 91-120.

van Sant AF, Newton RA (1989) Description of adult rolling movements and hypothesis of developmental sequences. Physical Therapy 69: 63-71.

Verbrugge L, Jette AM (1994) The disablement process. Social Science and Medicine 331: 821-7.

Whipple RH (1998) Improving balance in older adults: identifying the significant training stimuli. In Masdeu JC, Sudarsky L, Wolfson L (Eds) Gait Disorders of Aging. Falls and Therapeutic Strategies. Philadelphia, PA: Lippincott-Raven, pp 355-80.

Zetusky WJ, Jankovic J, Pirozzolo FJ (1985) The heterogeneity of Parkinson's disease: clinical and prognostic implications. Neurology 35: 522-6.

Treatment and Management of a Patient with Parkinson's Disease (2)

KAREN BRIDGEWATER AND MARGIE SHARPE

Introduction

Parkinson's disease (PD) is a progressive, degenerative disease of the central nervous system. The role of physiotherapy in PD is twofold: educative and rehabilitive. The aim is to maximize patient function, thereby minimizing secondary effects. It is therefore imperative that physiotherapy is sought and implemented immediately following diagnosis.

Best practice is paramount and we advocate a multidisciplinary approach to the evaluation and treatment of people with Parkinson's disease. This is also critical for research in movement dysfunction, and effective therapeutic intervention programmes for this clinical population.

Prior to the advent of dopamine therapy, physiotherapy focused on the amelioration of the primary symptoms of PD. The secondary musculoskeletal problems may have been affected indirectly (Schenkman and Butler, 1989 **C**).

Most recently, rather than endeavouring to alter primary symptoms, the emphasis has been to prevent, delay or reverse the associated musculoskeletal sequelae and improve physical performance through exercise and patient and family education.

There is an urgency to underpin physiotherapy practice with sound, rigorous experimental studies to refine and sustain our role in the evalu-ation, treatment and management of the patient with Parkinson's disease.

Assessment

General Principles

The evaluation of patients with PD is multifaceted. It involves both the neurological and musculoskeletal systems. Owing to the inherent fluctuations of the disease and medication effects (Cutson et al., 1995 **A**), it is imperative that the initial and subsequent evaluations are conducted at the same time of day, during the effective phase of medication.

To ensure that appropriate treatment is provided, further questions must be asked regarding functional activities. Which activities does Mr LH wish to resume, maintain or improve? What is inhibiting these activities? For example, why does he drive his car only occasionally? Is this decision related to diminished cervical movement, a loss of self-confidence, tiredness and concerns regarding road safety, lack of co-ordination, or a combination of these factors? What symptoms of advanced PD might later influence performance of those activities? Answers to these questions will influence planning of both the objective examination and the treatment programme.

There may be a number of factors beyond the cardinal signs, and the neurological or musculoskeletal issues contributing to any specific disability. For example, whilst Mr LH has an identified balance problem, the other cardinal signs of PD are 'mild'. Therefore, other issues might contribute to functional difficulties (emotional, cognitive, social, independent musculoskeletal issues, and medication side-effects may be contributory). Independent contributing factors must be considered as well as direct and secondary effects of PD.

The direct effects of PD (tremor, rigidity, bradykinesia, postural instability) may precipitate secondary effects. Rigidity and bradykinesia may lead to a stooped posture. Postures of chronic flexion may precipitate joint contractures and altered muscle length. These factors will cause limitation of range of movement in the affected joints. Diminished muscle strength and flexibility have been purported to affect righting and balance reactions, and thus contribute to balance disturbances and falls (Schenkman and Butler, 1989 **C**). However, this hypothesis has yet to be tested in a clinical trial. Vestibular impairment and neck proprioceptive feedback, which may be altered by decreased cervical mobility, have also been implicated in balance and mobility problems, albeit by clinical observation for the most part. Secondary problems influencing balance may occur in addition to primary deficits of postural instability, alerting mechanisms and motor planning (Cutson et al., 1995 **A**).

Neurological Symptoms

Rigidity, tremor and bradykinesia may be assessed using sub-items of scales such as the Webster Rating Scale (Webster, 1968). Although the reliability of the sub-items of this scale has not been reported to date, use of sub-item scores provides opportunity for comparison across assessments for an individual patient.

Non-randomized controlled clinical trials (Pramstaller and Marsden, 1996 **A**) and case studies (Lakke, 1985 **A**) have reported apraxia in this clinical population. Apraxia may be a contributing factor to difficulty rolling over, sitting up, and dressing as experienced by Mr LH. The evaluation of trunk apraxia is described by Lakke (1985 **B**).

Mr LH's clinical symptoms have been reported as only mild. Clinical reasoning processes regarding potential reasons for diminishing function should therefore include consideration of this fact.

Posture

Posture is frequently affected in PD, due to muscle weakness, decreased physiological range of motion, biomechanical spinal changes, rigidity and depression.

Mr LH has an erect posture, tending to flexion when tired. Posture should be observed, cognizant of progressed PD, and considered together with joint range (discussed in Assessment: Musculoskeletal Status). Assessment of standing posture with a Debrunner kyphometer is reliable in PD (Schenkman et al., 1997 **A**). However, a photograph of the patient standing just beyond a plumb line or standing before a posture grid provides adequate information for reassessment.

Balance

Mr LH is rated Stage III on the Hoehn and Yahr Scale (1967), which indicates deficient balance and righting reflexes, unsteady standing and gait. Patients with Parkinson's disease often fall; two-thirds sustain injury and are hospitalized and institutionalized (Koller, 1984 **A**). Numerous factors contribute to falls. To design an appropriate management programme, the environment(s) where Mr LH has fallen and concurrent PD symptoms need to be established. For example, he may have fallen due to distraction (Chen et al., 1996 **C**), a common problem in PD.

Vestibular dysfunction has been reported in PD (Reichart et al., 1982 **A**). Moreover, the vestibulo-ocular reflex (VOR) deteriorates with ageing, as do the adaptive plastic mechanisms which normally maintain VOR performance when altered responses result in visual-vestibular mismatch during head rotation (Paige, 1991 **C**, 1992 **C**). It is therefore important to evaluate the VOR as described by Herdman (1997 **C**).

Patients in Hoehn and Yahr Stages I and II are typically somatosensory dependent for maintaining balance. Patients of stages III and IV are more reliant on visual cues (Bronstein et al., 1990 **A**). Dependence on each cue can be assessed using the Sharpe Sway Unit.

Muscle strength and physiological range of movement have been implicated in balance (Whipple et al., 1987 **C**). It has been reported that weak dorsiflexors contribute to loss of balance in the elderly (Whipple et al., 1987 **C**). Assessment of muscle strength is considered later (in Assessment: Musculoskeletal Status).

Numerous balance tests have been found to be reliable in PD; time maintained in single and double leg stance positions (Smithson et al., 1998), the functional reach test (Schenkman et al., 1997; Smithson et al., 1998), responses to external perturbation (Pastor et al., 1993), performance of functional activities (Tinetti, 1986), the Timed 'Up and Go' Test (Podsiadlo and Richardson, 1991 **C**), and the Sharpe Sway Test. Such tests are appropriate for Mr LH.

Gait

As PD progresses, the gait deteriorates with an increase in the risk of falls (Aita et al., 1982 **A**). The patient is often stooped, taking small steps, with a poor heel-strike and diminished arm-swing (Poser and Ronthal, 1991 **C**). Mr LH typifies these features.

Musculoskeletal factors which may influence Mr LH's gait include hip, knee and ankle muscle tightness (particularly flexors) and weakness, poor trunk counter-rotation and trunk lateral flexors. If he has full lower limb range of motion, trunk range and strength should be examined and their potential contribution to his gait pattern considered.

Cao and associates (1997 **C**) have shown that in elderly people most falls occur when turning. This may be related to vestibular dysfunction and a deteriorated VOR. This patient demonstrates a wide-base ataxic gait, and lack of trunk rotation due to bracing of the neck and trunk. This decreases sensory input into the cerebellum and basal ganglia, enabling maintenance of an upright posture (Lance and McLeod, 1981 **C**). Consequently, decreased trunk rotation and arm-swing may not be due solely to rigidity and bradykinesia, or secondary musculoskeletal problems. It is thus necessary for therapists to assess the VOR in static and dynamic situations (Herdman, 1997 **C**).

The slow, shuffling gait of patients with PD is due to reduced stride length (Pedersen et al., 1997 **A**) and the inability to internally regulate stride length (Morris, Iansek et al., 1996 **A**). Difficulty in weight transference may also contribute to short, shuffling steps. Spatiotemporal measures have been shown to be reliable in gait analysis of PD patients (Morris, Matyas et al., 1996 **A**) and may be assessed in the clinic using a 12 metre walkway and stopwatch (Morris, Matyas et al., 1996; Schenkman et al., 1997 **A**). Assessment of speed, cadence and basic calculations of step length (number of steps/distance walked) are thereby possible.

Fine Motor Skills

Mr LH has problems with writing and dressing (possible difficulty with buttons or zips). These activities require a functional assessment, which includes the time taken to complete tasks, and qualitative statements regarding observed causes of difficulty. The involvement of an occupational therapist would be appropriate.

Musculoskeletal Status

Mr LH has normal lower limb range, but decreased bilateral rotation of the cervical spine, and low back pain. Both require a detailed examination (including flexibility and strength).

Loss of trunk mobility has been shown to occur early in the disease (Bridgewater and Sharpe, 1998 **A**). Clinical opinion suggests that muscles of the trunk (Schenkman and Butler, 1989 **C**) and periphery become contracted, and possibly also weak as PD progresses. The extensor muscles become weak and range of extension decreases.

Spinal assessment considering physiological, accessory and intervertebral movement may be conducted using techniques devised by Maitland (1986 **C**), and peripheral joints with a standard goniometer (American Academy of Orthopaedic Surgeons, 1965; Maitland, 1977). The Cervical and Back Range of Motion instruments have been shown to be reliable in PD (Schenkman et al., 1997 **A**). Chest expansion can be assessed using a tape measure (Burgos-Vargas et al., 1993).

Muscle weakness was first reported by James Parkinson in his essay 'An Essay on the Shaking Palsy' (1817 **C**). Since then, several controlled non-randomized studies have reported muscle weakness (Pedersen et al., 1997 **A**; Bridgewater and Sharpe, 1998 **A**) and alterations in muscle contraction parameters in PD (Pedersen et al., 1997 **A**). Muscle weakness may be due to a central nervous system mechanism, disuse atrophy, age-related changes in skeletal muscle, or a combination of these factors. In the absence of isokinetic equipment, manual muscle testing (Kendall and McCreary, 1983), a hand-held dynamometer (Schenkman et al., 1997) or free weights (Fiatarone et al., 1994) may be used to assess muscle strength.

Muscle length must also be assessed, particularly that of joint flexors and two- or multi-joint muscles, including the shoulder girdle muscles (Kendall and McCreary, 1983 **C**).

Activities of Daily Living

Difficulties turning over in bed, dressing, getting into and out of a bath and rising from low chairs are common in PD, and are part of Mr LH's symptom complex. Muscle weakness and stiffness, decreased range of motion and soft tissue contractures, although unlikely in this case, fine motor and balance impairment and apraxia in any combination may also contribute to these difficulties.

Functional activities tasks – for example, moving from supine to stand, or stand to supine – may be reliably assessed by timing with a stopwatch (Schenkman et al., 1997 **A**). Use of a function-based assessment scale, such as the Northwestern University Disability Scale (Canter et al., 1961), rather than a scale based on cardinal signs, may also be appropriate. Owing to potential difficulty in moving his centre of gravity, patterns of movement should also be observed, and considered in conjunction with Mr LH's balance assessment.

Cardiorespiratory Aerobic Function

Respiratory abnormalities, for example, reduced forced vital capacity, maximal pressures on inspiration and expiration, and functional capacity, have been demonstrated in people with PD when compared with age and gender matched normal controls (Hooker et al., 1996 **A**; Sabate et al., 1996 **A**; Canning et al., 1997 **A**). It would seem that both the cardinal signs and secondary effects of PD have a role to play in respiratory abnormalities. Given the nature of PD, a sedentary lifestyle is perpetuated. This leads to muscle weakness, loss of lean muscle mass and cardiorespiratory deconditioning (Protas et al., 1996 **A**). This compounds the disability directly resulting from the disease process.

Given his diminishing activity and the understanding that this is common in PD (Fertl et al., 1993 **A**), this patient's aerobic capacity is threatened. As aerobic capacity is vital for daily activities, it needs to be considered. Aerobic assessment has been conducted safely, maximally (Bridgewater and Sharpe, 1996 **A**; Hooker et al., 1996 **A**; Canning et al., 1997 **A**) and submaximally (Protas et al., 1996 **A**), by cycle ergometry (Canning et al., 1997 **A**) and walking on a treadmill (Bridgewater and Sharpe, 1996 **A**). In the trials of Canning and associates (1997 **A**) and Protas and associates (1996 **A**), only the maximal results were similar to results of normal populations.

Mr LH is taking nifedipine (Adalat), implying cardiovascular disease. Consultation with his doctor prior to aerobic assessment, and subsequent training are therefore imperative.

Depression

Depression has been shown to be widely associated with PD (Cummings, 1992 **A**). Contributing factors may include biochemical and organic changes, side-effects of medication or reaction to disability (Cummings, 1992 **A**). Because of the complexity of depression, and the challenge of its assessment (features common to both PD and depression include slowness of movement and postural changes), Mr LH may require referral to a psychiatrist.

Medication and Physiotherapy or Exercise

Physical performance can vary depending on the duration of time between medication and exercise, and the intensity of physical activity during that time (Goetz et al., 1993 **A**). Such variations may influence exercise safety, particularly when exercising unsupervised; the patient may manage an exercise in the clinic, but fall when attempting the same exercise at home. Patients with balance problems must be advised to be cautious.

Recording the type and dosage of PD and non-PD medications is required, because both motor function and cognition may be affected by medication. The physiotherapist must be aware of the patient's response to any medication.

An understanding of the effects and side-effects of medications will assist the physiotherapist in their analyses of functional difficulties, and indicate potential barriers to assessment, intervention and improvement. For example, the use of Adalat would caution us regarding strenuous aerobic assessment. Functional activities may also be impaired by medications. Sinemet is associated with postural hypotension, diplopia and blurred vision, Adalat with hypotension and temazepam may cause blurred vision with the effect of increasing Mr LH's unsteadiness in walking, and his tendency to fall. Mr LH's dizziness may also be made worse by Sinemet (dizziness; faintness; diplopia) and Adalat (dizziness; light-headedness), or temazepam (dizziness; faintness; vertigo). Depression may be worsened by Sinemet or temazepam, and fatigue by Adalat, temazepam and Sinemet. If such side-effects are suspected, discussion with Mr LH's doctor would be helpful.

Concepts of Treatment

There are a number of non-randomized controlled studies, descriptive and theoretical studies, and reports of opinions of respected physiotherapists that provide evidence to underpin physiotherapy practice in this clinical population. Typically the controlled clinical studies incorporate numerous 'treatments', and assess many variables (Formisano et al., 1992 **A**; Comella et al., 1994 **A**; Patti et al., 1996 **A**). Consequently, it is impossible to attribute improvements in particular tasks to particular interventions.

Neurological Symptoms

Comella and associates (1994 **A**), as a result of a randomized, single-blind, crossover study, reported that their battery of exercises decreased rigidity and bradykinesia, supporting the use of exercise regimens in the treatment of PD. Anecdotal evidence suggests that slow rhythmical, rotational, active assisted treatments result in freer movement, perhaps by decreasing rigidity (McNiven, 1986 **C**). Whilst unlikely to affect the pathology of PD directly (MacKay-Lyons and Turnbull, 1995 **A**), or provide long-term effects, such treatments may create a window of opportunity during which the patient can experience and practise normal movement patterns. However, a cost benefit analysis may preclude this treatment approach.

Posture

Owing to the inevitable posture of flexion, and its detrimental effect on function, treatment directed at posture is important, whether posture is affected by PD yet or not (Franklyn, 1986 **C**). Treatment (education, stretching and muscle strengthening) needs to be directed according to the typical posture of progressed PD: stooped, increased thoracic kyphosis, decreased lumbar lordosis, flexion at the hips and knees, and rounded shoulders. Thus muscles of the trunk, upper and lower extremities all need attention.

Trunk flexibility needs to be ensured. If trunk flexibility is inadequate to allow extension, muscle training and postural education will be ineffective in improving posture. In the case of Mr LH, trunk flexibility may be adequate, as it is said he can attain an upright posture. Therefore training of back extensors is the first priority, given that strength of these muscles has been shown to be diminished even in early PD (Bridgewater and Sharpe, 1998 **A**). Twice-weekly back extension exercises have been shown, in a non-randomized controlled trial, to improve back extension strength (Bridgewater and Sharpe, 1997 **A**). Cervical and thoracic exercises to correct or delay the 'poking chin' may also be useful (Kendall and McCreary, 1983 **C**).

Mr LH could be advised to stand with his back against a wall, aiming to touch heels, buttocks, shoulders and occiput against the wall without undue upper cervical extension (Banks, 1991 **C**). If he feels his ability to attain this position to be diminishing, review by a physiotherapist would be considered appropriate.

To prevent excessive cervical flexion, Mr LH could be encouraged to try to use only one pillow when sleeping on his back. In addition, some time could be spent daily lying flat on his back in order to maintain the ability to achieve at least neutral postural extension. His most common daily postures, such as sitting in his preferred chair, should also be considered (Banks, 1991 **C**), ensuring that prolonged spinal flexion is avoided.

Balance

Postural instability is a hallmark of PD. Balance should be addressed by considering the secondary effects of PD, and the provision of advice regarding compensatory strategies, for example the use of assistive devices, and avoiding precarious situations.

Mr LH's flexibility, both spinal and peripheral, should be considered and treated first. It must also be determined that both trunk and peripheral muscle strength are adequate to maintain and regain balance (Fiatarone et al., 1994 **C**). For example, weakness in the dorsiflexors has been noted in the frail elderly and implicated in balance problems (Whipple et al., 1987 **C**). Progressive resistance exercise programmes in the frail elderly have been shown in randomized controlled trials to improve balance, walking, leg muscle strength and lean muscle mass (Fiatarone et al., 1994 **C**). Given that PD patients have demonstrated an increase in muscle strength of the trunk in response to an exercise programme (Bridgewater and Sharpe, 1997 **A**), it is reasonable to postulate that the same may be achieved in the arms and legs, with a resultant impact on balance and gait.

On a basis of adequate flexibility and strength, Mr LH's balance can be further addressed. He requires a context-specific intervention programme addressing static and dynamic postural stability during both self-initiated displacement of his centre of movement, and in response to external perturbations (Schenkman and Butler, 1989 **C**). For example, simple functional tasks such as bending over to put on his socks, standing up to pull up his trousers, reaching forward to pick up a book from a shelf, walking, turning around, twisting and getting out of a chair are self-initiated functional activities. In contrast, being jostled in a crowd, tripping over an uneven pavement, and walking on an uneven or compliant surface are external perturbations.

Sensory conditions during exercise and treatment may be systematically varied for Mr LH, by manipulating the use or combinations of type of support surface, visual environment and type of perturbation (Sharpe and Corrigan, submitted **A**; Horak, 1987 **A**). The co-ordination of motor strategies with voluntary movement is yet another important aspect of treatment to improve Mr LH's postural stability. Given he has dizziness, vestibular compensation exercises for the vestibular-ocular reflex (VOR) may be a valuable adjunct (Herdman, 1997 **C**).

These intervention strategies have been selected for their potential role in the prevention of falls and injury. This security in turn will improve Mr LH's self-confidence and quality of life. The strategies proposed are based on findings of non-randomized clinical controlled trials of PD patients.

Gait

If diminished range of motion, loss of strength and postural imbalance are contributing to poor gait, those deficiencies need to be addressed first, in order to gain benefit from the following strategies.

The typical gait of PD is one of small shuffling steps. A non-randomized controlled clinical trial showed that people with PD are able to achieve normal stride length when facilitated by visual cues (Morris, Iansek et al., 1996 **A**). The increased stride length has been shown to carry over, lasting for the maximum examination time of two hours beyond treatment time (Morris, Iansek et al., 1996 **A**). Approaches detailed by Morris, Iansek et al. (1996 **A**) are therefore appropriate if Mr LH's stride length is shortened.

It has also been reported in non-randomized clinical controlled trials that the performance of simultaneous activities during gait, for example, talking to the patient whilst walking, reduces stride length (Morris, Iansek et al., 1996 **A**), and therefore should be avoided during any aspect of gait training and in everyday living. This difficulty with simultaneous tasks is attributed to a deficit in divided attention in people with PD (Sharpe, 1990 **A**).

In a randomized controlled study, Patti and associates (1996 **A**) have shown that repetitive practice of accentuated arm-swing, and turning, improves gait. Clinical opinion has also suggested that music with a rhythmic beat, or simple counting or tapping of a cane, enhances gait (Quintyn and Cross, 1986 **C**).

Mr LH's carer should be advised that pulling him when he is hesitant may cause a fall. Hesitation at doorways has been treated using visual, auditory and tactile external input to assist the patient to move. Such techniques have been based on non-randomized controlled trials (Stefaniwsky and Bilowit, 1973 **A**). Polysensory cueing (Homberg, 1993 **A**) has also been clinically proposed to assist with these hypokinetic situations. Mr LH's carer may utilize verbal and tactile cues, for example a light touch on the shoulder or occiput, or a simple one-stage command, for example 'go'. His carer may assist in object visualization, reminding Mr LH to imagine an object in his path, which he must 'clear'. Increased awareness of carpet patterns or a beam of light has clinically been proposed to effect movement (Quintyn and Cross, 1986 **C**). Finally, the carer may assist by providing a model for imitation. Clinically it has been seen that if the desired movement is exaggerated, the response is further enhanced (Quintyn and Cross, 1986 **C**).

Both Mr LH and his carer must be aware of the importance of regaining and maintaining a heel–toe gait. Clinically, the rhythmic verbalization of 'heel, heel' has been found to facilitate heel-strike, whether said by or to the patient (Franklyn, 1986 **C**).

Fine Motor Skills

While dexterity exercises have been shown to improve fine motor skill (Gauthier et al., 1987 **A**), difficulties with fine motor skills may better be addressed by an occupational therapist. Modification of clothing and choice of eating and writing utensils may make daily tasks more manageable.

Advice to time activities with the 'on phase' of medication and to seek opportunities to complete tasks in a stress-free environment (for example, signing important documents at home), may assist Mr LH and reduce both his and his carer's frustration.

Musculoskeletal Status

Prior to exercise intervention, Mr LH's back pain should be thoroughly investigated musculoskeletally (Maitland, 1986 **C**) and treated accordingly.

Prescription of exercises needs to be prompt and given at the time of diagnosis to prevent musculoskeletal problems and pain. It will also provide support and reassurance to both patient and caregivers.

For Mr LH, maintenance of, or regaining, musculoskeletal flexibility will provide a base upon which to strengthen those muscles required for maximal ease of function in posture, gait and physical performance. One immediate focus for Mr LH, according to his profile, would be the decreased range of motion in his cervical spine. As appropriate, treatment of his cervical spine, or any body area, may include any or all of the following treatment ploys: relaxation, passive mobilization, stretches and strengthening exercises.

Relaxation has been clinically advocated, potentially providing a foundation upon which to perform stretches (Schenkman and Butler, 1989 **C**). Self-relaxation, by cognitively focusing on relaxation and breathing out deeply, or using a top-to-toe approach of voluntary relaxation, has been advocated by Franklyn (1986 **C**).

Passive mobilization has also been shown to have a role in preventing contractures (Formisano et al., 1992 **A**), and treating pain and stiffness (Maitland, 1986 **C**). Muscle-strengthening exercises have also been shown to prevent contractures and stiffness, and to reduce pain (Ettinger et al., 1997 **C**).

Whilst exercising for flexibility two or three times weekly has been shown, by controlled trial, to improve flexibility in non-diseased aged individuals (Raab et al., 1988 **C**), the same cannot be presumed true in PD. To ensure maintenance of flexibility it may be more appropriate for Mr LH to perform selected exercises daily, particularly if his daily routine is becoming sedentary. Dorsiflexion, knee and hip extension, spinal extension, rotation, and lateral flexion, thoracic expansion and shoulder horizontal extension range all require range exercises. Combined with this is the importance of recognizing the role of two or multi-joint muscles. With respect to thoracic expansion, aerobic exercise will facilitate natural mobility. However, Mr LH should also be taught how to perform basal expansion inspiration exercises, to be repeated frequently throughout the day.

It has been shown that progressive resistance training induces skeletal muscle hypertrophy in the frail elderly (Fiatarone et al., 1994 **C**) and increases voluntary neural drive to muscles on both sides of the body (Yue et al., 1996 **C**). It is therefore reasonable to postulate that this approach may be beneficial in PD. The findings of Bridgewater and Sharpe (1997 **A**), in a controlled non-randomized clinical trial of PD patients, lends support to this hypothesis, showing a training effect of trunk muscle strength. Further cross-sectional and longitudinal randomized controlled trials are essential to determine the relationships between strength training, and functional and cognitive outcomes.

As Mr LH is rated Hoehn and Yahr stage III, exercises should be prescribed with increased awareness of his imbalance and thus increased probability of falls. Exercise machines that physically support the patient during exercise, and therefore do not require the patient to have perfect balance, may be appropriate.

Facial Expression

Proprioceptive neuromuscular facilitation, using the physiotherapist's fingertip pressure, quick stretches, and resistance, light brushing, icing and range-of-motion exercises have been shown through a clinical trial to improve facial mobility and alter expression (Katsikitis and Pilowsky, 1996 **A**). This approach may be helpful for Mr LH. Range of motion exercises in front of a mirror and mimicking of expressions have also been examined in a non-randomized controlled trial (Formisano et al., 1992 **A**). However, that study did not examine the efficacy of this intervention in isolation from other treatment techniques and therefore the findings are inconclusive.

Activities of Daily Living

Mr LH's difficulties with physical performance activities – for example, rising from low chairs – may be attributed to difficulty in moving his centre of gravity. Functional training, incorporating an improved range of motion into more efficient movement patterns, has been shown to be clinically appropriate for improving physical performance (Cutson et al., 1995 **A**). Treatment should include demonstration and practice, with simple sequences of activities that present difficulties, as described by Gauthier and associates (1987 **A**) in their clinical trial. Mrs LH may also be taught verbal or tactile cues which she can use to assist her husband with maximum safety.

When rolling over in bed it is possible that the uppermost hip may be insufficiently flexed to pull the lower trunk into side lying. By teaching Mr LH to flex his hip sufficiently, he may be able to complete movement successfully (proposed by Franklyn in 1986 **C**). Use of satin bed sheets, or sheets with a central insert of satin, and slippery night attire may also aid bed mobility. Temporary bed poles or bed rails may assist him when getting out of bed, as well as assisting in the prevention of falling out of bed (Sharp, 1991 **C**).

Teaching and assisting a patient's practice of whole-body movements in standing, sitting, kneeling and half kneeling, and balance activities, both in single leg stance and walking, have also been shown through a non-randomized controlled clinical trial to improve the ability of sit-to-stand, stand-to-sit, and rising from supine (Yekutiel et al., 1991 **A**). Whilst it is unclear which element of the intervention in this controlled trial (if any in isolation) elicited the improvement, incorporating the exercises of that study into Mr LH's routine may produce improvements.

It is quite possible that Mr LH is having difficulty negotiating stairs, rising from a chair, rolling over, dressing, and getting into and out of the bath, due to muscle weakness resulting from disuse atrophy. Therefore, the importance of progressive resistance training is rehighlighted. This patient's difficulty rolling over may be due to trunk apraxia. Visual tracking of an object and simultaneously reaching for the same object may facilitate rolling in this patient.

Equipment and options for bathing should also be discussed with an occupational therapist, given the dangerous nature of wet areas and the potential for falls.

Improved breathing control may improve the volume of his speech. Consultation with a speech pathologist would be the most appropriate course of action if seeking to improve this aspect of Mr LH's functional difficulty.

Aerobic Cardiorespiratory Endurance Training

The prescription of breathing exercises to maintain or improve respiratory function is frequently documented (Schenkman and Butler, 1989 **C**;

Formisano et al., 1992 **A**; Patti et al., 1996 **A**), but the specific effect of such exercises (for example, basal expansion or endurance training) has seldom been examined in clinical trials.

With aerobic class activity, aerobic ability can be increased in early PD in as little as 12 weeks, as shown in a controlled trial (Bridgewater and Sharpe, 1996 **A**). It has also been shown in a clinical trial with retrospective consideration of activity level that, as with non-diseased ageing individuals, aerobic capacity and therefore general activity level can be maintained in PD with ongoing aerobic activity (Canning et al., 1997 **A**). These results add credence to the suggestion that individuals with PD should be encouraged to undertake aerobic exercise and endurance training on a regular basis – for example twice a week for periods of at least 30 minutes – to improve or maintain cardiovascular fitness (Bridgewater and Sharpe, 1996 **A**). If walking is unsafe due to balance and gait disturbances, a stationary bicycle, hydrotherapy, swimming or circuit gym work may be used to increase heart rate.

Exercise prescription for improving and maintaining aerobic fitness is based on an individual's exercise capacity as determined at aerobic assessment (American College of Sports Medicine, 1991 **A**). The appropriate intensity for improving aerobic capacity is determined by a heart rate that corresponds to between 60% and 85% of VO_2 max (American College of Sports Medicine, 1991 **A**). Ratings of perceived exertion, for example, the Borg Category Ratio (Borg, 1982 **C**), can also serve as accurate indicators of exercise intensity in people with PD who are involved in training programmes. Moreover, recent evidence suggests that progressive resistance training provides more benefits than aerobic training alone (Shephard, 1990 **C**; Fiatarone et al., 1994 **C**).

Cognition

Depression, which is accompanied by tiredness, is common in the elderly and often poorly treated (Singh et al., 1997 **C**). Nevertheless, several recent studies have suggested that there are benefits of resistance training in the treatment of depression in non-Parkinsonian individuals (Ismail and El-Naggar, 1981 **C**; Valliant and Asu, 1985 **C**; Singh et al., 1997 **C**).

Exercise has been shown in a randomized controlled clinical trial to assist those who are depressed (Singh et al., 1997 **C**). Clinical trials have reported improvement of the emotional well-being of patients with PD when the patients are involved in group therapy (Palmer et al., 1986 **A**; Gauthier et al., 1987 **A**). Without analysis of control groups, it is unclear whether these effects are due to exercise or the nature of a group setting. Whatever the reason, Mr LH may benefit emotionally from participation in group exercise.

Goal Orientation, Motivation and Adherence

The benefits gained from one to one physiotherapy intervention programmes need to be maintained by continued long-term exercise either in community groups or at home. Without an organized programme, instructions to 'continue exercises' have previously failed to maintain gains made from an exercise programme (Comella et al., 1994 **A**). Although anecdotal, periodic one-to-one treatment enables the physiotherapist to reassess and remotivate the patient and modify the treatment programme. Since there is a high probability of non-adherence to exercise programmes, these programmes need to be tailored to each patient's needs, goals and lifestyle to promote a sense of programme ownership and meaningfulness. Detailing the home programme on videotape, paper or both have been proposed to enhance adherence (MacKay-Lyons and Turnbull, 1995 **A**). Lifelong exercise is important, given its influence on the survival rate of people with PD (Kuroda et al., 1992 **A**).

Encouragement from physicians, families and friends has also been proposed as important (Poser and Ronthall, 1991) despite the lack of evidence from clinical trials support this tenet. Both patient and caregivers need to understand the benefits of one to one physiotherapy, home exercises and the need for long-term commitment to their programme, because detraining occurs even in young individuals (Fringer and Stull, 1974 **C**).

Implications

There is a clear identification of the extent and limitations of the scientific background which currently underpins physiotherapy practice in PD. With the increasing demand for physiotherapy intervention in the management of this clinical population and the increasing pressures to produce positive outcomes quickly, it is imperative that a sound body of research-based knowledge supporting physiotherapy practice in PD is further developed with well-controlled clinical trials. Anecdotal evidence, unsubstantiated by either present scientific scrutiny or theoretical models, presents research challenges for the profession well into the new millennium.

References

Aita JF (1982) Why patients with Parkinson's disease fall. Journal of the American Medical Association 247: 515–16.

American Academy of Orthopaedic Surgeons (1965) Joint Motion: Method of Measuring and Recording. Edinburgh: Churchill Livingstone.

American College of Sports Medicine (1991) Guidelines for Exercise Testing and Prescription, 4th edn. Philadelphia, PA: Lea & Febiger.

Banks M (1991) Physiotherapy. In Caird FI (Ed) Rehabilitation in Parkinson's Disease, Therapy in Practice 25. London: Chapman & Hall.

Borg GA (1982) Rating of perceived exertion. Medicine and Science in Sports and Exercise 14: 377–87.

Bridgewater KJ, Sharpe MH (1996) Aerobic exercise and early Parkinson's disease. Journal of Neurologic Rehabilitation 10: 233–41.

Bridgewater KJ, Sharpe MH (1997) MH trunk muscle training and early Parkinson's disease. Physiotherapy Theory and Practice 13: 139–53.

Bridgewater KJ, Sharpe MH (1998) Trunk muscle performance and early Parkinson's disease. Physical Therapy 78: 566–76.

Bronstein AM, Hood JD, Grest MA, Panagi C (1990) Visual control of balance in cerebellar and parkinsonian syndromes. Brain 113: 767–79.

Burgos-Vargas R, Castelazo-Duarte G, Orozco JA, Garduno-Espinosa J, Clark P, Sanabria L (1993) Chest expansion in healthy adolescents and patients with the seronegative enthesopathy and arthropathy syndrome or juvenile ankylosing spondylitis. Rheumatology 20: 1967–70.

Canning CG, Alison JA, Allen NE, Groeller H (1997) Parkinson's disease: an investigation of exercise capacity, respiratory function, and gait. Archives of Physical Medicine and Rehabilitation 78: 199–207.

Canter GJ, de La Torre R, Mier M (1961) A method for evaluating disability in patients with Parkinson's disease. Journal of Nervous and Mental Diseases 133: 143–7.

Cao C, Ashton-Miller JA, Schultz AB, Alexander NB (1997) Abilities to turn suddenly while walking: effects of age, gender, and available response time. Journal of Gerontology, Series A, Biological Sciences and Medical Sciences 52: M88–M93.

Chen HC, Schultz AB, Ashton-Miller JA, Giordani B, Alexander NB, Guire KE (1996) Stepping over obstacles: dividing attention impairs performance of old more than young adults. Journal of Gerontology. Series A, Biological Sciences and Medical Sciences 51: M116–22.

Comella CL, Stebbins GT, Brown-Toms N, Goetz CG (1994) Physical therapy and Parkinson's disease: a controlled clinical trial. Neurology 44: 376–8.

Cummings JL (1992) Depression and Parkinson's disease. American Journal of Psychiatry 149: 443–54.

Cutson TM, Laub KC, Schenkman M (1995) Pharmacological and nonpharmacological interventions in the treatment of Parkinson's disease. Physical Therapy 75: 363–73.

Ettinger WH Jr, Burns R, Messier SP, Applegate W, Rejeski WJ, Morgan T, Shumaker S, Berry MJ, O'Toole M, Monu J, Craven T (1997) A randomized trial comparing aerobic exercise and resistance exercise with a health education program in older adults with knee osteoarthritis. The Fitness Arthritis and Seniors Trial (FAST). Journal of the American Medical Association 277: 25–31.

Fertl E, Doppelbauer A, Auff E (1993) Physical activity and sports in patients suffering from Parkinson's disease in comparison with healthy seniors. Journal of Neural Transmission, Parkinson's Disease and Dementia Section 5: 157–61.

Fiatarone MA, O'Neill EF, Ryan ND, Clements KM, Solares GR, Nelson ME, Roberts SB, Kehayias JJ, Lipsitz LA, Evans WJ (1994) Exercise training and nutritional supplementation for physical frailty in very elderly people. New England Journal of Medicine 330: 1769–75.

Formisano R, Pratesi L, Modarelli FT, Bonifati V, Meco G (1992) Rehabilitation and Parkinson's disease. Scandinavian Journal of Rehabilitation Medicine 24: 157–60.

Franklyn S (1986) An introduction to physiotherapy for Parkinson's disease. Physiotherapy 72: 379–80.

Fringer MN, Stull AG (1974) Changes in cardiorespiratory parameters during periods of training and detraining in young adult females. Medicine and Science in Sports and Exercise 6: 20–5.

Gauthier L, Dalziel S, Gauthier S (1987) The benefits of group occupational therapy for patients with Parkinson's disease. American Journal of Occupational Therapy 41: 360–5.

Goetz CG, Thelen JA, MacLeod CM, Carvey PM, Bartley EA, Stebbins GT (1993) Blood levodopa levels and Unified Parkinson's Disease Rating Scale function: with and without exercise. Neurology 43: 1040–2.

Herdman SJ (1997) Advances in the treatment of vestibular disorders. Physical Therapy 77: 602–18.

Hoehn MM, Yahr MD (1967) Parkinsonism: onset, progression, and mortality. Neurology 17: 427–42.

Homberg V (1993) Motor training in the therapy of Parkinson's disease. Neurology 43(Suppl 6), 45–6.

Hooker SP, Foudray CK, McKay LA, Pasquil CM, Seitzinger LS, Welsh MD, Waters CH (1996) Heart rate and perceived exertion measures during exercise in people with Parkinson's disease. Journal of Neurologic Rehabilitation 10: 101–5.

Horak F (1987) Clinical measurement of postural control in adults. Physical Therapy 70: 1881–5.

Ismail AH, El-Naggar AM (1981) Effect of exercise on cognitive processing in adult men. Journal of Human Ergology 10: 83–91.

Katsikitis M, Pilowsky I (1996) A controlled study of facial mobility treatment in Parkinson's disease. Journal of Psychosomatic Research 40: 387–96.

Kendall FP, McCreary EK (1983) Muscles. Testing and Function, 3rd edn. Baltimore: Williams & Wilkins.

Koller W (1984) Sensory symptoms in Parkinson's disease. Neurology 34: 957–9.

Kuroda K, Tatara K, Takatorige T, Shinsho F (1992) Effect of physical exercise on mortality in patients with Parkinson's disease. Acta Neurologica Scandinavica 86: 55–9.

Lakke JPWF (1985) Axial apraxia in Parkinson's disease. Journal of the Neurological Sciences 59: 37–46.

Lance JW, McLeod JG (1981) A Physiological Approach to Clinical Neurology, 3rd edn. London: Butterworths.

MacKay-Lyons M, Turnbull G (1995) Physical therapy in Parkinson's disease. Neurology 45: 205.

Maitland GD (1977) Peripheral Manipulation, 2nd edn. Sydney: Butterworths.

Maitland GD (1986) Vertebral Manipulation, 5th edn. Sydney: Butterworths.

McNiven DR (1986) Rotational impairment of movement in the Parkinsonian patient. Physiotherapy 72: 381–2.

Morris ME, Matyas TA, Iansek R, Summers JJ (1996) Temporal stability of gait in Parkinson's disease. Physical Therapy 76: 763–77.

Morris ME, Iansek R, Matyas TA, Summers JJ (1996) Stride length regulation in Parkinson's disease: normalization strategies and underlying mechanisms. Brain 119: 551–68.

Paige GD (1991) The aging vestibulo-ocular reflex (VOR) and adaptive plasticity. Acta Oto-laryngologica 481(Suppl): 297–300.

Paige GD (1992) Senescence of human visual-vestibular interactions, 1: Vestibulo-ocular reflex and adaptive plasticity with aging. Journal of Vestibular Research 2: 133–51.

Palmer SS, Mortimer JA, Webster DD, Bistevins R, Dickinson GL (1986) Exercise therapy for Parkinson's disease. Archives of Physical Medicine and Rehabilitation 67: 741–5.

Parkinson J (1817) An Essay on the Shaking Palsy. London, Sherwood: Nesly & Jones.

Pastor MA, Day BL, Marsden CD (1993) Vestibular induced postural responses in Parkinson's disease. Brain 116: 1177–90.

Patti R, Reggio A, Nicoletti F, Sellaroli T, Deinite G, Nicoletti F (1996) Effects of rehabilitation therapy on Parkinsonians' disability and functional independence. Journal of Neurologic Rehabilitation 10: 223–31.

Pedersen SW, Oberg B, Larsson L-E, Lindval B (1997) Gait analysis, isokinetic muscle strength measurement in patients with Parkinson's disease. Scandinavian Journal of Rehabilitation Medicine 29: 67–74.

Podsiadlo D, Richardson S (1991) The timed 'Up and Go': a test of basic functional mobility for frail elderly persons. Journal of the American Geriatrics Society 39: 142–8.

Poser CM, Ronthal M (1991) Exercise and Alzheimer's disease, Parkinson's disease, and multiple sclerosis. The Physician and Sportsmedicine 19: 85–92.

Pramstaller PP, Marsden CD (1996) The basal ganglia and apraxia. Brain 119: 319–40.

Protas EJ, Stanley RK, Jankovic J, MacNeill B (1996) Cardiovascular and metabolic responses to upper- and lower-extremity exercise in men with idiopathic Parkinson's disease. Physical Therapy 76: 34–40.

Quintyn M, Cross E (1986) Factors affecting the ability to initiate movement in Parkinson's disease. Physical and Occupational Therapy in Geriatrics 4: 51–60.

Raab DM, Agre JC, McAdam M, Smith EL (1988) Light resistance and stretching exercise in elderly women: effect upon flexibility. Archives of Physical Medicine and Rehabilitation 69: 268–72.

Reichart WH, Doolittle J, Philby M, McDowell FH (1982) Vestibular dysfunction in Parkinson's disease. Neurology 32: 1133–8.

Sabate M, Rodriguez M, Mendez E, Enriquez E, Gonzalez I (1996) Obstructive and restrictive pulmonary dysfunction increases disability in Parkinson's disease. Archives of Physical Medicine and Rehabilitation 77: 29–34.

Schenkman MS, Butler RB (1989) A model for multisystem evaluation and treatment of individuals with Parkinson's disease. Physical Therapy 69: 932–43.

Schenkman M, Cutson TM, Kuchibhatla M, Chandler J, Pieper C (1997) Reliability of impairment and physical performance measures for persons with Parkinson's disease. Physical Therapy 77: 19–27.

Sharp BK (1991) Nursing care. In Caird FI (Ed) Rehabilitation in Parkinson's Disease, Therapy in Practice 25. London: Chapman & Hall.

Sharpe MH (1990) Distractibility in early Parkinson's disease. Cortex 26: 239–46.

Shephard RJ (1990) Exercise for the frail elderly. Sports Training, Medicine and Rehabilitation 1: 263–77.

Singh NA, Clements KM, Fiatarone MA (1997) A randomised controlled trial of progressive resistance training in depressed elders. Journal of Gerontology, Series A, Biological Sciences and Medical Sciences 52: M27–35.

Smithson F, Morris ME, Iansek R (1998) Performance on clinical tests of balance in Parkinson's disease. Physical Therapy 78: 577–92.

Stefaniwski L, Bilowit DS (1973) Parkinsonism: facilitation of motion by sensory stimulation. Archives of Physical Medicine and Rehabilitation 54: 75–7, 90.

Tinetti ME (1986) Performance-oriented assessment of mobility problems in elderly patients. Journal of the American Geriatrics Society 34: 119.

Valliant PM, Asu ME (1985) Exercise and its effects on cognition and physiology in older adults. Perceptual and Motor Skills 61: 1031–8.

Webster DD (1968) Critical analysis of the disability in Parkinson's disease. Modern Treatment 5: 257–82.

Whipple RH, Wolfson LI, Amerman PM (1987) The relationship of knee and ankle weakness to falls in nursing home residents: an isokinetic study. Journal of the American Geriatrics Society 35: 13–20.

Yekutiel MP, Pinhasov A, Shahar G, Sroka HA (1991) Clinical trial of the re-education of movement in patients with Parkinson's disease. Clinical Rehabilitation 5: 207–14.

Yue GH, Wilson SL, Cole KJ, Darling WG, Yuh WTC (1996) Imagined muscle contraction training increases voluntary neural drive to muscle. Journal of Psychophysiology 10: 198–208.

Multiple Sclerosis

Case Report – Mrs LW

Background

Mrs LW was a 46-year-old divorced woman living alone in an unsuitable home environment. She had been working as a medical secretary and had reduced her working time to nine hours per week prior to her recent deterioration. She had five cats and lived in a ground floor maisonette, which she was unable to access unaided. She received meals twice daily and had help with housework three times weekly. This was provided by Social Services. She attended Church weekly and was also visited weekly by her mother.

Prior to admission to the rehabilitation unit, Mrs LW had been able to walk for short distances around her home with one walking stick. She had previously had low back pain and also a hysterectomy operation. She had also recently suffered a personal bereavement.

Two months prior to admission to the rehabilitation unit Mrs LW had fallen, and one week later she had also been involved in a road traffic accident in which she suffered a minor soft tissue injury to her right knee. She was seen in the multidisciplinary clinic and admitted for intensive rehabilitation. On admission she was using a self-propelling lightweight wheelchair for all mobility. She reported fatigue, low mood and suicidal thoughts.

Main Diagnosis

Secondary progressive multiple sclerosis with a recent sudden deterioration.

Presenting Problems

- Spastic paraparesis with severe flexor spasms in both lower limbs, right > left.

- Compensatory overuse of both upper limbs and shoulder girdles.
- Stiff low-toned asymmetrical trunk.
- Low back pain.
- Lower leg pain due to spasms.
- Bladder and bowel dysfunction.
- Soft tissue shortening right hamstrings and hip flexors.
- Oedematous left foot and ankle.
- Cognitive impairment.

Reported restriction of activity and participation:

- Unable to stand fully erect or walk due to pain and spasm.
- Cannot stand independently for more than a few minutes.
- Adequate management of tone.
- Poor bed mobility technique exacerbating adverse tone.
- Unsafe transfer techniques.
- Asymmetrical wheelchair posture with reduced ability to accept feet as a base of support.
- Dependent on self-propelling wheelchair for indoor mobility and unable to manage wheelchair outdoors.
- Difficulty with some self-care (washing, dressing and preparation of meals).
- Dependent on ISC pads for bladder management.
- Unable to drive or work.

Physical Examination

Sitting Posture

- Unable to accept base of support in sitting.
- Pelvis rotated to left, posteriorly tilted and laterally tilted to the left.
- Spinal scoliosis concave to the left but correctable with verbal cues.
- Overuse of right arm, fixing with elevation of right shoulder and head protraction.
- Both legs in painful flexor spasms, made worse by numerous triggers including external stimuli and handling.
- Increased flexor tone in feet and ankles producing hypersensitivity.
- Able to maintain static, flexed sitting posture and able to move to both sides although flexion but unable to transfer weight through extension.

Standing

- Lower limb posture flexed, adducted and internally rotated at the hips due to a combination of soft tissue shortening and tone.
- Able to achieve sit-to-stand independently but unable to maintain for periods greater than a few minutes.
- Some selective extensor activity present in trunk and lower limbs, best accessed automatically through sitting to standing.
- Unable to use arms functionally when standing.

Supine

- Unable to 'accept base of support'. Requires use of wedge or pillows under knees to achieve contact with supporting surface.
- Reduced frequency of spasms.
- Improved use of arms – no fixing in shoulders.

Function

Transfers:

- Able to achieve bed mobility independently but poor pelvis and truncal interplay reflected in decreased ability to roll selectively.
- Bed to chair: unable to lean forwards, using upper limbs and balls of feet to pivot into chair.
- Poor wheelchair drill although manages independently but with reduced safety awareness.
- Unable to walk independently.

At the end of the period in hospital (three weeks), out-patient physiotherapy was arranged and Mrs LW was referred for a trial of intrathecal baclofen.

Treatment and Management of a Patient with Multiple Sclerosis (1)

DIANE MADRAS

Multiple sclerosis (MS) is a condition that is characterized as a 'changing and fluctuating condition' (Thompson, 1998 **C**) and is typically progressive and degenerative in nature. It is unique to each patient owing to the patchy demyelination of the white matter of the central nervous system. MS follows an unpredictable course and needs a flexible approach by the physical therapist. When treating a patient with MS, the primary goal is to maximize function in the face of increasing disability. This is a different view from the more typical rehabilitation purpose of biding time for the initial insult to resolve, and then helping the patient heal and return to their previous functional state. The mindset of maximizing function corresponds well with the 'need for adaptation of therapy to a progressive neurological disease with an uncertain future course' (Kraft et al., 1996 **C**). There is a considerable variation both between patients and within any one patient at different stages of the disease, so the results of one study may not be directly comparable with other studies, or accurately reflect the response by any particular patient.

Inferences can be drawn from other similar patient populations and applied to the patient with MS. Due to the nature of the disorder, the outcomes related to rehabilitation revolve around decreasing disability and improving functional status, aerobic capacity and quality of life.

General Principles

The 'typical' patient with MS must 'overcome difficulties encountered due to the co-existence of weakness, spasticity, and cerebellar and cognitive dysfunction' (Kraft, 1996 **C**). Not every patient presents with all of these problems, but this combination presents a challenge to the treating therapist.

The primary rehabilitation aims being treated by physical therapy, regardless of the extent of the patient's disease, include:

- Providing comprehensive assessment of physical needs.
- Promotion of physical adaptation to disability and handicap.
- Facilitating independence in daily activities.
- Encouraging self-management.
- Preventing secondary complications such as contractures, pressure areas and pain (Thompson, 1998 **C**).

In the medical model of acute disease, the goal of therapy is to cure the disease and return patients to their previous state of health. This goal is not realistic in the treatment of patients with MS in the year 2000. Although some medications are designed to alter aspects of the *consequences* of the disease process, such as spasticity, these treatments do not change the disease itself, and the degenerative course continues unaffected.

When reviewing the case of Mrs LW, classifying her myriad problems may help to decide on an approach to treatment that can be both efficient and efficacious. Using a modification of the Nagi model, themes may be discovered. This model proposes a continuum from disease to impairment that leads to functional limitations. These functional limitations give rise to disabilities that become handicaps when taken within the social context (Jette, 1994 **C**).

Finding connections between Mrs LW's neuromuscular, musculoskeletal and cardiopulmonary problems and the activities she is not capable of

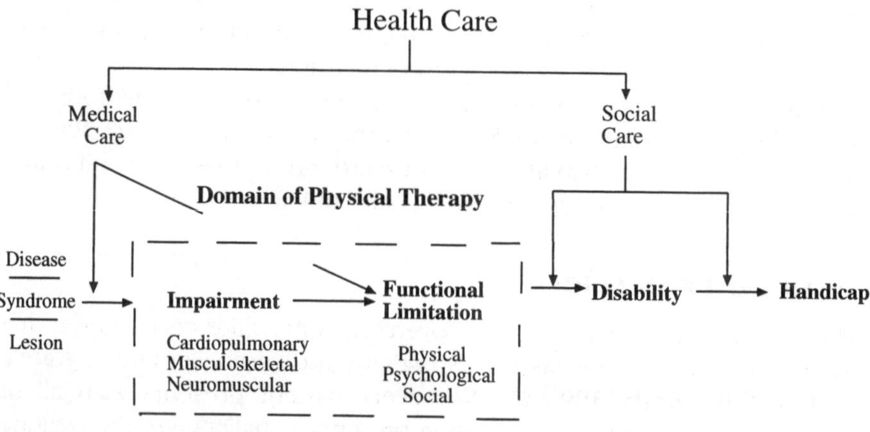

Figure 1: Guccione (1991) Copyright APTA permission given to reproduce.

performing due to either physical, psychological, or social limitations may be the most appropriate place for physical therapists to intervene.

Many factors influence the connection between impairments and functional limitations such as co-morbid conditions, the individual's health habits, personal motivation, social support, and architectural barriers (Guccione, 1991 **C**), which in the case of Mrs LW may prove to be major influences on her function.

It is important to find out how the patient perceives her problems. By understanding the patient's perspective, priority can be given in the evaluation to the problems that are having the greatest impact on everyday life; patients do not usually complain about problems at the level of impairment, rather they report functional limitations that they experience as they attempt to live their everyday lives. By acknowledging the functional problems of the patient, themes can be discovered that will guide treatment approaches. Specific treatment choices vary between therapists, depending on the resources available within their specific departments. Following the assessment, the physical therapist can move forward through the model, since the assumption is made that by decreasing the impairment and related functional limitation, disability and handicap can also be impacted favourably.

As Mrs LW's goals are not stated in the case presentation, I shall assume that her goals are to maximize her ability to perform activities of daily living (ADL) and instrumental activities of daily living. A person's ability to perform basic ADLs is influenced by their impairments, which result in functional limitations such as Mrs LW's upper extremity spasticity, impairing her ability to feed or dress herself independently. Other functional limitations may result from the same impairment, such as incontinence due to her inability to deal with her clothing in a timely manner to reach the toilet before she becomes incontinent. When reviewing her case, overall themes can be found which will guide treatment priorities that will address many functional limitations by treating the impairment.

There may be complicating factors in the treatment of Mrs LW that fall outside the realm of physical therapy treatment but which may be addressed indirectly through patient education or referral to the appropriate disciplines or services. Many of these referrals must be followed up by Mrs LW or the physical therapist to ensure proper problem management. This role is typically undertaken by a case manager, but many patients with MS must be their own advocate to ensure they receive proper services as they are needed.

Assessment of Functional Limitations

A thorough assessment of the patient with MS includes a medical and social assessment to ensure a comprehensive picture is formed. The medical assessment includes a review of the patient's physical status as well as adjustment of any medications to optimize function. The social assessment is an inventory of the patient's social support structure, including the availability of community services. This comprehensive evaluation should give a realistic picture of the resources the patient can draw from as well as identifying areas of deficit that the healthcare team may need to address or attempt to circumvent.

From the case history, we know that Mrs LW is a 46 year old female who has recently experienced a fall and was involved in a motor vehicle accident that injured her left knee. She has recently begun using a lightweight wheelchair for mobility.

According to the Nagi model, her disabilities and handicaps can be categorized into the domains of medical care and social care. The disabilities that fall into social care relate to her limited mobility in the wheelchair and car, her home environment and her difficulty with some ADLs. The disabilities and handicaps that are more appropriate to be addressed by the medical community include those related to her muscle tone and the functional limitations resulting from hypertonicity, impaired mobility and transfer techniques, incontinence and sexual dysfunction.

Therefore, comprehensive assessments of patients with MS by physical therapists must include all facets of the patient's complaints and provide a full description of their physical, cognitive and mental capabilities and difficulties. This assessment may need to take place over a number of days if the fatigue level of the patient is severe. As the initial evaluation makes use of many different examinations, the therapist may be able to choose an order of examination that allows for rest periods interspersed with activity assessments. The major areas of assessment include gait or wheelchair mobility, ability to transfer and the level of assistance required for each task. Gross muscle strength is important to assess deficits and their impact on mobility. Evaluation of sensation in all modalities, such as light and deep touch, proprioception and balance, is important to assess, keeping in mind that cerebellar and cognitive dysfunction are strong predictors of outcome (Thompson, 1998 **C**). The social interaction and support available to the patient must be assessed to gain a well-rounded profile. A complete assessment provides a snapshot of the patient's functioning at the time of the evaluation, but may change with time, so periodic reassessment is necessary.

Some aspects of the evaluation are performed by the physical therapist, and some by other members of the healthcare team, to provide a comprehensive view of the patient. The primary aspects evaluated by the physical therapist include functional activities, anthropometric measures and functional status for ADL. In the case of Mrs LW, a number of issues have been identified.

Priorities for Assessment and Interventions

To prioritize the components of interventions to address Mrs LW's complaints, I would assess the importance of the activities in her life and how the disease has impacted on her ability to carry them out. There are four major themes that arise from the study of Mrs LW's list of impairments: problems with spasticity, strength, endurance and psychosocial issues. The assessment of her spasticity would help delineate the origin of her low back pain and poor trunk control, either of which may be caused or aggravated by weakness and shoulder dysfunction. The assessment of her strength may help to pinpoint the underlying problems related to trunk control, balance and incontinence. The weakness in her skeletal muscles could also contribute to her poor trunk control, contributing to low back pain, poor balance and other muscle weakness impacting adversely on her bowel and bladder control. The lack of endurance is shown by her complaints of fatigue and is often a difficult problem for patients with MS. The increased energy expenditure necessary to propel her body through space and counteract spasticity could contribute to fatigue, which could contribute to depression. Fatigue can result from a host of causes, including the increased energy expenditure caused by spasticity, weakness or depression. The psychosocial aspects of Mrs LW's life show that she has moderately good support from her mother and uses some community services such as meals on wheels, but other sources of support could help fill the time when she used to be working. Breaking up her assessment into themes may help in choosing effective treatments that address more than one functional limitation at the same time.

The functional limitations that Mrs LW has, appear to stem from the musculoskeletal as well as the neuromuscular system. She complains of low back pain, which is typically categorized as musculoskeletal, although here it appears that the cause is neuromuscular, from increased spasticity as the precipitating problem.

From her history, one is struck by the magnitude of muscular spasticity. This impairs her ability to perform basic activities that may include getting to the bathroom in time to prevent incontinence. This can be extremely troublesome for some patients, and Mrs LW's other impairments related to trunk control such as low tone and low back pain can contribute to the problem of incontinence. Therefore, one of the first priorities is to gain control of her spasticity, so that she is not 'fighting against herself' to perform basic activities of daily living. Since she has poor trunk control, her low back pain may be exacerbated by uncontrolled or uncoordinated movement. A common problem coincident with low back pain is muscle spasm, creating a cycle of pain leading to protective muscle spasm which manifests in a decreased range of motion, which when stretched, leads to pain, maintaining the pain cycle (Figure 2).

By decreasing the muscle spasm in her low back musculature the cycle may be broken, and allow strengthening of the muscles that support the back. By increasing strength in the low back musculature, Mrs LW may regain or improve control of her trunk. Increased trunk control will help her sit in a more biomechanically optimal position that may allow better co-ordination of motion and easier performance of functional activities such as propelling her wheelchair, transferring to the toilet, reaching and other activities (Curtis et al., 1995 **A**; Hart et al., 1984 **B**). Therefore, her increased muscle tone and lack of control of her skeletal muscles take precedence as the highest priorities for assessment and intervention.

A limitation in strength of muscles with abnormalities in tone, either hypertonicity or hypotonicity, can prove a challenge to the physical therapist but in Mrs LW's case control of her high-tone extremities will help her become more mobile and able to provide for herself more easily. There is some controversy about the ability to strengthen spastic muscles but if the patient has enough control to contract her muscles volitionally, low-level strengthening activities can be performed (DeSouza and Ashburn, 1996 **A**; Petajan et al., 1996 **A**). Additional strength may be gained slowly over time, leading to improved muscle function; this translates into enhanced control and decreased oxygen consumed with smaller tasks. By increasing Mrs LW's ability to move by decreasing her tone and strengthening her weak muscles, her ability to move through space will be improved.

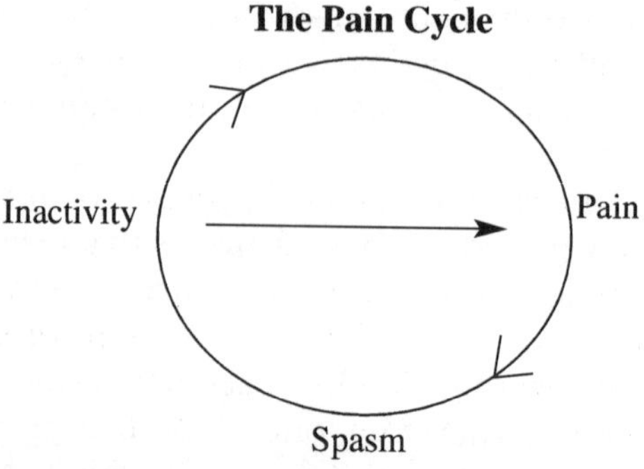

Figure 2: The pain cycle.

Most tasks performed in the upright position require a degree of balance. A lack of balance probably underlies her complaint of an inability to manage her wheelchair outdoors. Balance incorporates aspects of muscle strength, proprioception and motor control. Without adequate co-ordination of any of these components balance can be difficult, impairing the ability to perform activities when both sitting and standing. Mrs LW does not complain specifically of impaired balance, but her inability to sit properly in her wheelchair and independently propel her chair may result from a balance deficit and impact on her ability to perform activities of daily living.

As Mrs LW lives alone, she must perform many activities for herself, although she receives meals daily and visits from her mother weekly. Therefore cooking is not a major priority for her except to make snacks for between meals to meet her caloric needs.

A functional impairment that carries physical, psychological and social implications for Mrs LW is her complaint of fatigue. The onset of fatigue varies between MS patients, with some being very debilitated by minor activity, while others do not appear to be troubled by inordinate fatigue. The answer to the question 'How much is too much?' can be quite variable from patient to patient and from day to day. Fatigue is a problem with many potential sources, including poor nutrition (Grindel, 1994 **C**). As Mrs LW receives only two meals a day, the caloric content of those meals may not be adequate to sustain her, or she may be trying to perform too many activities in a day; in this case the source of her fatigue is unknown. Another problem that patients with MS have is the inability to relax. Relaxation techniques are often helpful strategies to cope with stress of the disease and depression (Maguire, 1996 **B**). The efficacy of prolonged stretching with MS mechanism of action remains unknown. Many patients with multiple sclerosis are also diagnosed with depression (Acorn and Anderson, 1990 **C**). Psychiatric interventions can be effective in helping people combat depression and increase their general sense of well-being and quality of life, which can reduce their level of disability.

Interventions

Physical therapists are best equipped to address problems in the physical domain, but physical therapy also increases the quality of life of patients with MS (DiFabio et al., 1997 **A**; Freeman et al., 1996 **A**, 1997 **A**; Solari et al., 1999 **A**).

Mrs LW's physical problems can be divided into neuromuscular and musculoskeletal but these are most probably interlinked. Interventions that address one aspect directly may indirectly impact on others. Her neuromuscular problems include spasticity, which may be causing low back pain, tight hamstrings and poor trunk control. Spasticity could be directly related to her bowel and bladder dysfunction by affecting her sphincter control or indirectly by prolonging the time necessary to reach the bathroom in time to avoid incontinence. Increased tone will also increase the energy expenditure when performing activities (Olgiati et al., 1988 **A**), contributing to fatigue. The combination of the physical problems could contribute to Mrs LW's depression, magnifying the physical impairments by adding an emotional component.

Spasticity

Spasticity is defined as hypertonia that responds to movement in a velocity-dependent manner such that increased velocity of motion increases the strength of muscle contraction (Thomas, 1983 **C**). Spasticity impairs function of patients with MS by increasing the energy expenditure required when performing activities (Olgiati et al., 1988 **A**), and causing pain (Hinderer and Gupta, 1996 **C**). Attempts to control spasticity in patients with MS are usually pharmacological, administered by physicians. There are many agents available, such as baclofen (Azouvi et al., 1996 **A**) and gabapentin (Dunevsky and Perel, 1998 **A**). The route of delivery of these antispasm drugs ranges from oral to intrathecal pumps. Mrs LW will be undergoing a trial of intrathecal baclofen; if she proves refractory to baclofen some physical techniques may be worth trying. Physical therapists can use physical techniques to complement the medication, or on their own if the patient cannot tolerate the medication.

Techniques that I would employ in the treatment of spasticity include: cooling (Kinnman et al., 1997 **A**; Price et al., 1993 **A**; Bell and Lehmann, 1987 **A**), prolonged stretching (Al Zamil et al., 1995 **A**; Hale ad Goodman, 1995 **B**), slow stroking (Brouwer and deAndrade, 1995 **A**), electric-stimulation (King, 1996 **B**), and acupuncture (Miller, 1996 **B**).

Some of these treatment techniques for spasticity have limited research to substantiate their use whereas for others efficacy is well documented. Cooling in the form of cryotherapy has been well documented for use in MS (Price et al., 1993 **A**) although to a lesser degree than personal cooling (Ku et al., 1999 **A**;, Kinnman et al., 1997 **A**; Flensner and Lindencrona, 1999 **A**; Robinson et al., 1997 **A**). Stretching is often the treatment of choice for the physical therapist because the requirement for equipment is minimal. Prolonged stretching may be time consuming and physically exhausting for the treating therapist, especially if the patient is difficult to position to apply the stretch. Questions that remain with prolonged stretching are: the duration of the applied stretch, and the duration of the positive effects from stretching. Hale (Hale and Goodman, 1995 **B**) suggests the duration of the applied stretch should be 10 minutes for reducing spasticity in patients after head injury or cerebrovascular accidents.

Less well-documented treatments for spasticity include slow stroking, acupuncure and electrical stimulation. Slow stroking was performed for three minutes on 10 patients with MS resulting in decreased H-reflex amplitude of the gastrocnemius muscle 30 minutes post-stroking. Subjectively the patients also reported feeling more relaxed after receiving treatment. The authors concluded that stroking reduced alpha-motorneuron excitability in MS patients (Brouwer and deAndrade, 1995 **A**). Electrical stimulation of spastic muscles has received attention, as regards both increasing functional abilities using functional stimulation and decreasing the hypertonicity of the muscles by inducing muscular fatigue (King, 1996 **B**). Patients with increased tone in their wrist flexors were treated with 10 minutes of electrical simulation (250μ microsecond at 45 Hz with a pulse width ramp up/down 3/0 seconds with an on/off time of 10 seconds). The amplitude of stimulation the subjects were able to tolerate ranged from 15 to 20 mA. The resistance to stretch applied to the wrist was decreased after electric stimulation (King, 1996 **B**). Thus, coupling electrical stimulation with prolonged stretching may provide some relief from Mrs LW's spasticity. Interest in acupuncture has been growing in the United States but so far only one study has examined the efficacy of this treatment modality and found encouraging results (Miller, 1996 **B**).

There is no evidence that direct pressure over the tendons influences muscle tone. Neurophysiology teaches that golgi tendon organs can be stimulated to increase relaxation of the antagonist muscle with direct pressure.

Therefore, the approach to address Mrs LW's spasticity of her upper extremities would be a combination of cryotherapy, electrical stimulation and static stretching. Cryotherapy would take the form of a cold pack administered for 10 minutes coupled with a static stretch of the biceps during the application of cold. Adjunctive electrical stimulation would then be applied to the muscles in their lengthened position. The stretching would continue after electrical stimulation until her elbow is extended to its full range of motion. If she exhibits increased tone after removal of the cold pack (as shown by increased resistance to stretch), I would substitute electrical stimulation for the cold pack. The entire duration of her stretching would not exceed 30 minutes, depending on the pain experienced and the progress made by Mrs LW. The same type of treatment would be administered to her hamstrings, except her positioning would be in the prone position. If she could not tolerate lying prone, she would be positioned lying on her side with her lower extremities supported, and stretching would be undertaken on the top leg. To stretch the other leg, Mrs LW would need to roll over, which might increase her tone when she attempted to move, so the therapist would need to assess how quickly she reverted to high tone before attempting this treatment. The education of the therapist could occur along with education of the patient.

Patient education refers to the transmittal of information from the healthcare provider to the patient with the intent of increasing the patient's ability to manage her disease (Hellstrom, 1995 **C**). With regard to Mrs LW's self-management of her spasticity, positions that decrease her tone may be viable self-treatment approaches between therapy sessions. Very little is published regarding self-management of spasticity for patients with multiple sclerosis without the use of medications to decrease hypertonicity.

The functional limitations that Mrs LW complains about are probably related to her spasticity. Those that will improve with decreases in spasticity include her low back pain, and tight hamstrings. The increased tone in her hamstrings may be contributing to her poor trunk control and poor trunk control may also be related to weakness.

Weakness

Weakness in MS results from the demyelination process, which cannot be treated effectively today, although medications are available to slow the rate of progression of the demyelination (Rudick et al., 1997 **A**). As the motorneurons lose myelin, the conduction velocity to the muscles slows, and is perceived as weakness by the patient. Weakness of muscles used in everyday activities can result in an overuse syndrome with pain, nerve compression and tendinitis. Each of these possible aetiologies may be present in the case of Mrs LW, and treatment choices made by the physical therapist would depend on the differential diagnosis of the cause of her overuse syndrome.

There are many diagnostic possibilities for the pain resulting from Mrs LW's overuse of her upper extremities, including nerve entrapments, nerve compression, impingement, tendinitis, or cervical nerve root problems resulting from faulty neck posture while propelling her wheelchair. Without a clear picture of her posture, determination of faults is difficult. As we know that Mrs LW has increased tone in her upper extremity flexors, I shall assume that she is also spastic in her pectoralis muscles and therefore has a muscle imbalance around her scapulae (Norkin and Levangie, 1992 **C**), resulting in protracted shoulders and lengthened rhomboids and levator scapulae (Andersen, 1983 **C**). To address this problem, selective stretching of Mrs LW's pectoral muscles and strengthening of her scapular retractors is necessary.

Currently, physical therapy interventions cannot impact on demyelination as the cause of the weakness, but the effects of the weakness can be addressed through training (Kraft, 1996 **A**) and patient education.

Treatment options for training weak muscles include progressive resistive exercises, with or without added weight increase strength (Fiatarone et al., 1990 **B**; Whaley et al., 1992 **B**; Ades et al., 1995 **B**; McCartney et al., 1995 **G**; Kraft et al., 1996 **C**). Interventions commonly employed to increase strength are applicable with Mrs LW, and include progressive resistive training (Rall et al., 1996 **B**), and targeted strengthening for the trunk (Butler, 1998 **A**). Patients with MS who had mild disease showed greater absolute increases in lifting ability than patients with severe disease, although both increased their strength. The importance of long-term performance of strength training has not been investigated in the MS patient population. In the case of Mrs LW, the activities she performs result in compensatory overuse of the shoulder girdle stabilizing musculature and poor trunk control. Shoulder girdle musculature can be strengthened, and posture improved with strength training, decreasing her propensity towards an overuse injury of her upper extremities.

Other weaknesses that are seen in patients with MS, but not necessarily with Mrs LW, include foot drop, and other weaknesses that may or may not be related to mobility. In the case of foot drop, dynamic electrical stimulation can be used to apply intermittent exogenous electrical stimulation to the tibialis anterior muscle to provide adequate contraction to allow clearance of the foot during gait. Studies performed on patients with paraplegia showed that functional electrical simulation (FES) may aid walking, but whether FES aided gait is efficient remains open to question (Kobetic et al., 1997 **B**; Zupan et al., 1995 **A**). Other weaknesses not related to mobility may be contributing to Mrs LW's incontinence and fatigue level, and may be influenced by intensive exercise training, to increase mobility and ADL ability (Fuller et al., 1996 **A**).

Weakness or spasticity could be playing a role in Mrs LW's bowel and bladder dysfunction. Treatments for incontinence range from some form of diaper to intermittent catheterization to muscle strengthening. Use of a diaper-like solution currently being used by Mrs LW can become costly, with frequent spillage of urine which may impact on social functioning. Intermittent catheterization helps place the bladder on a schedule, which may result in a lesser occurrence of incontinence (Brown, 1994a **A**; Brown, 1994b **A**). To strengthen the muscles of the pelvic floor, Vahtera (Vahtera et al., 1997 **A**) advocates the use of electric stimulation (ES). He found that ES was effective in patients with bladder dysfunction when applied with a carrier frequency of 2000 Hz and treatment frequencies of 5–10 Hz,

10–50 Hz, and 50 Hz (7 s pulse/25 s pause) delivered via intra-anal (men) or intra-vaginal (women) electrodes. He applied this treatment for 10 minutes at each frequency followed by a three-minute rest. ES was applied for six sessions, and each patient received two sessions of biofeedback for instructions in pelvic floor exercises. There were significantly fewer symptoms of storage dysfunction in those treated at three weeks and two months (Vahtera et al., 1997 **A**).

Although Mrs LW uses a wheelchair for mobility, other patients with MS weakness who are less severely impaired may have the goal of walking as a primary outcome. The methods employed to assist patients to improve efficiency or mobility when walking was examined in a study by Lord et al. (1998 **A**). Two approaches to rehabilitation were taken: a task-oriented approach and a facilitated approach. In the task-oriented approach, the authors required the patients to carry out a programme of functional exercises written by the PT and based on the necessary components required for walking and functional mobility. Compensatory strategies were not specifically avoided. Tasks included functional exercises rather than component-practice tasks. This approach focuses on the patient's disability rather than their ability, and 'anticipates that impairments might be minimized as a consequence of improved function' (Lord et al., 1998, p. 479).

With the facilitation approach, reduction of impairments was 'identified at the initial assessment, and recorded in terms of postural control, balance responses, the ability to recruit motor activity in different parts of the range, muscle length, tonus change and bony malalignment' (Lord et al., 1998, p. 479). This approach used both passive and active techniques, and progression was determined by the rate of change in impairment and function and was reassessed as necessary. This approach was 'attempting to reduce the patient's impairments, expecting disability to be improved as a direct consequence' (p. 479).

Both approaches involved the patient in goal setting and progression of the programme, provided verbal feedback, and supplied the patients with orthotics and walking aids as necessary. The PT treatments occurred in one-hour bouts with 15–19 treatments administered over a period of 5–7 weeks. They found no statistically significant difference between the two approaches, but both groups improved in balance, when measured on the Berg balance scale, and gait as measured by stride length, walking time and a global gait score. Unfortunately, the sample size was small, and the differences noted were not large.

Fatigue

The functional impairment that impacts not only on Mrs LW's physical well-being but also on her psychological and social functioning is fatigue. As the precipitating factors of her fatigue are unknown, I shall put her in the moderate fatigue category, which means Mrs LW can stay awake throughout the day, but requires naps in stressful situations or with moderate amounts of activity. By incorporating rest periods throughout the day's activities, Gerber et al. (1987 **B**) showed an increase in the time of activity in patients with rheumatoid arthritis. Patients with MS may well respond in the same way.

Interventions to address Mrs LW's fatigue levels throughout the day require lifestyle management. One of the most difficult lessons for patients with MS to learn is their physical limits. A standard intervention for fatigue is work simplification that allows patients to perform their activities of daily living in a more efficient and less taxing manner. Patients forget (or have never been told) that many activities can be performed while sitting, for instance ironing or peeling vegetables. Many people stand by their kitchen sinks while preparing meals, whereas a small stool placed in the kitchen can allow them to sit and perform these activities. As Mrs LW has recently become non-ambulatory, she may be spending an excessive amount of energy transferring to a standing position to perform activities she was able to perform standing previously. Although education does not always translate into lifestyle changes, it is a beginning step.

A lifestyle change that can positively affect Mrs LW's fatigue is aerobic exercise. This does not mean that she must run for 20 minutes; activities that raise the heart rate for a sustained amount of time are beneficial. Pescatello and Murphy (1998 **B**) performed an observational study and found an improvement in fat distribution and blood glucose in viscerally obese older adults who performed activity. Although longer exercise intervals are advocated with changing fat distribution, there is anecdotal evidence that shorter or less intense bouts of activity are better than no activity. By increasing Mrs LW's tolerance to activity, her fatigue may be positively impacted (Svensson et al., 1994 **A**), thereby decreasing that functional limitation.

If Mrs LW has difficulty finding an activity she enjoys, an alternative is extended outpatient rehabilitation (DiFabio et al., 1988 **A**). Participation in rehabilitation activities for one day each week, if extended over a year, decreases symptom frequency and fatigue in patients with MS. The rehabilitation programme DiFabio advocates is an integrated physical therapy (balance training, co-ordination, gait, transfer, endurance training and ROM) and occupational therapy (feeding, dressing and grooming) approach. Included with the physical and occupational therapy components is patient education regarding: prevention of falls, skin breakdown, urinary tract infection, depression and premature nursing home placement. There was no discernible change in impairment, or preservation of functional status

(DiFabio et al., 1998 **A**). Other potential avenues to address Mrs LW's fatigue include the use of orthotic devices for upper extremity work, transferring equipment, electric scooters or wheelchairs (manual and electric), and modified cars and vans for mobility (Buchanan and Lewis, 1997 **C**). As we know that Mrs LW's home is unsuitable for her at this time, modification to increase accessibility or safety is helpful. Some suggestions for home modifications include: call systems, adjustable furniture, electric beds, temperature controls, accessible or adapted bathrooms, barrier-free, height-adjusted or disability-adjusted facilities, adapted telephones, ramps, WC accessibility, automatic doors, rails and grab bars (Buchanan and Lewis, 1997 **C**).

Fatigue, being a multi-factorial condition, may also result from improper nutrition (Grindel, 1994 **C**). A dietary consultation could help determine whether malnutrition is playing a role in her fatigue levels, and may be simple to remedy.

Education to address energy conservation and efficiency may decrease the patient's fatigue levels, although no studies have addressed this directly. Gerber (Gerber et al., 1987 **B**) examined the effectiveness of a patient education workbook or traditional occupational therapy for joint protection and energy conservation. The workbook consisted of didactic information regarding energy, rest and fatigue. The following chapters described behaviour modification techniques and health education strategies with examples of real and hypothetical situations for illustration. Traditional occupational therapy techniques included videotapes, written materials, individualized teaching and reviews of difficulties encountered daily. Outcome measures consisted of questionnaire data from the Psychological Adjustment to Illness Scale and the Health Assessment Questionnaire. There were no significant differences found between the two groups in the trial, and fatigue was not assessed as an outcome (Gerber et al., 1987 **B**).

Depression

Depression is a functional limitation that is defined as the most prevalent psychiatric disturbance and is characterized by mood, cognitive and motivation alterations and changes in physical and psychological functioning (Acorn and Andersen, 1990 **C**). Although the direct treatment of depression is best left in the hands of those trained in psychology or counselling, exercises offered by physical therapists can offer some remediation of the depression, but by no means solve the problem. DiFabio et al. (1997 **A**) showed improvement in health-related quality of life in patients with progressive multiple sclerosis after physical therapy treatments. Wellbeing was also the topic of Moore and Bracegirdle's (1994 **A**) investigation of the effects of a short-term, low-intensity exercise programme on community-dwelling elderly women. Although these women did not necessarily have MS, they did show significant improvements in wellbeing ratings after a six week exercise protocol.

Other problems that may result from Mrs LW's MS include cognitive deficits, and depression which may be positively addressed indirectly through physical therapy treatments, but is out of the sphere of expertise of the therapist.

Improvement in Levels of Disability

Disability relates to the performance of tasks and roles, as defined in the Nagi model. Both the medical and social care of the individual can impact on the level of disability of the patient. Contained within the roles and tasks performed by the individual are aspects that contribute to or detract from each patient's quality of life. Freeman (Freeman et al., 1996 **A**) studied the effect of multiple sclerosis on the quality of life using Kurtzke's Functional Systems Scale (FSS; Kurtzke, 1970) and Expanded Disability Status Scale (EDSS; Kurtzke, 1983), the SF 36 (Ware et al., 1993), the Functional Independence Measure (FIM; Linacre et al., 1991), and the General Health Questionnaire (GHQ; Goldberg and Williams, 1988). Freeman found the median EDSS score to be 6.5, defined as intermittent or unilateral constant assistance to walk 100 metres, which is a high degree of physical disability. According to the SF 36, the patients reported a poorer level of health, physical functioning and greater role limitations due to physical or emotional health problems. From the GHQ, 74% of the MS population scores reflected the presence of emotional disturbance while 49% of the patients studied showed depressive symptomatology (Freeman et al., 1996 **A**).

In a later study, Freeman (Freeman et al., 1997 **A**) evaluated the entire therapy package using a model of comprehensive care that emphasizes achievement in quality of life within the limits of the disease. The input the patients received from a multidisciplinary team as inpatients consisted of medical, nursing, occupational therapy and physical therapy. Goal setting occurred jointly with the medical care team and the patient. Patients participated in physical therapy for two 45-minute sessions and occupational therapy for one session per day for an average of 20 days. Although Freeman found no change in functional status, overall motor domain scores improved significantly with regard to transfers, sphincter control and locomotion in those who used wheelchairs, but not for those who were able to walk. Outcomes measured using the FIM showed an improvement in the overall level of disability in 72% of the participants while 29% of the control group showed improvement. Mrs LW might benefit from a similar programme as her functional limitations include transferring difficulty and sphincter control. When considering the handicap of the participants in the study, the treatment group made small improvements in their level of handicap compared with the control group that showed a small decline in their level of handicap. Unfortunately, Freeman did not examine carry-over to determine whether the positive changes could remain after discharge from the programme (Freeman et al., 1997 **A**).

Delivery and Timing of Intervention

There is debate about the optimum location where rehabilitation services should be delivered. Are patients best rehabilitated during admission to hospital, or are they better served being maintained in their own homes and undergoing treatment on an outpatient basis? Some authors state that admission to a rehabilitation facility results in improvement of physical functioning (Solari et al., 1999 **A**), although success has also been documented by DiFabio et al. (1998 **A**) who used an outpatient model. In Solari's study, 50 patients with MS were admitted to hospital and received rehabilitation twice daily for three weeks. Each patient received individualized treatment. At the end of three weeks, the patients reported a lower level of impairment, as measured by the EDSS (Kurtzke, 1983) and the FIM (Granger et al., 1990). Solari (Solari et al., 1999 **A**) did not control for the severity of disease with his study. DiFabio studied 46 patients with chronic progressive MS, offering one five-hour treatment each week for one year, and found that receiving treatment was a predictor of reduced symptom frequency of fatigue but not functional status at the one-year follow-up. Therefore, evidence exists regarding the efficacy of rehabilitation, but neither DiFabio nor Solari appears to present a stronger case for their protocol for rendering rehabilitation.

The length of treatment (long term or short term) is also an issue of debate. Conventional wisdom states 'more is better', but the question of the truthfulness of that statement must always be considered. In the United States, the typical method of predicting length of inpatient or outpatient stay depends on the acuity of the patient as well as the support systems of the patient and the community. If an individual has good family support and the community offers resources the patient can utilize, admission to hospital may not be necessary. The typical mode of rehabilitation begins with intensive early therapy with a progressive weaning of visits. Discharge from therapy occurs when the patient is able to perform ADLs in a timely manner to their satisfaction.

Outcome Assessment at the End of Therapy

The defining of outcomes for the patient with MS is problematic for the therapist because the typical 'return to previous function' outcome may not be appropriate for these patients. Some outcome measures used with MS patients include the FIM (Freeman et al., 1997 **A**; Solari et al., 1999 **A**), SF-36 (Freeman et al., 1996 **A**; DiFabio et al., 1997 **A**), Health Related Quality of Life scale (HRQOL) (Schwartz et al., 1999 **C**; Melin et al., 1995), the Multiple Sclerosis Quality of Life scale (MSQOL) (DiFabio et al., 1997), and the Minimal Rating of Disability scale (MRD) (Cervera-Deval et al., 1994) in addition to the Kurtzke Expanded Status Scale (Freeman et al., 1996 **A**, 1997 **A**; Schwartz et al., 1999 **C**). Only the MSQOL was designed specifically for patients with MS although the other outcome measures have been used for patients with MS. Schwartz defines the outcomes of treating MS as 'a symptom inventory, a performance measure with eight domains of function. The domains of function included: mobility, hand function, vision, fatigue, cognition, bladder and bowel, sensory, and spasticity' (Schwartz et al., 1999, p. 63 **C**). In the case of Mrs LW, it is apparent that her impairments have changed following her motor vehicle accident, increasing her functional limitations and adding to increased disability and handicap.

The goals for patients with MS are of necessity functional, and serve as a temporary marker of functional achievement. Owing to the nature of the disorder, discharge from therapy may occur at seemingly arbitrary points.

Implications

The treatment associated with the case of Mrs LW was presented within the framework of the Nagi model of disability, with the intention of uncovering themes within her disabilities and handicaps that could be linked to functional limitations resulting from impairments caused by her MS. She exhibits many potential complications of MS that tend to accumulate as years since diagnosis pass, although no one case of MS is truly representative of the disease. She presents with many impairments that can be manifest in many functional limitations. The themes in her pattern of limitations can help direct her therapy toward a positive outcome while possibly not directly addressing all of her concerns. The major impairments to which many of her complaints can be tied are spasticity, weakness, poor motor control, depression and fatigue. The evidence is for the physical therapy interventions of stretching, cryotherapy and electrical stimulation to address spasticity. What is the optimal position, duration and frequency of stretching for reducing spasticity? Is there an optimal regimen, or is every patient unique? With regard to weakness, does long-term strength training provide different results from short term strengthening? Does the location of the patient (inpatient or outpatient) matter in the overall outcome of the patient with MS? While physical therapists may not be able to impact directly on the disease, diminution of the functional limitations by addressing specific impairments and providing symptomatic relief becomes the priority. It is hoped that by careful treatment planning and continued research regarding treatment efficacy, the patient will enjoy an accompanying improvement in disability and handicap outcomes.

References

Acorn S, Andersen S (1990) Depression in multiple sclerosis: critique of the research literature. Journal of Neuroscience in Nursing 22: 209–14.

Ades P, Waldmann M, Gillespie C (1995) A controlled trial of exercise training in older coronary patients. Journal of Gerontology 50A: M7–M11.

Al Zamil A, Hassan N, Hassan W (1995) Reduction of elbow flexor and extensor spasticity following muscle stretch. Journal of Neurological Rehabilitation 9: 161–5.

Andersen J (1983) Grant's Atlas of Anatomy, 8th edn. Baltimore, MD: Williams & Wilkins.

Azouvi P, Mane M, Thiebaut J, Denys P, Remy-Neris O, Bussel B (1996) Intrathecal baclofen administration for control of severe spinal spasticity: functional improvement and long-term follow-up. Archives of Physical Medicine Rehabilitation 77: 35–9.

Bell K, Lehmann J (1987) Effect of cooling on H- and T-reflexes in normal subjects. Archives of Physical Medicine Rehabilitation 68: 490–3.

Brouwer B, deAndrade V (1995) The effects of slow stroking on spasticity in patients with multiple sclerosis; a pilot study. Physiotherapy Theory and Practice 11: 13–21.

Brown D (1994a) Diapers and underpads, part 1: Skin integrity outcomes. Ostomy Wound Management 40: 20–2, 24–6, 28.

Brown D (1994b) Diapers and underpads, part 2: Cost outcomes. Ostomy Wound Management 40: 34–6, 38, 40.

Buchanan R, Lewis K (1997) Services that nursing facilities should provide to residents with MS: a survey of health professionals. Rehabilitation Nursing 22: 67–72.

Butler P (1998) A preliminary report on the effectiveness of trunk targeting in achieving independent sitting balance in children with cerebral palsy. Clinical Rehabilitation 12: 281–93.

Cervera-Deval J, Morant-Guillen M, Fenollosa-Vasquez P, Serra-Escorihuela M, Vilchez-Padilla J, Burguera J (1994) Social handicaps of multiple sclerosis and their relation to neurological alterations. Archives of Physical Medicine Rehabilitation 75: 1223–7.

Curtis K, Kindlin C, Reich K, White D (1995) Functional reach in wheelchair users: the effects of trunk and lower extremity stabilization. Archives of Physical Medicine Rehabilitation 76: 360–7.

DeSouza L, Ashburn A (1996) Assessment of motor function in people with multiple sclerosis. Physiotherapy Research International 1: 98–111.

DiFabio R, Choi T, Soderberg J, Hansen C (1997) Health-related quality of life for patients with progressive multiple sclerosis: influence of rehabilitation. Physical Therapy 77: 1704–16.

DiFabio R, Soderberg J, Choi T, Hansen C, Schapiro R (1998) Extended outpatient rehabilitation: its influence on symptom frequency, fatigue, and functional status for persons with progressive multiple sclerosis. Archives of Physical Medicine Rehabilitation 79: 141–6.

Dunevsky A, Perel A (1998) Gabapentin for relief of spasticity associated with multiple sclerosis. American Journal of Physical Medicine Rehabilitation 77: 451–4.

Fiatarone M, Marks E, Ryan N, Meredith C, Lipsitz L, Evans W (1990) High-intensity strength training in nonagenarians. Journal of the American Medical Association 263: 3029–34.

Flensner G, Lindencrona C (1999) The cooling suit: a study of ten multiple sclerosis patients' experiences in daily life [corrected] [published erratum appears in Journal of Advanced Nursing 1999, 30(3): 775]. Journal of Advanced Nursing 29(6): 1444–53.

Freeman J, Langdon D, Hobart J, Thompson A (1996) Health-related quality of life in people with multiple sclerosis undergoing inpatient rehabilitation. Journal of Neurological Rehabilitation 10: 185–94.

Freeman J, Langdon D, Hobart J, Thompson A (1997) The impact of inpatient rehabilitation of progressive multiple sclerosis. Annals of Neurology 42: 236–44.

Fuller K, Dawson K, Wiles C (1996) Physiotherapy in chronic multiple sclerosis: a controlled trial. Clinical Rehabilitation 39: 91–7.

Gerber L, Furst G, Shulman B et al. (1987) Patient education program to teach energy conservation behaviors to patients with rheumatoid arthritis: a pilot study. Archives of Physical Medicine Rehabilitation 68: 442–5.

Goldberg DP, Williams PA (1988) Users' Guide to the General Health Questionnaire. Windsor: NFER-Nelson, p 129.

Granger C, Cotter A, Hamilton B, Fiedler R, Hens M (1990) Functional assessment scales: a study of persons with multiple sclerosis. Archives of Physical Medicine Rehabilitation 71: 870–5.

Grindel C (1994) Fatigue and nutrition. Medical and Surgical Nursing 3: 475–81, 499.

Guccione A (1991) Physical therapy diagnosis and the relationship between impairments and function. Physical Therapy 71: 499–503.

Hale LFV, Goodman M (1995) Prolonged static muscle stretch reduces spasticity. South African Journal of Physiotherapy 51: 3–6.

Hart D, Stobbe T, Till C, Plummer R (1984) Effect of trunk stabilization on quadriceps femoris muscle torque. Physical Therapy 64: 1375–80.

Hellstrom O (1995) Health promotion and clinical dialogue. Patient Education and Counselling. 25: 247–56.

Hinderer S, Gupta S (1996) Functional outcome measures to assess interventions for spasticity. Archives of Physical Medicine Rehabilitation 77: 1083–9.

Jette A (1994) Physical disablement concepts for physical therapy research and practice. Physical Therapy 74: 380–6.

King T (1996) The effect of neuromuscular electrical stimulation in reducing tone. American Journal of Occupational Therapy 50: 62–4.

Kinnman J, Andersson U, Kinnman Y, Wetterqvist L (1997) Temporary improvement of motor function in patients with multiple sclerosis after treatment with a cooling suit. Journal of Neurological Rehabilitation 11: 109–14.

Kobetic R, Triolo R, Marsolais E (1997) Muscle selection and walking performance of multichannel FES systems for ambulation in paraplegia. IEEE-Trans Rehabilitation Engineering 5: 23–9.

Kraft G (1996) Rehabilitation principles for patients with multiple sclerosis. Journal of Spinal Cord Medicine 21: 117–20.

Kraft G, Alquist A, deLateur B (1996) Effect of resistive exercise on function in multiple sclerosis. Archives of Physical Medicine Rehabilitation 77: 984.

Ku YE, Montgomery LD, Wenzel KC, Webbon BW, Burks JS (1999) Physiologic and thermal responses of male and female patients with multiple sclerosis to head and neck cooling. American Journal of Physical Medicine and Rehabilitation 78(5): 447–56, 470–3, 499.

Kurtzke J (1970) Neurologic impairment in multiple sclerosis and the Disability Status Scale. Acta Neurologica Scandinavica 46: 493–512.

Kurtzke J (1983) Rating neurological impairment in multiple sclerosis: an expanded disability status scale (EDSS). Neurology 33: 1444–52.

Linacre JM, Heinemann AW, Wright BD, Granger C, Hamilton BB (1991) The functional independence measure as a measure of disability, Research report 91-01. Chicago: Chicago Rehabilitation Services Evaluation Unit, Rehabilitation Institute of Chicago.

Lord S, Wade D, Halligan P (1998) A comparison of two physiotherapy treatment approaches to improve walking in multiple sclerosis: a pilot randomized controlled study. Clinical Rehabilitation 12: 477–86.

Maguire BI (1996) The effects of imagery on attitudes and moods in multiple sclerosis patients. Alternative Therapies in Health and Medicine 2(5): 75–9.

McCartney N, Hicks A, Martin J, Webber C (1995) Long-term resistance training in the elderly: effects on dynamic strength, exercise capacity, muscle and bone. Journal of Gerontolology 50A: B97–B104.

Melin A, Wieland D, Harker J, Bygren L (1995) Health outcomes of post-hospital-at-home care: secondary analysis of a Swedish trial. Journal of the American Geriatric Society 43: 301–7.

Miller R (1996) Physiotherapy. An investigation into the management of the spasticity experienced by some patients with multiple sclerosis using acupuncture. Complementary Therapies in Medicine 4: 58–62.

Moore C, Bracegirdle H (1994) The effects of a short-term, low-intensity exercise programme on the psychological well-being of community-dwelling elderly women. British Journal of Occupational Therapy 57: 213–16.

Norkin C, Levangie PK (1992) Joint Structure and Function, 2nd edn. Philadelphia, PA: FA Davis.

Olgiati R, Burgunder J, Mumenthaler M (1988) Increased energy cost of walking in multiple sclerosis: effect of spasticity, ataxia, and weakness. Archives of Physical Medicine and Rehabilitation 69: 846–9.

Pescatello L, Murphy D (1998) Lower intensity physical activity is advantageous for fat distribution and blood glucose among viscerally obese older adults. Medicine and Science in Sports and Exercise 30: 1408–13.

Petajan J, Gappmaier E, White A, Spencer M, Mino L, Hicks R (1996) Impact of aerobic training on fitness and quality of life in multiple sclerosis. Annals of Neurology 39: 432–41.

Price R, Lehman J, Boswello-Bessette S, Burleight A, deLateur B (1993) Influence of cryotherapy on spasticity at the human ankle. Archives of Physical Medicine and Rehabilitation 74: 300–4.

Rall L, Roubenoff R, Cannon J, Abad L, Dinarello C, Meydani S (1996) Effects of progressive resistance training on immune response in aging and chronic inflammation. Medicine and Science in Sports and Exercise 28: 1356–65.

Robinson LR, Kraft GH, Fitts SS, Schneider V (1997) Body cooling may not improve somatosensory pathway function in multiple sclerosis, presented in part at the Xth International Congress of Electrophysiology, Kyoto Japan, October 1995. American Journal of Physical Medicine and Rehabilitation 76(3): 191–6.

Rudick R, Goodkin D, Jacobs L et al. (1997) Impact of interferon beta 1a on neurologic disability in relapsing multiple sclerosis. The Multiple Sclerosis Collaborative Research Group (MSCRG). Neurology 49: 358–63.

Schwartz C, Vollmer T, Lee H, North American Research Consortium on Multiple Sclerosis Outcomes Study Group (1999) Reliability and validity of two self-report measures of impairment and disability for MS. Neurology 52: 63–70.

Solari A, Filippini G, Gasco P et al. (1999) Physical rehabilitation has a positive effect on disability in multiple sclerosis patients. Neurology 52: 57–62.

Svensson B, Gerdle B, Elert J (1994) Endurance training in patients with multiple sclerosis: five case studies. Physical Therapy 74: 1017–26.

Thomas CL (Ed) (1983) Taber's Cyclopedic Medical Dictionary, 14th edn. Philadelphia: FA Davis, p S-69.

Thompson A (1988) Multiple sclerosis: rehabilitation measures. Seminars in Neurology 18: 397–403.

Thompson A (1998) Symptomatic treatment in multiple sclerosis. Current Opinions in Neurology 11: 305–9.

Vahtera T, Haaranen M, Viramo-Koskela A, Ruutiainen J (1997) Pelvic floor rehabilitation is effective in patients with multiple sclerosis. Clinical Rehabilitation 11: 211–19.

Ware J, Snow K, Kosinski M, Gandek B (1993) SF-36 Health Survey Manual and Interpretation Guide. Boston, MA: Health Institute, New England Medical Center.

Whaley M, Kaminsky L, Getchell B, Treloar J, Kelly M (1992) Change in total cholesterol after endurance training: a function of pretraining concentration. Journal of Cardiopulmonary Rehabilitation 12: 42–50.

Zupan A, Gregoric M, Valencic V (1995) Long-lasting effects of electrical stimulation upon muscles of patients suffering from progressive muscular dystrophy. Clinical Rehabilitation 9: 102–9.

Treatment and Management of a Patient with Multiple Sclerosis (2)

JENNIFER FREEMAN

Relatively few clinical trials have been undertaken to evaluate the effectiveness of physiotherapy interventions in people with multiple sclerosis (MS). Most of the literature describes, rather than evaluates, the aims and process of different rehabilitation interventions, and outcome is frequently determined in anecdotal terms. Despite this, physiotherapy for MS is advocated in articles (Bohannon, 1993a **C**), textbooks (Mertin, 1997 **C**), and guidelines from medical (BSRM, 1993 **C**) and charitable organizations (Freeman et al., 1997b **C**). Importantly, a number of patient surveys strongly express the need for increases in physiotherapy provision, with many lamenting the paucity of services available (Perry, 1994 **A**; Robinson et al., 1996 **A**).

While objective evidence of effectiveness from clinical trials is essential, information from rigorously undertaken qualitative studies is also crucial in informing clinical practice. A series of indepth interviews and focus groups undertaken by Robinson and colleagues (1996 **A**) found that people with MS often regarded physiotherapy in a very different way from the physiotherapists themselves. People with MS viewed it 'as a way of maintaining body flexibility, and for dealing with muscular and other difficulties on a continuous basis, considering the physiotherapist and themselves as a team in which the physiotherapist needs to be present to initiate and support exercise'. They expected a continuing relationship as part of their lifelong approach to MS, utilizing services and therapies on a continuous, rather than short term or palliative basis. In contrast, the physiotherapists perceived this relationship as temporary and limited, focused on ensuring that the patient worked independently, so that in a short period of time they could effectively maintain an exercise programme without returning frequently for further treatment.

In this chapter I aim to draw upon a variety of sources, including my own clinical experience, to rationalize how I might work with Mrs LW if she were to arrive on my ward tomorrow morning.

General Principles

Of utmost importance is the recognition that MS is characterized by a multiplicity of signs and symptoms that interact in a variety of ways to create a wide range of often complex physical, psychological and cognitive problems. Furthermore, the disease course is characteristically unpredictable and variable, although generally progressive. When you combine these features, together with the fact that the average age of onset for MS is 30 years (Sadovnik and Ebers, 1993 **A**), then it becomes increasingly apparent that the needs of these people will evolve over many decades. Effective ongoing assessment and intervention is therefore particularly important, and extremely challenging.

Given the multiplicity and diversity of problems it is widely agreed that a coordinated multidisciplinary team approach is central to effective management (Ko Ko, 1999 **C**). Numerous papers and books describe this approach, and identify the key components of its success as including: expert assessment (Johnson and Thompson, 1996 **C**); tailoring of programmes to meet the needs of the individual (Thompson, 1996 **C**); effective teamworking (Barnes, 1993 **C**); and a patient centred goal setting approach (Schut and Stam, 1994 **C**). A number of clinical trials have recently demonstrated the effectiveness of this multidisciplinary 'package of care' in reducing levels of disability and handicap, both with regard to inpatient rehabilitation (Freeman et al., 1997b **A**; Solari et al., 1999 **A**) and outpatient rehabilitation (Di Fabio et al., 1997 **A**). In contrast, the evidence from studies evaluating physiotherapy intervention in isolation from other disciplines remains equivocal. Although some studies have demonstrated positive benefits in minimizing disability and improving walking (De Souza and Worthington, 1988 **A**; Lord et al., 1998 **A**), others have shown disappointing results in these outcomes (Vowels and Pelosi, 1983 **A**; Fuller et al., 1996 **A**). Little evidence is available regarding which precise components within these packages of care contribute to the outcome. Some of this evidence will be referred to later.

It is reported that current physiotherapy practice tends to be dominated by two distinct treatment approaches, which can be termed 'facilitation' (impairment based) or 'task-oriented' (disability based) (Horak, 1991 **C**). While there is much discussion amongst therapists about which approach is most effective, little research has been undertaken to investigate this in MS.

A recent study by Lord (Lord et al., 1998 **A**) compared these two approaches in treatment to improve walking and found no significant differences in effectiveness between the two methods. Both were associated with improved mobility. In my experience, clinicians in the United Kingdom often incorporate both within their treatment programmes.

Self-management and education is considered to be the cornerstone of any successful treatment strategy (Hatch, 1997 **C**). If a patient has a better understanding of the nature of their symptoms (such as spasms and spasticity) and the rationale behind the treatment approach (for example the importance of good posture; of maintaining full range of movement in soft tissues and joints; and adopting patterns of movement which do not aggravate spasms), then they will have better control of their symptoms and a clearer idea of when to seek help. Education and collaboration with the person's spouse and carers is also important in this process (Rossiter et al., 1998 **A**). Mrs LW is divorced and living alone, and hence self-management is especially important. It would also be beneficial to collaborate with her social service carers and her mother, on whom she may depend for more assistance in the future.

Therapy should be relevant and meaningful to the patient (Payton and Nelson, 1998 **A**). It should be goal-oriented (Schut and Stam, 1994 **C**). Therapists sometimes express concern about resistance by people with MS to professional advice – non-compliance in professional terms. It has been suggested that this often arises out of a failure by professionals to understand the complicated agendas of the lives of disabled people (Robinson et al., 1996 **A**). In MS for instance almost every aspect of the person's life may be affected; not only do they face the prospect and reality of increasing disability, but also the uncertainty of when new relapses will occur or when established disability will set in. I would therefore aim to incorporate 'physiotherapy exercises' into Mrs LW's normal daily routine, ensuring that her home exercise programme was sufficiently flexible to accommodate to changes in her condition, (for example fatigue) and lifestyle (for example a busy day at work). In my opinion, this is crucial for Mrs LW who, despite significant impairments, is juggling a number of difficulties in her life including working, dealing with a personal bereavement, and recovering from a recent car accident. All of this, in addition to dealing with and adjusting to the progressive nature of her condition, means that the 'goal posts' in terms of her abilities, her needs and desires are likely to move.

Finally, it is necessary to acknowledge the impact that cognitive impairment may have on the success of physiotherapy management (Langdon, 1996 **B**). This is important as cognitive deterioration is estimated to occur in 45–65% of people with MS (McIntosh-Michaelis et al., 1991 **A**). Specifically, deficits occur regularly on measures of recent memory, attention, concentration, information-processing speed and executive functions (Rao, 1995 **A**). Such deficits will affect the learning of new skills and therefore the success of carry-over between therapy sessions. Close liaison with a neuropsychologist is fundamental to highlight the specific problems and to understand which cognitive strategies should be incorporated to optimize learning and carry-over. These strategies are often simple and easy to incorp-orate into physiotherapy sessions. They include providing brief, clear and concrete oral instructions; practising activities in separate, smaller components; and providing written information as an *aide-mémoire* (Langdon, 1996 **B**).

Physiotherapy Intervention

As with any patient, my first priority would be to undertake an initial comprehensive assessment that considers the spectrum of physical, cognitive and psychosocial issues with which Mrs LW presents. I would use a problem-solving approach to identify the aims of intervention (Edwards, 1996 **C**). Integral to this would be a range of baseline objective measurements against which my future assessments could be compared. In terms of outcomes, I would use the framework advocated by the World Health Organization whereby the consequences of disease are measured at a number of different levels: impairments, activities and participations (World Health Organization, 1997). In measuring impairments I would undertake goniometry measurements of lower limb joint range (Norkin and White, 1975); a spasm frequency score (Penn et al., 1989); and a self-rating visual analogue scale to quantify low back pain (Wade, 1992). As Mrs LW is currently in an inpatient rehabilitation unit I would rate her level of functional ability, in conjunction with other team members, using either the Functional Independence Measure or the Barthel Index (Wade, 1992). Both of these measures have proved to be reliable, valid and responsive for MS within a variety of hospital and community settings (Granger et al., 1990 **A**; Brosseau and Wolfson, 1994 **A**; Freeman et al., 1997b **A**). If Mrs LW were undertaking physiotherapy in relative isolation from other disciplines (for example on an out-patient basis) then I would choose a measure which was more specific to my input; either the Rivermead Motor Assessment Scale (Wade, 1992) or the Amended Motor Club Assessment (De Souza and Ashburn, 1996). The setting of goals would be integral to Mrs LW's management, and would be also used to measure effectiveness. Ideally these would be incorporated within an integrated care pathway, a system which has been demonstrated to improve the effectiveness of goal setting and to coordinate the provision of services for people with MS (Rossiter et al., 1998 **A**).

Based on this assessment my overall aims would be to:

- improve safety and performance in everyday activities;
- wherever possible reverse the secondary complications (pain, joint and soft tissue stiffness and contractures, oedema) and prevent further complications from developing;
- optimize quality of life.

More specifically my physiotherapy management programme would aim to:

- achieve as efficient and normal movement patterns as possible;
- provide strategies to reduce the frequency and severity of spasms and spasticity;
- preserve integrity of the musculoskeletal system;
- implement a standing regimen;
- improve posture and comfort when sitting and lying;
- refine the compensatory strategies being used;
- provide advice on management of tone and fatigue;
- assess the potential for walking;
- liaise with colleagues regarding continence, sexual, cognitive, emotional, employment, self-care and environmental issues.

The following section describes aspects of this management programme.

Strategies to Reduce the Frequency of Spasms and the Severity of Spasticity

The severe flexor spasms and spasticity experienced by Mrs LW are typical of patients with advanced MS where spinal cord plaques result in a lack of opposition of the descending excitatory systems (Brown, 1994 **B**). As illustrated by this case study, this often impacts dramatically on many aspects of the patient's daily function and places them at risk of contracture (Sheean, 1998 **B**). Although it is generally accepted that physiotherapy can be an effective treatment for spasticity, the evidence is largely anecdotal. Issues such as the optimal duration and frequency of treatment have not been addressed.

Eliminating Aggravating Factors of Spasticity and Spasms

The exclusion or reduction of noxious factors that might aggravate spasticity is the first step in its management (Gracies et al., 1997). Attention to these factors is the responsibility of all members of the multidisciplinary team. I would therefore collaborate closely with other staff members about factors such as Mrs LW's pain, bladder and bowel dysfunction, and potential tightness of shoes caused by her oedematous feet.

Liaison with medical colleagues with regard to pharmacological management of spasticity would be essential. Pharmacological intervention to reduce spasticity with agents such as baclofen, dantrolene or tinazidine is common (Lawson, 1998). There is widespread evidence from randomized controlled trials to support their effectiveness in reducing spasticity and painful spasms (refer to Bakheit, 1996 for a review). Although no specific details of current drug management are provided in the case notes, it is highly likely that Mrs LW will be taking some form of oral anti-spastic medication. The negative impact that these drugs may have on muscle strength and function is widely documented (Gracies et al., 1997 **A**); for example baclofen has been shown to cause deterioration in walking ability in ambulatory MS patients (From and Heltberg, 1975 **A**). It is generally recognized that neurophysiotherapists are key players in determining the impact that a drug has on movement and function. Some suggest that anti-spasticity medication should not be given unless it is in association with, and monitored by, a physiotherapist (Thompson, 1998 **C**). A significant part of my role would therefore be to liaise closely with medical staff about the impact any alterations in medications were having on her motor performance. Such impacts might include increasing weakness, extra effort required in propelling her wheelchair or transferring, or respiratory depression.

In Mrs LW's case oral medication in combination with physiotherapy intervention was inadequate in controlling her spasms and spasticity, hence the referral for assessment of intrathecal baclofen (Penn et al., 1989 **A**). This more invasive approach has been found to be effective in managing severe spasms and spasticity in people with MS, without many of the adverse side-effects of oral medications (Latash et al., 1990 **A**; Coffey et al., 1993 **A**; Abel and Smith, 1994 **A**). Physiotherapists have a major role to play in this procedure, from initial assessment through to long term follow-up (Thompson, 1998 **C**). If Mrs LW needed to be transferred to the acute hospital for this procedure I would facilitate continuity of care by liaising with my colleagues, and providing a written and oral summary of my assessment and treatment to date.

Preserving the Integrity of the Musculoskeletal System

There is a growing body of literature that describes the importance of maintaining the integrity of the musculoskeletal system in neurological conditions (for a summary refer to Carr and Shepherd, 1998 **B**). In progressive conditions such as MS, deterioration of the musculoskeletal system often progresses gradually in an insidious fashion over a number of years. These secondary complications of soft tissue shortening, joint stiffness and disuse weakness arise from both immobility (for example prolonged periods of sitting in a chair) and repetitive abnormal postures and movement. A key aim of my programme would be to reverse these and to prevent the development of further complications. In my experience, when the pathology and consequent impairments are severe, this is not always possible.

I would use a variety of methods as part of the management programme. I would teach Mrs LW specific soft-tissue stretches to practise daily (Carr et al., 1995) and educate her about ways in which she could incorporate positioning within routine activities such as sleeping and sitting to improve and maintain the range in her muscles and joints (Edwards, 1996 **C**). Within therapy sessions I would use a range of techniques to correct the muscle imbalance and skeletal malalignment by concurrently mobilizing the joints, lengthening the shortened soft tissues and strengthening the weak muscles. I would use techniques such as passive stretching (Carr and Shepherd, 1998 **B**); the gymnastic ball (Edwards **C**); trunk mobilizations (Davies, 1990 **C**); and positioning (Pope, 1992 **C**). Although there is evidence to support the usefulness of serial splinting (refer to Bakheit, 1996 for a summary **A**), I would not use this method in Mrs LW's case because of the severity of her spasms.

Implementing a Standing Regimen

Implementation of a regular standing programme would be an important goal for Mrs LW's long-term management. Ideally I would aim for standing to be achieved independently, in good anatomical alignment. Given the apparent severity of the spastic paraparesis and lower limb flexor spasms I think that this is unlikely to be achieved, at least in the short term. I would therefore use equipment such as the Oswestry Standing Frame (OSF; Tussler, 1998) to achieve standing, on a daily basis, in as normal alignment as possible for graduated periods of up to 30–45 minutes. My intention would be for this to continue in the community following discharge. I would therefore liaise with community services, arranging a joint session with them at home to ensure that this was feasible.

The rationale behind a standing programme is that it stimulates more normal tonus, thereby facilitating postural adjustments (Brown, 1994 **C**); helps to maintain normal joint movement by providing stretch to joint capsules, ligaments and musculo-tendinous units; reduces the risk of disuse osteoporosis; and improves psychological well-being (Tussler, 1998 **C**). Although used widely by physiotherapists throughout the United Kingdom (Edwards, 1996 **C**) evidence of the therapeutic benefits of standing programmes on these varied outcomes remains equivocal, with no research support for its use in MS. A number of single case studies have demonstrated benefits in reducing lower limb spasticity in patients with spinal cord injury (Bohannon, 1993b **A**), head injury (Richardson, 1991 **A**) and cerebral palsy (Tremblay et al., 1990 **A**). These effects have been shown to last from about 30 minutes to one day. A reduction in osteoporosis has also been demonstrated in spinal cord injured patients (Goemare et al., 1994 **A**). Conflicting evidence, however, is provided by Kunkel and colleagues (1993 **A**). In their small sample of six wheelchair-bound males (four spinal cord injured and two MS, half of whom demonstrated spasticity), standing twice daily over six months was not shown to be effective in reducing spasticity, osteoporosis or contractures. A positive psychological impact was demonstrated, however, with 67% continuing the standing programme following completion of the trial. It is important to note that the majority of these studies used a tilt table for standing. I believe that the OSF is less restrictive, providing a more dynamic means of assisted standing than the tilt table, thereby allowing more normal postural reactions and a better outcome. Similarly, when possible, facilitation of standing by using one therapist in front to support the knees and another behind to provide a 'mobile support' is, in my experience, preferable to using external support from equipment. The literature does not provide evidence to either support or refute these beliefs.

Sufficient range of movement at the hip, pelvis and lower limb is a prerequisite to achieving standing in good anatomical alignment (Edwards, 1996 **C**). Standing Mrs LW without first achieving adequate range may cause pain or compensation at adjacent body segments. This is likely to exacerbate rather than alleviate spasticity. Prior to standing Mrs LW, I would therefore use the methods described previously to achieve sufficient range of movement. In addition, throughout the standing programme I would take care to ensure correct alignment and weight bearing. This might require me to give personal assistance to the trunk from behind, or external support from equipment such as a foam wedge positioned on the tabletop in front.

Improving Posture and Comfort when Sitting and Lying

Mrs LW's sitting posture is abnormal: her pelvis is rotated, posteriorly tilted and laterally tilted to the left; her lower limbs remain flexed, adducted and internally rotated. When lying she requires a wedge under the knees to achieve contact with the supporting surface. This postural malalignment is a direct consequence of the combined impairments of soft tissue shortening, weakness, spasticity and spasms. Discomfort and pain will directly and negatively impact on these impairments (Gracies et al., 1997 **A**). An immediate priority of my treatment would therefore be to improve Mrs LW's posture and comfort both in her wheelchair and when lying. This is for three reasons. First, Mrs LW relies on a wheelchair for mobility, which means that she will spend considerable amounts of time in the chair. Much of the remaining time is likely to be spent lying in bed. If abnormal postures are sustained over time, the tissues will adapt, and lead to 'preferred' postures and postural deformities (Mayer et al., 1997 **C**). Second, effective carry-over between treatment sessions depends, at least in part, on achieving optimal posture over the 24-hour cycle. Third, there is increasing evidence that spasticity and spasms can be modified through control of posture in terms of stability and alignment (for a summary of evidence see Pope, 1992 **B**).

I would undertake a seating assessment, in conjunction with an occupational therapist, to determine the key factors that interfere with her ability to achieve a relaxed and symmetrical sitting position. The fact that Mrs LW 'overuses' her upper limbs when sitting and standing but not when lying indicates that trunk weakness may be an important contributing factor. The use of external support, through specialist equipment such as contoured back supports or tilt-in-space mechanisms, may prove helpful in increasing her trunk stability, and thereby improve her posture and function when seated in a chair. Similarly, a pressure-relieving cushion will help to minimize the risk of pressure sores, which are a potential complication given her reduced mobility, asymmetrical posture (and therefore asymmetrical load bearing), and the shearing forces produced by spasms (Pope, 1996 **C**). I would also investigate whether the provision of an adapted electric wheelchair might bring further benefits in terms of achieving autonomy in outdoor mobility, reduced fatigue, and a reduction in the compensatory 'overuse' of her upper limbs, upon which she is currently reliant to maintain a static posture.

In my experience, achieving optimal seating takes time. The seating requirements evolve as alterations in the musculoskeletal and neural impairments occur. Ideally therefore there must be flexibility with the provision of wheelchair adaptations. Within an inpatient setting this is relatively easy to achieve, as different products may be trialled. This becomes less practicable in other settings. In my own experience, financial constraints rather than need often dictate the types of equipment issued to patients. Clinical consensus is that seating needs should be regularly reviewed, especially in progressive conditions where the person's needs will inevitably change over time.

Close liaison with the nursing staff will be particularly important to achieve a lying position for Mrs LW that is both comfortable and of maximum therapeutic benefit in terms of symmetry and alignment. I would undertake joint sessions with staff, as well as using visual aids such as positioning posters, to facilitate continuity of care. Where necessary I would use equipment such as pillows, foam wedges, or T-rolls to achieve this position (Edwards, 1996 **C**). When using the wedge under the legs in the supine position I would aim for Mrs LW to gradually accommodate to a more extended position, by graduating from a larger to a smaller wedge.

Refining Compensatory Strategies to Enable Safe and Optimal Function

Not all compensatory strategies are useful. Sometimes they are counterproductive and may reinforce poor patterns of movement. The primary concern of my intervention would be to maintain function at an optimum level, with as efficient and normal movement patterns as possible. Given Mrs LW's physical status, together with the progressive nature of her condition, she will invariably need to use some compensatory strategies to function (Carr and Shepherd, 1998 **B**). I would aim, wherever possible, to minimize these compensations as, if they become marked and repetitive, they may actually begin to 'mask' the ability of the patient (Pope, 1992 **C**). Furthermore they may aggravate the intensity of the spasms and spasticity, and are frequently more energy consuming.

I would increase Mrs LW's awareness of the strategies she is currently using; this alone may go some way to reduce the 'overuse' described in the case study. Alongside this I would attempt to improve the underlying cause for her compensations, namely her difficulty in moving as a result of weakness, soft tissue contractures, spasticity and spasms. In the early stages of intervention, while these issues are being addressed, I would assist (facilitate) the patient's movement to enable as normal a pattern of movement as possible, gradually reducing the amount of assistance provided as appropriate. I would use a range of methods to achieve this, including handling and modification of the environment (Edwards, 1996 **C**). Theoretically this would provide the system with the opportunity to relearn a more normal pattern of neuromotor activity (for a summary see Carr and Shepherd, 1998 **B**). Finally, given that Mrs LW is unsafe in transfers I would teach her new techniques such as the use of a sliding board, liaising closely with nursing staff to ensure this technique is effectively carried over into the ward setting.

Assessing the Potential for Walking

Factors detailed in the case study that indicate a poor prognosis for walking include Mrs LW's inability to stand independently for more than a few minutes, her inability to walk for the past two months, and the severity of the spastic paraparesis and flexor spasms which have remained resistant to three weeks' intensive inpatient rehabilitation. I would, however, refrain from making a judgement about her potential to walk until after her trial of intrathecal baclofen. Positive results have been demonstrated in clinical trials of intrathecal baclofen with regard to regaining walking ability in patients whose severe spasms and spasticity were resistant to oral medication (Lewis and Mueller, 1993 **A**).

The goal of walking may be an important motivational factor for Mrs LW. Surveys of people with MS demonstrate that 'the transition from walking, with whatever difficulty, to the use of a wheelchair is seen by many people with MS, and their family, as a major life transition' (Perry, 1994 **A**). As a consequence, 'there are often conflicts at this point between different views of the need for a wheelchair and their consequences' (Robinson, 1996, p. 30 **A**). While remaining very sensitive to this, I would, however, ask Mrs LW about her own expectations, and would introduce her to some of the pros and cons of using a wheelchair in comparison with struggling to 'stay on her feet'. Some of the benefits might include increased autonomy in mobility, and a reduction in fatigue, spasms and pain. To my knowledge there are no clinical trials that provide evidence to support this decision.

Delivery and Timing of Intervention

Clinical consensus is that early intervention is most effective at managing symptoms and preventing secondary complications from developing. Of equal importance is the need for regular and ongoing review in order that problems are anticipated and addressed quickly rather than left to evolve unchecked. I would ensure that, following discharge from hospital, Mrs LW was reviewed by a physiotherapist on a regular basis. The individual variability of MS means that it is difficult to prescribe specific time frames for review. Clinical consensus is that reviews at six-monthly intervals are generally appropriate. In my opinion an open access self-referral system, which enables contact when needs require, is best suited to MS. There are, of course, potential disadvantages to this system. First, and perhaps most importantly, it is reliant upon the patient, or an advocate recognizing their problems, being capable and motivated to contact the relevant therapist. A further concern is sometimes expressed that physiotherapists would be inundated with excessive and sometimes inappropriate referrals. While no evidence currently exists about such a system for MS patients, evaluation of a musculoskeletal self-referral service demonstrated that these fears were not realized (Ferguson et al., 1999). Recently in the United Kingdom an increasing number of MS clinical nurse specialist posts have been developed which may facilitate more timely and appropriate referrals to disciplines such as physiotherapy (Johnson, 1997 **C**).

Implications

Relatively little research has evaluated physiotherapy interventions for people with MS. As clinicians seeking to provide evidence for what we do it is therefore necessary to apply findings from studies of other disease groups and from basic scientific research. It is difficult to know for certain whether these results are generalizable to people with MS. The potential for applied research within this area is therefore enormous. Topics might include evaluation of specific interventions such as the effect of standing regimens on hypertonicity and lower limb spasms; the impact of general strengthening programmes on functional abilities; or the impact of aerobic exercise programmes on levels of fitness, functional ability and fatigue. Evaluation of both the process and outcome of service delivery is also required; for example, determining the effectiveness of an open access physiotherapy service. Finally, but certainly not of least importance, we must explore what people with MS want from physiotherapists. It is easy to become focused on aspects of pathology, or the specific details of our intervention from a professional perspective, and forget whom we are providing the service for. This is challenging. If we are to gain a comprehensive understanding of this complex disease it is essential that we foster interaction between neuroscience, clinical neurology and the views of people with MS at both investigative and practice levels.

References

Abel N, Smith RA (1994) Intrathecal baclofen for treatment of intractable spinal spasticity. Archives of Physical Medicine and Rehabilitation 75: 54-58.

Bakheit AMO (1996) Management of muscle spasticity. Critical Reviews in Physical and Rehabilitation Medicine 8(3): 235–52.

Barnes M (1993) Multiple sclerosis. In Greenwood R, Barnes MP, McLellan TM (Eds) Neurological Rehabilitation. Edinburgh: Churchill Livingstone, pp 485–504.

Bohannon RW (1993a) Physical rehabilitation in neurologic diseases. Current Opinion in Neurology 6: 765–72.

Bohannon RW (1993b) Tilt table standing for reducing spasticity after spinal cord injury. Archives of Physical Medicine and Rehabilitation 74: 1121–2.

British Society of Rehabilitation Medicine (1993) Multiple Sclerosis (Working Party Report). London: Royal College of Physicians.

Brosseau L, Wolfson C (1994) The inter-rater reliability and construct validity of the functional independence measure for multiple sclerosis subjects. Clinical Rehabilitation 8: 107–15.

Brown P (1994) Pathophysiology of spasticity. Journal of Neurology, Neurosurgery and Psychiatry 57: 773–7.

Carr J, Shepherd R (1998) Neurological Rehabilitation: Optimising Motor Performance. Oxford: Butterworth Heinemann.

Carr JH, Shepherd RB, Ada L (1995) Spasticity: research findings and implications for intervention. Physiotherapy 81(8): 421–8.

Coffey RJ, Cahill D, Steers W et al. (1993) Intrathecal baclofen for intractable spasticity of spinal origin: results of a long-term multi centre study. Journal of Neurosurgery 78: 226–32.

Davies PM (1990) Right in the Middle: Selective Trunk Activity in the Treatment of Adult Hemiplegia. London: Springer-Verlag.

De Souza LH, Ashburn A (1996) Assessment of motor function in people with multiple sclerosis. Physiotherapy Research International 1(2): 98–111.

De Souza LH, Worthington JA (1988) Rehabilitation of multiple sclerosis patients using movements re-education (abstract). Scandinavian Journal of Rehabilitation Medical Supplement 17: 165.

Di Fabio RP, Choi T, Soderberg J, Hansen CR (1997) Health-related quality of life for patients with progressive multiple sclerosis: influence of rehabilitation. Physical Therapy 77(12): 1704–16.

Edwards S (1996) Neurological Physiotherapy: A Problem Solving Approach. London: Churchill Livingstone, pp 189–206.

Edwards S (1998) Physiotherapy management of established spasticity. In Sheean G (Ed) Spasticity Rehabilitation. London: Churchill Communications, pp 71–91.

Ferguson A, Griffin E, Mulcahy C (1999) Patient self-referral to physiotherapy in general practice: a model for the new NHS? Physiotherapy 85(1): 13–20.

Freeman J, Johnson J, Rollinson S, Thompson A, Hatch J (1997a) Standards of Healthcare for People with Multiple Sclerosis. London: Multiple Sclerosis Society of Great Britain and Northern Ireland, and the National Hospital for Neurology and Neurosurgery.

Freeman JA, Langdon DW, Hobart JC, Thompson AJ (1997b) The impact of inpatient rehabilitation on progressive multiple sclerosis. Annals of Neurology 42(2): 236–44.

Freeman JA, Langdon DW, Hobart JC, Thompson AJ (1999) Inpatient rehabilitation in multiple sclerosis. Do the benefits carry over into the community? Neurology 52: 50–6.

From A, Heltberg A (1975) A double blind trial with baclofen and diazepam in spasticity due to multiple sclerosis. Acta Neurologica Scandinavia 51: 158–66.

Fuller KJ, Dawson K, Wiles CM (1996) Physiotherapy in chronic multiple sclerosis: a controlled trial. Clinical Rehabilitation 10: 195–204.

Goemare S, Van Laere M, De Neve P, Kaufman JM (1994) Bone mineral status in paraplegic patients who do or do not perform standing. Osteoporosis International 4(3): 138–43.

Gracies JM, Elovic E, McGuire J, Simpson D (1997) Traditional pharmacological treatments for spasticity, Part 1: local treatments. Muscle and Nerve (Suppl 6) S61–S91.

Granger CV, Cotter AC, Hamilton BB, Fiedler RC, Hens MM (1990) Functional assessment scales: a study of persons with multiple sclerosis. Archives of Physical Medicine and Rehabilitation 71: 870–5.

Hatch J (1997) Building partnerships. In Thompson AJ, Polman CO, Hohlfeld R (Eds) Multiple Sclerosis: Clinical Challenges and Controversies. London: Martin Dunitz, pp 345–51.

Horak FB (1991) Assumptions underlying motor control for neurologic rehabilitation. In Lister MJ, Washington DC (Eds) II Step: Contemporary Management of Motor Control Problems. London: Foundation for Physical Therapy, pp 11–28.

Johnson J (1997) What can specialist nurses offer in caring for people with Multiple Sclerosis? In Thompson AJ, Polman CO, Hohlfeld R (Eds) MS: Clinical Challenges and Controversies. London: Martin Dunitz.

Johnson J, Thompson AJ (1996) Rehabilitation in a neuroscience centre: the role of expert assessment and selection. British Journal of Therapy and Rehabilitation 3(6): 303–8.

Ko Ko C (1999) Effectiveness of rehabilitation for multiple sclerosis. Clinical Rehabilitation 13(Suppl 1): 33–41.

Kunkel CF, Scremin AM, Eisenberg B, Garcia JF, Roberts S, Martinez S (1993) Effect of 'standing' on spasticity, contracture, and osteoporosis in paralysed males. Archives of Physical Medicine and Rehabilitation 74: 73–8.

Langdon DW (1996) Neuropsychological problems and solutions. In Edwards S (Ed) Neurological Physiotherapy: A Problem Solving Approach. London: Churchill Livingstone, pp 41–63.

La Rocca NG, Kalb RC (1992) Efficacy of rehabilitation in multiple sclerosis. Journal of Neurologic Rehabilitation 6: 147–55.

Latash ML, Penn RD, Corcos DM, Gottlieb GL (1990) Effects of intrathecal baclofen on voluntary motor control in spastic paresis. Journal of Neurosurgery 72: 388–92.

Lawson K (1998) Tizanidine: a therapeutic weapon for spasticity? Physiotherapy 84(9): 418–20.

Lewis KS, Mueller WM (1993) Intrathecal baclofen for severe spasticity secondary to spinal cord injury. Annals of Pharmacotherapy 27: 767–74.

Lord SE, Wade DT, Halligan PW (1998) A comparison of two physiotherapy treatment approaches to improve walking in multiple sclerosis: a pilot randomised controlled study. Clinical Rehabilitation 12: 477–86.

Mayer NH, Esquenazi A, Childers MK (1997) Common patterns of clinical motor dysfunction. Muscle and Nerve Suppl 6: 21–35.

McIntosh-Michaelis SA, Roberts MH, Wilkinson SM, Diamond ID, McLellan DL, Martin JP, Spackman AJ (1991) The prevalence of cognitive impairment in a community survey of multiple sclerosis. British Journal of Clinical Psychology 30: 333–48.

Mertin J (1997) In Kesselring J (ed.) Multiple Sclerosis. Cambridge: Cambridge University Press, Ch. 13, pp 136–40.

Norkin CC, White DJ (1975) Measurement of Joint Motion: A Guide to Goniometry. Philadelphia: FA Davies.

Payton OD, Nelson CE (1998) A preliminary study of patients' perceptions of certain aspects of their physical therapy experience. Physiotherapy Theory and Practice 12: 27–38.

Penn RD, Savoy SM, Corcos D, Latash M, Gottlieb G, et al. (1989) Intrathecal baclofen for severe spinal spasticity. New England Journal of Medicine 320: 1517–54.

Perry S (1994) Living with Multiple Sclerosis. Newcastle upon Tyne: Atheneum Press.

Pope PM (1992) Management of the physical condition in patients with chronic and severe neurological pathologies. Physiotherapy 78(12): 896–903.

Pope P (1996) In Edwards S. Neurological Physiotherapy: A Problem Solving Approach. London: Churchill Livingstone, Ch. 7, pp 135–60.

Rao SM (1995) Neuropsychology of multiple sclerosis. Current Opinion in Neurology 8: 216–20.

Richardson D (1991) The use of a tilt-table to effect passive tendo-achilles stretch in a patient with head injury. Physiotherapy Theory and Practice 7: 45–50.

Robinson I et al. (1996) A Dispatch from the Front Line: The Views of People with Multiple Sclerosis about their Needs. A Qualitative Approach. London: Brunel MS Research Unit.

Rossiter DA, Edmunsen A, Al Shahi R, Thompson AJ (1998) Integrated care pathways in multiple sclerosis: completing the audit cycle. Multiple Sclerosis 4: 85–9.

Sadovnik AD, Ebers GC (1993) Epidemiology of multiple sclerosis: a critical review. Canadian Journal of Neurological Science 20: 17–29.

Schut HA, Stam HJ (1994) Goals in rehabilitation teamwork. Disability and Rehabilitation 16(4): 223–6.

Sheean G (1998) Spasticity Rehabilitation, London: Churchill Communications Europe.

Solari A, Filippini G, Gasco P, Colla L, Salmaggi A, La Mantia L, Farinotti M, Medozzi L (1999) Physical rehabilitation has a positive effect on disability in multiple sclerosis patients. Neurology 52: 57–62.

Thompson AJ (1996) Multiple sclerosis: symptomatic treatment. Journal of Neurology 243: 559–65.

Thompson AJ (1998) Spasticity rehabilitation: a rational approach to clinical management. In Sheean G (Ed) Spasticity Rehabilitation. London: Churchill Communications Europe.

Tremblay F, Malouin F, Richards CL, Dumas F (1990) Effects of prolonged muscle stretch on reflex and voluntary muscle activations in children with spastic cerebral palsy. Scandinavian Journal of Rehabilitation Medicine 22: 171–80.

Tussler D (1998) The Oswestry standing frame: use following spinal cord injury. British Journal of Therapy and Rehabilitation 5(6): 292–4.

Vowels LM, Pelosi A (1983) An Evaluation of Physiotherapy in Chronic and Deteriorating Neurological Conditions. Melbourne, Australia: MS Society Publications.

Wade DT (1992) Measurement in Neurological Rehabilitation. Oxford: Oxford University Press.

World Health Organization (1997) ICIDH-2 International Classification of Impairments, Activities and Participations. A Manual of Dimensions of Disablement and Functioning. Beta-1 Draft for Field Trials. Geneva: WHO.

Coda

In this series we have looked specifically at physiotherapy, but it was acknowledged by all the authors that the treatment and management of people with neurological conditions is best undertaken through collaboration between different health professionals. Our concentration on the one profession here is important to try to disentangle the contribution of the different component parts of rehabilitation and to inform others about the current bases for our practice.

Physiotherapy is often derided for its lack of research underpinning practice and it was very good to see the number of references that were cited in each chapter. There was clearly more research undertaken in some conditions than others, but in all a start has been made to seek evidence on which to base practice. There has been a history in medicine, which is also reflected in physiotherapy, of depending heavily on authority figures. They have tended to predominate in decisions about current methods of treatment and management of different conditions, and have largely gone unchallenged. These people are extremely valuable to the profession but their opinions, as with all others, must be subject to critical appraisal and their ideas and methods tested experimentally.

There seems to be a belief that the more evidence we have the clearer things will be. However, anyone who is familiar with science knows that this is far from the case. As will be seen from these chapters, specialists do not always agree, may interpret the literature in different ways, and research findings may contradict each other. This means that both clinicans and researchers must be critical about published work, and in the end make up their own minds on the basis of personal experience and the best evidence available at the time.

Index

A

Q

R

S

T